# lonely planet

# British Columbia & the Canadian Rockies

Yukon
Territory
p180

British
Columbia
p108

Alberta
p146

Banff & Jasper
National Parks
p206

Vancouver
Island
p82

Vancouver
p50

**Bianca Bujan, Brendan Sainsbury,
Debbie Olsen, Jonny Bierman**

**Ucluelet Harbour, Vancouver Island (p101)**

# CONTENTS

Indigenous frame drum

## Land Acknowledgement

Lonely Planet respectfully acknowledges that Canada is the traditional territory of more than 630 First Nations communities as well as Inuit and Métis communities. We offer gratitude to the Indigenous Peoples for their care for, and teachings about, this land.

Maligne Canyon,
Jasper (p229)

Icefields Parkway (p220), Alberta

# BRITISH COLUMBIA & THE CANADIAN ROCKIES

## THE JOURNEY BEGINS HERE

When it comes to natural beauty, British Columbia (and the Canadian Rockies region) boasts the best of all biomes. From the warm waters of the West Coast to the towering trees of the Great Bear Rainforest to the snowy slopes of the Rocky Mountains, an outdoor playground awaits. Cultural diversity shines as bright as the diverse landscapes.

### Bianca Bujan

*@bitsofbee*

*Born and raised in Vancouver, Bianca loves to share the best of her city. She enjoys connecting with new cultures and experiencing destinations through the people who call each place home.*

**My favourite experience** is picnicking in Granville Island. I pop into the Public Market for snacks, stroll to Ron Basford Park, and settle in for a quiet picnic with harbor views.

4

# WHO GOES WHERE

Our writers and experts choose the places which, for them, define British Columbia & the Canadian Rockies.

For me, **Jasper** (p224) is like Banff without the wrapping paper. Everything's a bit more unkempt and laidback. Over 20 years I've experienced many of its different flavors, from getting evacuated from Maligne Lake during the 2015 Excelsior fire to skiing solo into the Tonquin Valley in winter.

### Brendan Sainsbury

*@sainsburyb*

*Brendan has written or co-written 66 Lonely Planet guidebooks.*

I learned to love hiking as a child when I scampered up the steep Bear's Hump trail with my cousins in **Waterton Lakes National Park** (p158). It's still one of my favorite places in the Canadian Rockies.

### Debbie Olsen

*wanderwoman.ca*

*Debbie has written several books and guidebooks. She's a Calgary Herald travel columnist, a freelancer and managing editor of Wander Woman Travel Magazine.*

The **Coast Mountains and Great Bear Rainforest** (p114) beckon me to explore their icy depths, emerald colors and thermal waters. On a quest to ski, soak and hike them all, I love exploring the region's boundless terrain to my heart's content.

### Jonny Bierman

*@ecoescape.travel*

*Jonny is a Vancouver-based sustainable travel journalist and photographer.*

400 km
200 miles

N

**Icefields Parkway**
Rubberneck along Canada's most scenic road trip (p220)

SASKATCHEWAN

NUNAVUT

*Victoria Island*

*Coronation Gulf*

*Lake Athabasca*

*Lake Claire*

*Wood Buffalo National Park*

● Yellowknife

**Jasper National Park**
Watch for wildlife and starry nights (p224)

*Great Slave Lake*

*Great Bear Lake*

NORTHWEST TERRITORIES

*Lac La Martre*

Fort Simpson ○

*Liard River*

Fort Nelson ○

**Dawson City**
Gallivant through a gold-rush town (p196)

*Franklin Mountains*

*Mackenzie River*

*Nahanni National Park Reserve △*

**Vancouver Island**
Watch for whales from breathtaking beaches (p83)

Tuktoyaktuk ○

Inuvik ○

*MacKenzie Mountains*

Watson Lake ○

**Kluane National Park & Reserve**
Marvel at Mount Logan, Canada's highest mountain (p195)

*Ivvavik National Park △*

*Yukon River*

YUKON TERRITORY

*Kluane Lake*

*Kluane National Park △*

● Whitehorse

*Teslin Lake*

*Atlin Lake*

■ Dawson City

ALASKA

USA | CANADA

Haines ○

Juneau ●

*Gulf of Alaska*

## Drumheller

Delight in Canada's dinosaur capital (p164)

## Banff National Park

View vibrant lakes and majestic landscapes (p210)

## Thompson Okanagan

Sip syrah in BC's biggest wine region (p130)

## Whistler

Seek adrenaline-pumping thrills on the ski slopes (p118)

## Great Bear Rainforest

Search for the rarest bear on Earth (p114)

## Haida Gwaii

Revel in rich heritage and rugged landscapes (p143)

## Stanley Park

Stroll the seawall of this massive urban park (p62)

## Vancouver

Indulge in Western Canada's dining capital (p50)

CANADA
USA

MONTANA

IDAHO

WASHINGTON

ALBERTA

BRITISH COLUMBIA

Athabasca River

Peace River

Lesser Slave Lake

Rocky Mountains

Coast Mountains

Spatsizi Plateau Provincial Wilderness Park

Tweedsmuir Provincial Park

Jasper National Park

Banff National Park

Glacier National Park

Kootenay National Park

Waterton Lakes National Park

Fraser River

Kinbasket Lake

Okanagan Lake

Ootsa Lake

Queen Charlotte Sound

Hecate Strait

Haida Gwaii

Vancouver Island

PACIFIC OCEAN

Edmonton
Red Deer
Drumheller
Calgary
Medicine Hat
Lethbridge
Banff
Lake Louise
Cranbrook
Silverton
Nelson
Kelowna
Penticton
Revelstoke
Hinton
Jasper
Grande Cache
Valemount
Williams Lake
Kamloops
Merritt
Hope
Vancouver
Bellingham
Seattle
Whistler
Victoria
Nanaimo
Tofino
Prince George
Tumbler Ridge
Dawson Creek
Fort St John
Kitwanga
Smithers
Terrace
Kitimat
Bella Coola
Port Hardy
Stewart
Prince Rupert

7

# WILDLIFE WATCHING

The landscape is vast and varied in BC and the Canadian Rockies region, where temperate rainforests, jagged mountain ranges and widespread waterways provide shelter and sustenance for the wildlife that call these areas home. Protected parks and reserves provide refuge for wildlife, allowing them to thrive and survive in their natural habitats, and human impacts and interactions are restricted to ensure the safety of Canada's creatures.

### Beautiful Beasts

Gawk at the gigantic grizzlies found in the wilds of northern BC, or meander among the massive moose that prance along the plains of Alberta.

### Wandering Whales

BC is a whale-watching wonderland. In spring, gray whales swim along western shores, and humpbacks can be spotted migrating to warmer waters during winter months.

### Endemic Species

Buck-toothed beavers are the obvious all-Canadian critter, but the country is home to several other endemic species, including the marmot (Vancouver Island) and the Yukon ungulates.

## BEST WILDLIFE EXPERIENCES

Ogle the native ungulates that inhabit huge natural enclosures at ❶ **Yukon Wildlife Preserve** (p191), just outside Whitehorse.

Sail the shores of the ❷ **Great Bear Rainforest** (p114) with Maple Leaf Adventures in search of the spirit bear, the rarest bear on Earth.

Join Prince Rupert Adventure Tours through the ❸ **Khutzeymateen Grizzly Sanctuary** (p121), Canada's only protected grizzly bear habitat.

Embark on a paddling tour with North Island Kayak Tours from ❹ **Telegraph Cove** (p105) and get up-close with whales and other marine life.

Take an Indigenous-led whale-watching tour through the waters of ❺ **Tofino** (p100) with Ahous Adventures in search of gray whales and humpbacks.

# CULTURAL CONNECTIONS

Authentic Indigenous experiences are offered throughout the region, inviting visitors to develop a deeper understanding of the cultural origins and continued contributions of the people who first called this land home. In BC alone, more than 200 different Indigenous communities and over 30 living languages exist, so the cultural offerings here are distinct and diverse. Be sure to download the interactive Indigenous BC app (indigenousbc.com) for immersive experiences found throughout the province.

### Immersive Experiences

Through shared stories and songs, and Indigenous-guided land and water tours, you can be immersed in the beauty of the cultures and languages of the region.

### Indigenous Cuisine

Take a local tour, visit a winery, or dine at a restaurant to savor cuisine composed of traditional Indigenous ingredients such as wild salmon, bannock, berries and game meats.

### Historic Sites

Admire artwork and artifacts at museums, galleries and cultural centers, and take guided tours through sacred lands and sites showcasing the region's diverse history.

## BEST INDIGENOUS EXPERIENCES

Investigate the history of the Tr'ondëk Hwëch'in (River People) First Nations, who pre-date the Klondike Gold Rush at ❶ **Dänojà Zho Cultural Centre** (p200) in Dawson City.

Experience Métis culture at ❷ **Métis Crossing** (p179), one of the few places in the world where you can see a sacred white bison.

See the world's oldest and best preserved buffalo jumps at ❸ **Head-Smashed-in Buffalo Jump** (p169), a Unesco World Heritage Site.

Witness the celebration of two nations – Squamish & Lil'wat Nation – at ❹ **Squamish Lil'wat Cultural Centre** (p115) through stunning exhibits and live demos.

Take an authentic, Indigenous-led fishing excursion in ❺ **Haida Gwaii** (p143) with Haida Style Expeditions.

# ALLURE OF THE ARTS

Museums, galleries, theaters, public art displays, and artisan shops – art is everywhere and accessible to all here. From massive urban murals that color the city's walls in Vancouver to a massive, multi-day, open-access arts festival in Edmonton, to a showcase of esteemed writers in Dawson City, creatives of all kinds are celebrated across Canada, where local and international talents take the spotlight, and many of the art offerings can be enjoyed for free.

### Aboriginal Art

Throughout BC and the Canadian Rockies, traditional and modern paintings, sculptures, jewelry and textiles are showcased by emerging and established Indigenous artists.

### Museums & Galleries

The region is home to architecturally and historically significant galleries and museums that house some of the country's largest collections of art by local, national and international artists.

### Festivals & Events

Arts enthusiasts flock to the fringe festivals that are hosted around the region, and music festivals, culture crawls and pop-up exhibits invite creative crowds year-round.

## BEST ARTS EXPERIENCES

Explore the ❶ **Art Gallery of Alberta** (p179), an architectural marvel in the heart of downtown Edmonton and one of Canada's largest galleries.

Snap photos of the stunning outdoor murals found throughout the city at the ❷ **Vancouver Mural Festival** (p74).

Visit the cabins of three erstwhile resident writers: Jack London, Robert Service and Pierre Berton on ❸ **Writer's Row** (p198) in Dawson City.

Check out the ❹ **Edmonton International Fringe Theatre Festival** (p179), the oldest and largest fringe theater festival in North America.

Admire fine art at the ❺ **Bill Reid Gallery of Northwest Coast Art** (p57), Canada's only public gallery dedicated to contemporary Indigenous art of the Northwest Coast.

# BITES & BREWS

From the fresh, wild salmon snatched from BC's cool coastal waters, to the top-quality beef and bison reared on Alberta's far-reaching, fertile farmlands, the region's culinary claim to fame lies in its freshly fished and farmed seafood and livestock. Paired with farm-fresh produce, international influences, homegrown hops and a world-renowned wine scene, it's no wonder the culinary scene across these two provinces is recognized and revered on a global scale.

### Craft Beer

BC has become the craft capital of Canada, and as a productive hop-growing region, craft breweries continue to sprout throughout the area.

### Simple Salmon

Unsurprisingly, given BC's easy access to the ocean, salmon is one of the most prominent foods. Freshly caught chinook, coho, pink and sockeye are best here.

### Asian Influence

Home to the largest population of Chinese residents found outside Asia, Vancouver has become a global go-to spot for regional Asian cuisine.

## BEST FOOD EXPERIENCES

Sample global street foods at the **❶ Richmond Night Market** (p80), North America's largest.

Stroll and snack your way through the food stalls of the **❷ Granville Island Public Market** (p67).

Sip on a caesar cocktail at **❸ Major Tom** (p42) in Calgary, the birthplace of the celebrated Canadian bevy.

Sample chardonnay and syrah at **❹ Nk'Mip Cellars** (p130), the first Indigenous-owned winery in North America.

Chomp on charred churrascaria and take in Brazilian traditions at **❺ Gaucho Brazilian BBQ** (p42) in Canmore.

# THRILLS & SPILLS

The stunning shorelines, massive mountain ranges, and towering trees of BC and the Canadian Rockies add up to unparalleled natural surroundings, setting the scene for endless outdoor fun. Adventure enthusiasts can enjoy it all in BC – from sea to sky – where it's possible to swim in the sea, ski the slopes and meander along mountain trails, all within close proximity. And the rugged landscapes of the Canadian Rockies take thrills to the next level with river rafting, backcountry hikes and heliskiing.

### Peak Pursuits

The Rocky Mountains are a top destination for backcountry adventures, while Vancouver's local peaks provide slopeside play closer to the city.

### Aquatic Adventures

Aquaphiles flock to this region for its abundance of water adventures. Whitewater rafting, waterfall walks, alpine-lake dips and sea kayaking are big here.

### Protected Parks

Canada's national and cultural heritage is protected. This takes the form of 171 national historic sites, 47 national parks and five national marine conservation areas.

## BEST HIKING EXPERIENCES

Head out on a hike at
**❶ Kluane National Park & Reserve** (p195) near Whitehorse, home to Canada's highest mountain.

Take an ice walk in winter at
**❷ Grotto Canyon** (p157), a family-friendly hike near Canmore that leads to two beautiful lakes.

Clip on crampons and challenge the Columbia Icefield at **❸ Jasper National Park** (p224) for a physically challenging hike along Athabasca Glacier.

Take the hike of a lifetime on a multi-day backpacking trek along the **❹ West Coast Trail** (p94) at Pacific Rim National Park.

Stroll the scenic trails of
**❺ Stanley Park** (p62), and look for local wildlife as you pass along the perimeter pathway of Lost Lagoon.

# REGIONS & CITIES

Find the places that tick all your boxes.

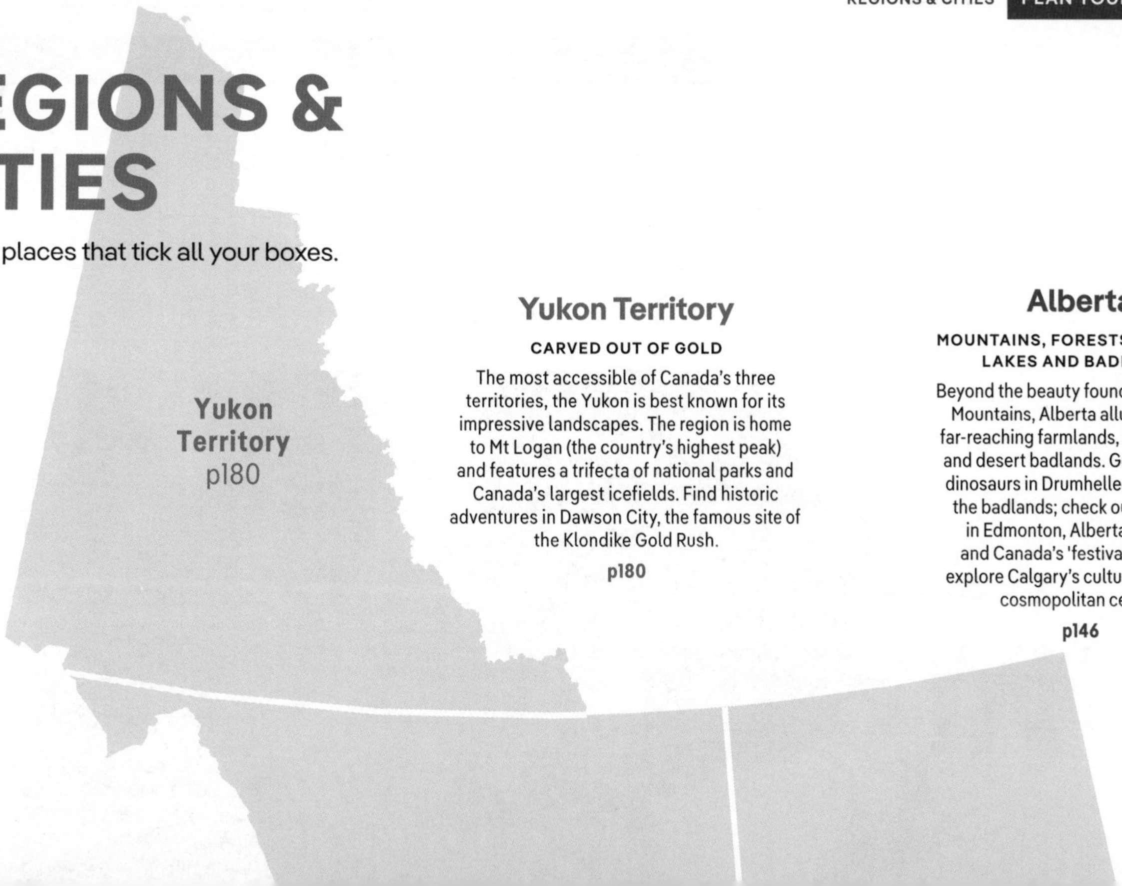

## Alberta

**MOUNTAINS, FORESTS, PRAIRIES, LAKES AND BADLANDS**

Beyond the beauty found in the Rocky Mountains, Alberta allures with its far-reaching farmlands, boreal forest and desert badlands. Go digging for dinosaurs in Drumheller, the best of the badlands; check out a festival in Edmonton, Alberta's capital and Canada's 'festival city'; and explore Calgary's culturally diverse cosmopolitan center.

**p146**

## Yukon Territory

**CARVED OUT OF GOLD**

The most accessible of Canada's three territories, the Yukon is best known for its impressive landscapes. The region is home to Mt Logan (the country's highest peak) and features a trifecta of national parks and Canada's largest icefields. Find historic adventures in Dawson City, the famous site of the Klondike Gold Rush.

**p180**

Yukon
Territory
p180

## British Columbia
### p108

### Alberta
### p146

### Banff & Jasper National Parks
### p206

**Vancouver Island**
### p82

**Vancouver**
### p50

## British Columbia

### AWE-INSPIRING MOUNTAINS SCULPTED IN TIME

BC dazzles with its dichotomy of nature and city. And while the West Coast boasts a balance of both, the places beyond the ocean's edge showcase some of BC's greatest beauty. Search the Great Bear Rainforest for the world's rarest bear, or head to Haida Gwaii to discover the roots of Indigenous Peoples.

**p108**

## Vancouver Island

### CHARMING COMMUNITIES AND WILDERNESS WONDERS

Best known for BC's capital city of Victoria, with its world-renowned brunch scene and reputation as Canada's 'garden city,' this immense isle attracts adventurers for its vast and varied landscapes too. Beyond Victoria you'll find a bevy of backcountry eco-adventures, as well as cold-water surfing, spelunking and bucket-list hiking trails.

**p82**

## Banff & Jasper National Parks

### THE CANADIAN ROCKIES' GREATEST HITS

Found along the crest of the Canadian Rockies, Banff and Jasper are home to some of the world's top alpine adventures. Hot springs, ski resorts, glacier hikes and wildlife sightings make this a top pick, and these adjacent national parks are linked by a road tripper's reverie: the spectacular Icefields Parkway.

**p206**

## Vancouver

### GREEN CITY BY THE SEA

The natural beauty and mild climate perfectly complement the cultural diversity and friendly people found here. Recognized as one of the world's best food cities, Vancouver's cuisine alone is worth a visit, and the Indigenous roots and international influences provide context for the stories behind this coastal city, which sits nestled in nature.

**p50**

19

# ITINERARIES

# Mainland to Mountaintop

**Allow:** 4 days          **Distance:** 147km

Take a deep dive into the best food spots, green spaces and cultural sites in and around Vancouver. Start in the gateway city of Richmond, explore your way through downtown and Vancouver's North Shore, and then head up the Sea-to-Sky Hwy to wrap it up in Whistler.

**Sea-to-Sky Highway**

**❶**
## RICHMOND ⏱ 1 DAY

Chinese-Canadian influences mean **Richmond** (p80) is home to some of the best Asian cuisine found in the world, which you can sample along the self-guided Dumpling Trail or at the Richmond Night Market, the largest of its kind in North America. Stop in the village of Steveston for fresh fish-and-chips and harbor views before heading downtown.

**❷**
## DOWNTOWN VANCOUVER ⏱ 1 DAY

Explore **Downtown Vancouver** (p56), where Stanley Park is only steps from the museums and galleries, boutiques and shops, and world-renowned restaurants and eateries line downtown streets. Start with a walking tour or a seawall stroll through the park, before sampling the city's best cultural and culinary highlights.
*Detour: Spend a few hours on the North Shore by taking the Seabus from downtown Vancouver to Lonsdale Quay. Return before heading to the next stop.*

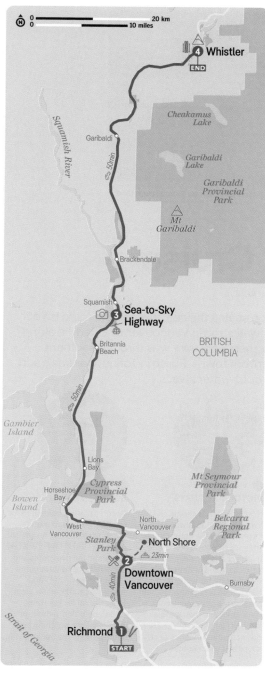

N

0                      20 km
0                 10 miles

**4 Whistler**
**END**

*Cheakamus Lake*

Garibaldi

🚗 50min

*Garibaldi Lake*

*Garibaldi Provincial Park*

*Mt Garibaldi*

Brackendale

Squamish
📷 **3** **Sea-to-Sky Highway**

**BRITISH COLUMBIA**

Britannia Beach

🚗 50min

*Squamish River*

*Gambier Island*

Lions Bay

*Cypress Provincial Park*

*Mt Seymour Provincial Park*

Horseshoe Bay

*Bowen Island*

West Vancouver
*Stanley Park*

North Vancouver

*Belcarra Regional Park*

🍴 **2** ● **North Shore**
🚟 23min

**Downtown Vancouver**

🚗 40min

Burnaby

*Strait of Georgia*

**Richmond 1** 🎿
**START**

**③**
## SEA-TO-SKY HIGHWAY
⏱1 DAY

Drive along the snaky Sea-to-Sky Hwy (also known as Hwy 99), a picturesque driving route that takes you past waterfalls, rivers and ocean views. Stop for a ride up the Sea-to-Sky Gondola, and be sure to pop into Squamish to fuel up on food (and gas) before completing your journey towards North America's biggest ski resort.

**④**
## WHISTLER ⏱1 DAY

Venture from the mainland to the peak of **Whistler** (p118) where a slopeside playground awaits. Year-round offerings make this the place to be in all seasons, whether you're looking to spend the day skiing the peaks, or enjoying a wellness stay in the woods.

PLAN YOUR TRIP ITINERARIES

Cox Bay, Tofino, Vancouver Island

## ITINERARIES

# Coastal Cruise

**Allow:** 10 days    **Distance:** 488km

If you've set your sights on seeing the sea, this coastal route is your best bet. Start with a seawall stroll in Vancouver, or a paddle along the city's coastal waters, then work your way through southern Vancouver Island's waterfront towns. Finish in Tofino, Canada's surf town, and challenge the cold-water swells.

### ❶ VANCOUVER ⏱ 1 DAY

Start your aquatic adventures with a day spent in **Granville Island** (p64), where you can stroll the seawall, stock up on snacks at the Public Market, and cool off with a splash at the water park – the largest of its kind in North America. Then dine dockside.

🛶 *Detour: Catch a mini-ferry from Granville Island dock to Science World, enjoying water views along the way. Visit for two or three hours.*

### ❷ VICTORIA ⏱ 2 DAYS

Next stop is BC's capital city, **Victoria** (p86), renowned for its natural beauty and cultural sites. Be sure to do brunch, as this city has been deemed the 'brunch capital of Canada.' In keeping with the water theme, take a stroll along Inner Harbour, passing the city's most iconic landmarks, and then wander through Fisherman's Wharf, a quaint floating community of shops and snack spots.

### ❸ SOOKE ⏱ 1 DAY

Spend a day in **Sooke** (p91) for boating, hiking and wildlife-spotting by the sea. A series of hikes for all skill levels will take you along the river pools and waterfalls found throughout Potholes Provincial Park, and Sooke Harbour is a great launch point for kayaking, paddleboarding, fishing, or guided whale-watching boat tours through the Sooke Basin.

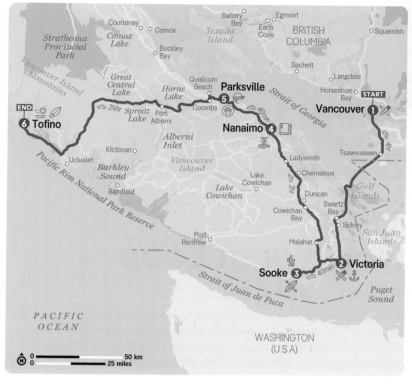

**④ NANAIMO** ⏱1 DAY

Waterfront playgrounds, Canada's tallest waterfall and the region's staple sweet treat can be found in **Nanaimo** (p95), known as Vancouver Island's 'second city' and another entry point by ferry from the mainland. Indigenous history and heritage run deep here, so be sure to stop in at a museum or cultural site to learn about the city's origins before moving on to your next stop.

**⑤ PARKSVILLE** ⏱2 DAYS

Spend two full days exploring **Parksville** (p97), with some time spent in the neighbouring town of **Qualicum Beach** (p95) too. Outdoor adventures await in this region, where you can go spelunking in underground caves, enjoy low-tide beach play, get up close with wildlife and dine on delectable seafood dishes caught fresh from the sea. A unique market with goats on the roof is also a must.

**⑥ TOFINO** ⏱3 DAYS

Wrap up your waterfront road trip with a few days in **Tofino** (p100), Canada's surf capital, where cold-water ocean swells are the biggest draw. Storm watching has also become a beloved pastime here. The city is home to the largest and longest beach found in the Pacific Rim National Park Reserve, and offers unparalleled landscapes for outdoor adventure among the rocky ocean shores and temperate rainforest.

LYNN A/SHUTTERSTOCK ©

**Spirit bear**

## ITINERARIES

# Northwest Loop

**Allow:** 8 Days    **Distance:** 1683km

For a deep dive into BC's central and northern regions, this road trip begins on the northwest coast, weaves into canyons and mountain ranges, through BC's cowboy country, and into the world's largest coastal temperate rainforest, where you can search for the rarest bear on Earth while being immersed in nature.

**1** **PRINCE RUPERT** ⏱1 DAY

Kick off your adventures in **Prince Rupert** (p122), a port city on BC's northwest coast. This is the departure point for adventures in the northern region of Vancouver Island, including access by ferry to Port Hardy, Bella Coola and Haida Gwaii. This is where the journey would begin for those heading to the Great Bear Rainforest. Explore the natural and cultural heritage around this small town before onward travel.

**2** **KITIMAT** ⏱1 DAY

For your next stop, dip into **Kitimat** (p122), a small town folded into a forested valley, for a day of backcountry hiking and freshwater fishing – Kitimat is said to have some of the best fishing on the West Coast. Take a private boat-access-only hot-springs tour, and be sure to learn about the Haisla Peoples, who first called this land home, on an Indigenous-led tour.

**3** **TERRACE** ⏱1 DAY

Scenic rivers, waterways and ocean inlets provide the perfect backdrop for jet-boat tours in **Terrace** (p122), where you can spot grizzlies, waterfalls and even hidden ghost towns along the way. Take time to tour the nearby Kitselas Canyon for an Indigenous-guided tour. Stock up on snacks and gas before you head out for the longest portion of this far-flung road trip.

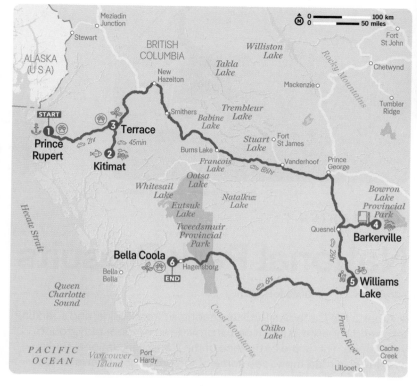

#### 4 BARKERVILLE ⏱1 DAY

Small towns speckle this stretch of highway, providing stop-in options for snacks and fuel, with Prince George the largest pass-through city. Don't miss **Barkerville** (p128), a tiny historic town recognized as the largest living history museum in western North America. A designated National Historic Site of Canada, Barkerville's heritage buildings and period displays transport visitors to the 1800s and the gold-rush era.

#### 5 WILLIAMS LAKE ⏱1 DAY

**Williams Lake** (p127) is considered 'cowboy country' in the Cariboo, where lesser-known mountain ranges, gold-rush history and immersive Indigenous experiences offer a glimpse into the region's past. Hiking and biking are popular pastimes here. Another long stretch of driving awaits, so be sure to stop and stretch your legs as you admire the lakes and creeks that line the route to your final destination.

#### 6 BELLA COOLA ⏱3 DAYS

The **Bella Coola Valley** (p119) is remote and rugged – a sacred place where Indigenous storytelling, wildlife excursions and natural wonders come together. See the Bella Coola fjord, scale the via ferrata, and search the Great Bear Rainforest – the world's largest coastal temperate rainforest – for a peek at the Kermode bear (or 'Spirit bear'), the world's rarest bear breed.

Sulphur Mountain Gondola, Banff

## ITINERARIES

# National Park Pursuits

**Allow:** 9 days      **Distance:** 931km

In Alberta the Canadian Rockies meet the Great Plains, and sparkling lakes and snowy mountain peaks provide an outdoor playground year-round. This is the birthplace of the Canadian National Parks system, so a road trip to see some of the province's best is a must. Note: this route includes highway tolls.

### ❶ WATERTON LAKES NATIONAL PARK ⏱ 2 DAYS

Start your journey at **Waterton Lakes National Park** (p160), arriving via the Lethbridge airport, or by boat from the US side. This was the first Canadian national park to take part in the Unesco heritage program, and the two national historic sites found in the area offer beautiful landscapes for outdoor adventure, combining clear lakes, whooshing waterfalls and magnificent mountain vistas.

### ❷ CALGARY ⏱ 1 DAY

**Calgary** (p170) is best known for the annual Calgary Stampede, but there's so much more to see and do here. The Bow River hosts rafting during the warmer months, and scenic riverside trails provide a large network of urban pathways for biking. Calgary also has award-winning culinary and cultural offerings that invite diverse populations to explore Alberta's largest urban center.

### ❸ DRUMHELLER ⏱ 1 DAY

Take a cruise through the Canadian Badlands, where otherworldly landscapes reveal deep canyons and prehistoric hoodoos. Spend a day in **Drumheller** (p164), where the world's largest deposits of dinosaur bones invite visitors to find fossils and learn about the prehistoric creatures that once roamed the Earth. Be sure to spend some time at the museum, where you can see the world's largest display of dinosaurs up close.

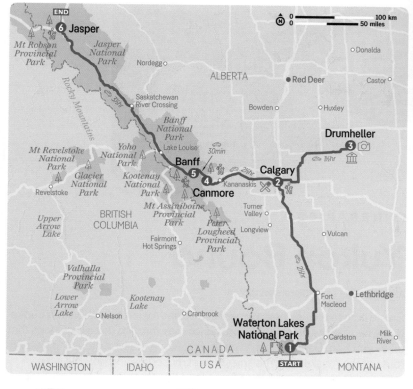

## ④ CANMORE ⏱ 1 DAY

Found just southeast of Banff, **Canmore** (p152) is worthy of a stop. Nine provincial parks are packed into this region, with winding trails that invite everything from hiking and biking to horseback riding and cross-country skiing (when the weather fits). Be sure to finish off your day of outdoor adventures with a scenic soak at the only Nordic Spa found in the Canadian Rockies.

## ⑤ BANFF ⏱ 2 DAYS

**Banff National Park** (p210) was Canada's first, and its allure comes in the combination of the cozy comforts found in the town of Banff and the rustic wilderness found nearby. Here you can paddle across sparkling lakes, cycle and hike the series of scenic multi-purpose trails, and ski the powdery slopes. Be sure to visit the Cave & Basin National Historic Site while you're there.

## ⑥ JASPER NATIONAL PARK ⏱ 2 DAYS

Journey along the Icefields Parkway, possibly the most beautiful stretch of highway in the world, to get to **Jasper National Park** (p224), the final stop on your journey. The slightly less popular Rocky Mountain Park has just as much to offer, with rugged landscapes, an abundance of wildlife, a sizable townsite and an alpine ski resort. Alberta's tallest mountain is found here.

THACHAKUL/SHUTTERSTOCK ©

Welcome to Yukon sign

## ITINERARIES

# Yukon Bound

**Allow:** 10 Days          **Distance:** 2039km

Cruise across the northern Canadian Rockies region from Alberta's capital to the capital city of the Yukon on this journey through three provinces that takes you from Edmonton to Whitehorse. Along the way, cross the historic route of the Alaska Hwy, making stops at museums and notable sites, suspension bridges and hot springs along this cross-provincial road trip.

**1**
### EDMONTON ⏱ 2 DAYS

Begin your journey in **Edmonton** (p175), Alberta's vibrant capital city. Best known as the home to West Edmonton Mall, North America's largest shopping center, Edmonton is also recognized for its galleries and museums, and for hosting the largest fringe festival in North America. The North Saskatchewan River Valley is a great urban park, and don't miss Edmonton's historic district.

**2**
### DAWSON CREEK ⏱ 1 DAY

Hop onto Yellowhead Hwy to cross into the next province, where your second stop is **Dawson Creek** (p144), found at the the edge of eastern BC. Check out the local art scene, take a step back in time at the pioneer village, explore the train museum and trek across the trestle bridge before proceeding to your next BC stop.

**3**
### FORT ST JOHN ⏱ 1 DAY

Continuing your exploration of eastern BC, stop at **Fort St John** (p144), both the largest city in the state's northeast and the largest BC city on the Alaska Hwy. Hang out in a city park, and purchase Indigenous art while you're there. Then, charge your phone, pack snacks, and prepare for the longest stretch of driving, with some areas completely off-grid as you head north towards the Yukon.

FROM LEFT: LISABOURGEAULT/SHUTTERSTOCK ©, TRINA BARNES/SHUTTERSTOCK ©,T.SCHOFIELD/SHUTTERSTOCK ©

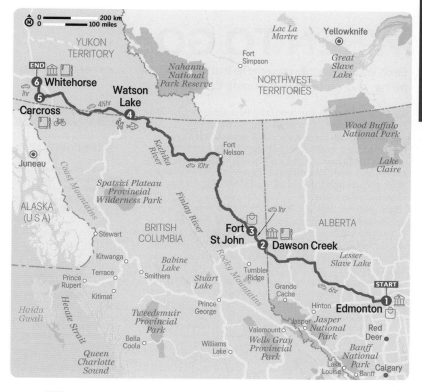

## ④ WATSON LAKE ⏱ 1 DAY

You've made it to the Yukon, congratulations! Spend a day wading your way through the **Watson Lake** (p190) area, the first town in the Yukon along the Alaska Hwy and a good rest stop after a long drive. Hike around the loop trails of Watson Lake, or fish for lake trout and northern pike. Pitch a tent for lakeside camping, or hunker down in a hotel.

## ⑤ CARCROSS ⏱ 1 DAY

As you move closer to your final destination, spend some time in **Carcross** (p190), a tourist village that was once a railway hub. Indigenous culture is big here, so be sure to take time to explore the totem poles and historic sites found in the area. For biking, head to Montana Mountain and explore the bike-trail network created in partnership with the Carcross-Tagish First Nation.

## ⑥ WHITEHORSE ⏱ 2 DAYS

Welcome to **Whitehorse** (p186), capital of the Yukon and your final stop. Walk along the waterfront, visit local museums and cultural centers, and teeter across the river on a suspension bridge. Inspect the historic SS *Klondike* steamboat while you're there. If you're up for a day trip, this city is the perfect base for beyond-Whitehorse excursions.

# WHEN **TO GO**

Each season has its own perks in this region, with summer hiking and biking, and winter skiing topping the list.

As a year-round destination, the best time to go really depends on what you want to do. Outdoor experiences are the main attraction, so you'll want to choose wisely: the blooms and beautifully clear lakes beckon travelers to the BC and Canadian Rockies region for hiking, biking and paddling during summer, while the snowy mountain peaks lure skiers and snowboarders to the slopes during winter.

Shoulder seasons are best for smaller crowds, lower prices and milder temps. For the ultimate crossover, visit Vancouver during shoulder season (May to June or September to October), where it's possible to go hiking, mountain biking, swimming and skiing all in one day, weather permitting.

Prices peak during high season (June to August), but during lower season (November to March) some outside attractions and accommodations may be closed, and there is a higher chance of rainy weather.

### I LIVE HERE

### BARKERVILLE

**Mike Retasket is an Indigenous Interpreter for Barkerville and a former chief of the Bonaparte Indian Band.**

'The main season for Barkerville is June to September, when the weather is warmer. Located on the shared territory of seven nations: Lhtako, Nazko, Lhoosk'uz, Ulkatcho, ?Esdilagh, Xatśūll, Simpcw and Lheidli, there are lots of stories to be shared. In tourism, we are responsible for the past, sharing about our history as Indigenous Peoples, the present, ensuring this history is not forgotten, and the future, by passing this knowledge on.'

LEFT: BRIAN A JACKSON/SHUTTERSTOCK ©
FAR RIGHT: ELISE MYETTE/SHUTTERSTOCK ©

### SUNNY SEASON

Across the region the warmest weather occurs between June and September, making the summer season the best time for warm-weather adventures outdoors. These are the best months for hiking, biking, paddling and swimming.

**Moraine Lake (p219), Banff**

## Weather Through the Year (Vancouver)

| JANUARY | FEBRUARY | MARCH | APRIL | MAY | JUNE |
|---|---|---|---|---|---|
|  |  |  |  |  |  |
| Avg daytime max: 6°C | Avg daytime max: 8°C | Avg daytime max: 12°C | Avg daytime max: 15°C | Avg daytime max: 16°C | Avg daytime max: 19°C |
| Days of rainfall: 20 | Days of rainfall: 16 | Days of rainfall: 20 | Days of rainfall: 18 | Days of rainfall: 13 | Days of rainfall: 14 |

## WEST COAST RAIN

Vancouver, or 'Raincouver,' is known for its soggy skies. Due to being located in a temperate rainforest, and its location on the northeast side of the Pacific Ocean, it rains an average of 170 days per year here. Alberta and the Yukon see significantly less rain.

## City Festivals

**Edmonton International Fringe Theatre Festival** (p179) For theater enthusiasts, this is not to be missed. It's the largest festival of its kind in North America. For 10 days, thousands of artists from around the world descend upon Alberta's capital city for a summer of live theater and entertainment. **August**

**Okanagan Wine Festivals** (p135) Sample wine from Nk'Mip, North America's first Indigenous-owned winery at this twice-yearly showcase of the best wines found in the Okanagan Valley. **June and October**

**Edmonton International Jazz Festival** (p179) This brings the best in jazz to the city during its run. **June**

**Adäka Cultural Festival** (p259) Join in the celebrated unity of the Northern Dene Nations and Yukon First Nations at this week-long festival full of art, music, stories, history and more. **June/July**

## Other Local Festivals

**Vancouver Mural Festival** (p74) A 10-day outdoor celebration of public art, where a street party showcases live performances, demos by artists, talks and food. **August**

**Edmonton Heritage Festival** (p179) Claims to be the 'world's largest three-day multiculturalism celebration.' Brings entertainment, culture, music and cuisine to Edmonton from destinations around the world. **August**

**Faro Crane & Sheep Festival** (p192) A Yukon festival in which visitors can join locals in observing Sandhill Cranes and Fanning Sheep as their migrations bring them through town. **May**

**Edmonton Folk Music Festival** (p179) Four days of toe-tapping performances at the amphitheater. Musicians from all over the world have performed at the festival, with most hailing from Canada, the US and the UK. **August**

⊙ **I LIVE HERE**

### BANFF

**Kim Logan is the Manager, Earned Media at Banff & Lake Louise Tourism. @kim.n.logan**

'I moved to the Canadian Rockies for the year-round mountain adventure. With 300 days of sunshine a year and endless adventures, there's no excuse to not be outside. I love hiking in the spectacular forests in fall. During our long, magical winters, you'll find me on a cross-country ski track or downhill skiing. There's a lifetime's worth of experiences here.'

**Larch Valley, Banff**

## SNOWY SLOPES

While Vancouver's local mountains don't get snow until mid-November, melting away by late February, you're likely to see snowy slopes in the Canadian Rockies region for a longer stretch of time, with snow in Banff often lasting from mid-September to late May.

| | JULY | AUGUST | SEPTEMBER | OCTOBER | NOVEMBER | DECEMBER |
|---|---|---|---|---|---|---|
| |  |  |  |  |  |  |
| Avg daytime max: | 21°C | 21°C | 18°C | 13°C | 6°C | 4°C |
| Days of rainfall: | 9 | 9 | 10 | 18 | 20 | 21 |

FLATFIVEFOTO/SHUTTERSTOCK ©

# GET PREPARED FOR BC & THE CANADIAN ROCKIES

Useful things to load in your bag, your ears and your brain.

## Clothes

**Layers** Whatever you're up to, layers are essential, as the weather can vary greatly throughout the day. Wear (or pack) a thin, waterproof jacket in case the wind picks up or it starts to rain.

**Footwear** Across the region, outdoor adventure is the biggest draw. With walkable cities, comfortable flat shoes are essential, and if you plan to hit the hiking trails, supportive sneakers or sturdy hiking boots are a must.

**Accessories** If you're visiting BC's West Coast, you'll want to pack a small umbrella, as it rains approximately 160

### Manners

**Politeness is paramount.** Canadians are commonly very friendly and value politeness, saying 'please,' 'thank you,' 'excuse me' and even 'sorry' (sometimes more often than necessary).

**Some conversation topics are taboo.** When it comes to politics, sex and religion, Canadians tend to keep their opinions to themselves.

**Know your ice hockey.** Especially in BC and Alberta, small talk tends to lead to this topic.

days per year here. For the colder regions in Alberta and the Yukon, carry warm gloves and a hat to cover your ears.

## 📖 READ

**This Place: 150 Years Retold** (Van Camp et al; 2019) Adult graphic novel anthology sharing Canada's past through an Indigenous lens.

**Inner Ranges: An Anthology of Mountain Thoughts and Mountain People** (Geoff Powter; 2018) On climbers and mountaineers.

**Klondike: The Last Great Gold Rush, 1896–1899** (Pierre Berton; 2001) History and entertainment merge in this account of the Canadian frontier.

**The 500 Hidden Secrets of Vancouver** (Shannon McLachlan; 2020) An insider's guide to Vancouver and its best hidden secrets.

## Words

**Unceded territory** This is land that was never legally given up through a treaty or agreement by the original Indigenous inhabitants of the land.

**Indigenous** The term used to refer to the original inhabitants of the land.

**Inuit** Refers to the Indigenous peoples who are found in Arctic Canada, including Inuvialuit (Northwest Territories and Yukon), Nunavik (Northern Quebec), Nunatsiavut (Labrador) and Nunavut.

**Métis** Refers to the Indigenous peoples of the Métis Nation, found in Manitoba, Saskatchewan, Alberta, northwest Ontario, northeast British Columbia, the southern Northwest Territories, northern Montana and North Dakota.

**First Nations** The term used to describe a group of Indigenous peoples who are not Inuit or Métis.

**Toque** The word Canadians use to refer to a warm, knitted hat, most often worn in winter.

**Loonie/Toonie** These are the names of the one-dollar coin (loonie) and two-dollar coin (toonie) in Canadian currency.

**Cowtown** Sometimes used to refer to the city of Calgary.

**Timmies/Tims/Timbits** Words often used to refer to Tim Horton's, a popular Canadian coffee chain. Timbits are donut holes sold there.

**Clicks** Canadians often use this term to refer to kilometers.

**Sourdough** In the Yukon this term may be heard when referring to someone who has made it through a Yukon winter.

**Cheechako** Refers to those in the Yukon who have yet to experience the cold season.

## 📹 WATCH

**British Columbia: An Untold History** (Kevin Eastwood; 2021) Doco miniseries on BC history.

**One Week** (Michael McGowan; 2008) Film about a man who motorcycles across Canada after being diagnosed with cancer.

**How a People Live** (Lisa Jackson; 2013) Doco on the Gwa-sala 'Nakwaxda'xw First Nations people.

**Gunless** (William Phillips, 2010) A Wild West outlaw is unable to goad locals into a gunfight (pictured).

**Still Standing** (Sebastian Cluer; 2015) Canadian comedian Jonny Harris visits far-flung small towns.

## 🎧 LISTEN

**The Story from Here** (Gloria Macarenko; 2021) Weekly radio show that showcases human-interest stories from Canada, coast to coast.

**Daybreak Alberta** (Paul Karchut; 2022) Live radio show on weekends, featuring local interviews, great music and regional news.

**Fireside Canada** (David Williams; 2023) A storytelling and history podcast that takes a deep dive into Canadian legends, lies and lore.

**This Is Vancolour** (Mo Amir; 2021) A local podcast that discusses relevant cultural and political issues with the city's most colourful personalities.

ANTON BIELOUSOV/SHUTTERSTOCK ©

A member of the Squamish Nation

# INDIGENOUS TOURISM

Indigenous tourism offers the opportunity to connect with the original inhabitants of the land through immersive tours, shared stories, legends and songs. Each territory across the region is unique both in landscape and human history, and as a result, no Indigenous experience is the same.

## FIRST NATIONS, MÉTIS & INUIT

The Indigenous peoples of BC and the Canadian Rockies are primarily of First Nations, Métis and Inuit descent. There are more than 200 distinct First Nations in BC alone, all with their own history, language and traditions. It's important to select tours and experiences that are Indigenous-owned and -operated so that your tourism dollars go back into the communities that take time to share their culture with visitors. Visit **indigenoustourism. ca** for a complete list of Indigenous-owned and -controlled tourism businesses found throughout the country.

## CULTURAL CENTERS

Cultural centers showcase arts, history and heritage through live events, hands-on workshops and temporary exhibits as well as by displaying artifacts. Throughout the country, cultural centers shine a spotlight on both the past and present-day Indigenous cultures. The **Squamish Lil'wat Cultural Centre** (p115) in Whistler, BC, is the only one of its kind, where the joining of two nations is showcased through stunning displays, tasty cuisine and live demonstrations. The **Dänojà Zho Cultural Centre** (p200) sits on the traditional territory of the Tr'ondëk Hwëch'in and shares the history and culture of the first people of the Klondike.

# UNDERSTANDING LAND ACKNOWLEDGEMENTS

The country we now know as Canada sits on land that was originally inhabited by Indigenous Peoples. As a way of showing respect for the people and cultures who first called the land home, territory-specific land acknowledgements are often spoken at the beginning of public events throughout the country. BC consists of 95% unceded territory, meaning the land was never legally given up to the Crown through a treaty or other agreement, so this is included in land acknowledgements around the province. In Alberta, treaties 6, 7 and 8 cover most of the land we now know as Alberta, and Métis, First Nations and Inuit peoples are respectfully acknowledged.

## CUISINE

To taste authentic Indigenous cuisine, head to **Salmon n' Bannock** (p78) in Vancouver, found both in the Vancouver International Airport (YVR) and as a standalone restaurant – the only Indigenous-owned Indigenous restaurant in the city. **Nk'Mip Cellars** (p130) is the first Indigenous-owned and -operated winery, and the vineyard's on-site restaurant, the Bear, the Fish, the Root & the Berry, celebrates the Indigenous roots of the Okanagan through delicious cuisine.

## ACCOMMODATIONS

Extend your Indigenous experience with an overnight stay at one of the country's many immersive accommodations. **Big Bar Guest Ranch** (p128) is an Indigenous-owned experience that combines Western culture with traditional knowledge, comfortable cabins and great food. In Haida Gwaii, check out **Heillen Village Longhouses** (p145), where you can enjoy an off-grid, overnight outdoor adventure, and **Haida House** (p145), which offers oceanside cabins with hot tubs, Haida cuisine and guided adventures.

### BEST INDIGENOUS TOURS

**Talaysay Tours** (p63) Take an engaging Talking Totems tour through Stanley Park and learn about Salish and Northwest Coast Indigenous art.

**Squamish Lil'wat Cultural Centre** (p115) Visit this center where two nations are celebrated through exhibits, food and live demonstrations.

**Copper Sun Journeys** (p119) Take a Petroglyph Tour through the sacred valley of Bella Coola and learn about the ancient history of the area from a Nuxalk guide.

**Haida Style Expeditions** (p143) Join a fishing expedition, cultural tour or wildlife-viewing excursion with this Haida-owned operation located in Haida Gwaii.

**Métis Crossing** (p179) Experience Indigenous culture at the first major Métis cultural center in Alberta, where you can take guided tours and see sacred white bisons.

**Carcross** (p190) Visit this town where you can take a self-guided tour and then tackle the world-class mountain-biking trail, conceived and maintained by the Tagish First Nation.

**Head-Smashed-In Buffalo Jump** (p169) Take a guided tour of this Unesco World Heritage Site, recognized as one of the world's oldest and best-preserved buffalo jumps.

**Dänojà Zho Cultural Centre** (p200) Learn about the Tr'ondëk Hwëch'in First Nation, whose peoples and culture predate the Klondike Gold Rush by thousands of years via this Dawson City center.

Statue, Osoyoos

ANDREA C. MILLER/SHUTTERSTOCK ©

**Southern bald eagle**

# WILDLIFE

The unique and diverse landscapes found throughout the three provinces that make up this widespread region make for an infinite number of wandering wildlife species. From deep-water marine life to massive roaming land mammals, to beautiful birds of all sizes, this is the place to see wildlife come alive in its natural habitat.

### BRAWNY BEARS

In the forests and mountains of the pacific northwest, including Whistler and Vancouver Island and up into parts of the Canadian Rockies, such as Banff National Park, a bounty of black bears can be found. For grizzly-gazing, more than half of Canada's grizzly bears reside in British Columbia, found primarily around Lillooet and the South Chilcotin Ranges, with the remainder residing in high-elevation alpine regions in Alberta, especially in Banff and Jasper. There's also the elusive white kermode bear ('Spirit bear'), found exclusively in BC's Great Bear Rainforest.

### UNIQUE UNGULATES

Canada is home to 11 species of ungulates, or hooved mammals, some found nowhere else in the world. The Yukon is the place to spot almost all of them, including Dall Sheep, a unique breed of ungulate found only in this region. Head to Kluane National Park and Reserve to spot mountain goats, caribou and North America's largest subspecies of moose. Waterton Lakes National Park in Alberta also has a plethora of the quadrupeds, including yellowtail deer and moose, and you can spot bighorn sheep and elk in Banff's Bow Valley Parkway. Deer, elk and moose can also be spotted throughout BC, especially in the Kootenay and Cariboo regions.

## BE BEAR AWARE

Whether you're hiking alone, or participating in a guided wildlife-viewing tour, it's important to know what to do if you encounter a bear. Many of the region's parks and protected areas provide unparalleled

bear-viewing opportunities, but as a wild species, bears can be potentially dangerous to humans. If you spot a bear in the wild, maintain an appropriate distance, minimize enticing scents, and if possible, carry

bear spray when wandering in the woods without a guide. If you see a bear up close, remain calm and do not run away. For more wildlife safety tips, visit wildsafebc.com.

## BEST WILDLIFE EXPERIENCES

### Watch Roaming Hooved Mammals

At the **Yukon Wildlife Preserve** (p191), found just outside of Whitehorse, over a dozen native ungulates inhabit huge natural enclosures, spread across 700 acres of land. This is Yukon's only wildlife rehabilitation facility, providing a safe and ethical space for animals such as elk, moose and deer to roam free and a great spot to view them from a safe distance.

### Get Up Close with Bald Eagles

Situated on 8 acres of land on Vancouver Island, **North Island Wildlife Recovery Centre** (p97 focuses on caring for injured animals, and housing those that are no longer fit to return to the wild. See the largest eagle flight enclosure of its kind in Canada, and get up close with black bear cubs, owls, hawks, turtles and even a rare white raven. If you time your visit just right, you can witness an Indigenous-led eagle release ceremony.

### Look at Lumbering Grizzlies

Located in the north coast region of BC, **Khutzeymateen Grizzly Sanctuary** (p121) is a boat-access-only area and is the first in Canada to be protected specifically for grizzly bears and their habitat. Tours must be with a permitted guide here, where you can observe grizzly bears as they roam through nature, and spot bald eagles, seals and other wildlife along the way.

## AQUATIC & AERIAL ANIMALS

Orcas, humpback whales, gray whales, harbor seals, steller sea lions, harbor porpoises and many other aquatic animals can be spotted in the waters off the coast of Vancouver and Vancouver Island, with Tofino and Telegraph Cove noted as the top spots to see orcas and other marine mammals. And for birdwatching, over 500 species of birds have been spotted in BC alone, with the Vancouver area known as the Pacific Flyway, due to the high volume of migratory birds that cross through. As a result, BC is home to some of the best birdwatching spots in North America. Bald eagles, herons, hummingbirds and swallows can be spotted in the sky. Check bcbirdtrail.ca for a self-guided birdwatching route through BC.

Orca

37

HOBSTER/SHUTTERSTOCK ©

**Street dancers, Vancouver**

# THE ARTS

As a country filled with natural beauty, it's no surprise that paintings of landscapes and locales around Canada are a popular art form here. From Indigenous artists sharing tales and traditions through totem poles and paintings to emerging artists painting murals around the city, Canada has a thriving arts scene that is showcased around the country.

## GALLERIES & MUSEUMS

Housed in a heritage building in the center of downtown, the **Vancouver Art Gallery** (p57) is the largest public art museum in Western Canada and an innovative arts institution lauded for its collection of groundbreaking contemporary works from global artists. Also found in downtown Vancouver, the **Bill Reid Gallery of Northwest Coast Art** (p57) is the only art gallery in Canada dedicated to Indigenous Northwest Coast art. It honors both the works of Bill Reid, one of Canada's most distinguished sculptors, and exhibits the works of contemporary Indigenous artists. The building that houses the **Art Gallery of Alberta**

(p179) is a work of art on its own. Inside, over 6000 works of art can be found, including a wide collection of Canadian abstract paintings and sculptures.

## ART WALKS

See the city through an artistic lens with a walk through the **Vancouver Mural Festival** (p74), where outdoor murals and public art displays, created by local and international artists, add color and culture to 11 neighborhoods throughout the city. A dirt street in Dawson City called **Writer's Row** (p198) showcases the old cabins that once housed three well-known resident writers: Jack London, Robert Ser-

## PACIFIC NORTHWEST COAST ART

Two of the most prominent Canadian artists to date, Bill Reid and Emily Carr, who both called BC home, put Pacific Northwest Coast art in the spotlight. Reid (1920–98) is lauded for bringing attention to both Haida art and Pacific Northwest Coast art through his renowned sculptures and paintings, and was a proponent for Indigenous rights in Canada. Carr (1871–1945), who was one of the few female artists of her period, was a 20th-century painter and writer whose works were heavily inspired by the Indigenous culture and communities found in the region in which she lived.

vice and Pierre Berton. Head to Calgary's **St Patrick's Island** (p174) in the East Village district and peruse Art in the Public Realm, a series of permanent public art installations, including computerized pop-art displays, sculptures and murals.

### MUSIC & THEATER

The **Edmonton International Fringe Festival** (p179) is the oldest and largest fringe theater festival in North America, and is a must for theater lovers. And the **Francis Winspear Centre for Music** (p179) is home to the Edmonton Symphony Orchestra, and hosts other concerts and events throughout the year. At the **Studio Bell – National Music Centre** (p172) in Calgary, you can explore Canadian music history and get hands-on with instruments in a contemporary space. In Vancouver, catch a play or performance at the **Stanley Theatre** (p76) the flagship stage for the Arts Club Theatre Company – the largest in Western Canada.

MMCINNEY PHOTOGRAPHY/SHUTTERSTOCK ©

Studio Bell, Calgary

### BEST PLACES TO SHOP FOR ART

**Vancouver's Granville Island** (p64) is a hub for arts and crafts, and where quirky carvings, framed photography, unique paintings and handcrafted keepsakes can be picked up. Watch artists in action, talk to them about their craft and then shop their galleries and stalls. This is also a great place to shop for arts supplies, with some of the city's best craft stores found here.

**BC's Sunshine Coast** (p117) is home to one of the largest populations of artists per capita in Canada, with a thriving arts community. Tours will take you to the homes and studios of local artists, where you can watch them work, take a try at their art form, and shop their art displays to take home. In Gibsons and Sechelt, artisan shops line the streets.

Calgary's **East Village** (p174) is a hip downtown spot with Indie music venues and galleries. This area is home to Central Library, where you can shop at the Library Store for great gifts for book lovers, writers and artists; and at Studio Bell, which has a shop filled with music-inspired gifts, art and jewelry.

**Edmonton's Old Strathcona** (p175) is a historic district filled with arts and entertainment facilities, and is a local shopping hub.

SEN YANG/SHUTTERSTOCK ©

**Steak dish, Vancouver**

# THE FOOD SCENE

International influences fuel the food scene here, but there are
Canadian-born bevvies and bites that have made a mark too.

Italy has pizza and pasta, and Mexico has tacos and tamales. Unlike other countries in the world, people are often stumped when it comes to naming iconic dishes that hail from Canada. And with so much land made of such diverse landscapes, it's not surprising that the foods found within this expansive country are diverse as well.

The far-reaching farmlands found in Alberta boast some of the best beef and bison in the world, thanks to the region's location and drier climate. The coastal waters found along the shores of BC spawn notable seafood, and the boreal forests and mountain ranges of the northern Rockies bring regional berries, mushrooms and herbs to the table.

These locally grown ingredients combined with international influences found through-

out the country make up Canada's unique and thriving culinary scene, where comfort foods like fries doused in cheese curds and gravy, sweet treats made of maple syrup, and freshly smoked salmon are just some of the tasty gems created and consumed here.

## Coastal Cuisine

Seafood is the star on the West Coast of BC, with five main species of wild salmon (pink, chinook, chum, sockeye and coho), as well as albacore tuna, Dungeness crab, Pacific halibut and spot prawns topping the list of fresh catches found in the coastal waters. As a result, you'll see seafood dishes scattered across most of the menus at restaurants found in and around Vancouver and Vancouver Island. From food stands offer-

| Best Canadian Dishes | SALMON & BANNOCK | TOURTIERE | HAWAIIAN PIZZA | MONTREAL-STYLE SMOKED MEAT SANDWICHES |
|---|---|---|---|---|
| | Traditional Indigenous meal. Wild salmon and pan-fried bread. | A savory French Canadian meat pie filled with pork and potatoes. | Yes, it's Canadian. Topped with pineapple and ham or bacon. | Beef brisket, best on Montreal bagel. |

ing fish-and-chips around city harbors to high-end sushi joints frequented by celebrities and top chefs, fish-forward eats are a must on the coast.

## Meaty Mains

Beef and bison are best in Alberta. High-quality beef is Alberta's primary culinary claim to fame, due largely to the cattle being farmed on the fertile grasslands and valleys found in the area, and the thriving community of cattle farmers and ranchers. Beef here is primarily grass-fed and grain-finished (as opposed to the common practice of corn-fed cattle found elsewhere). Half of Canada's beef supply comes from this region, and Alberta has a number of wagyu producers – a breed of cattle known to rival Kobe beef.

Bison is an Indigenous food staple in this province, and while it's been consumed for thousands of years by the original inhabitants of Alberta, it's become a popular modern-day menu item, with bison tenderloin, burgers and short ribs taking the culinary spotlight.

## Plant-Based Fare

Thanks to the abundance of farms found throughout the region, there's no shortage of vegetarian and vegan food offerings in BC and the Canadian Rockies. Many restaurants offer plant-based menu options, and vegan and vegetarian restaurants continue to pop up in major cities like Vancouver and Calgary, where some of the top restaurants offer meat-free menus with everything from casual comfort foods to high-end dishes. There's definitely more than just salads for those who prefer to consume a plant-based diet.

NALIDSA/SHUTTERSTOCK ©

### FOOD & WINE EVENTS

**Richmond Night Market** (p80; richmondnightmarket.com; summer) Summer night market held in Richmond, BC, where the best Asian and global cuisines take center stage. The largest market of its kind in North America.

**Victoria International Wine Festival** (vicwf.com; September) A weeklong event, this festival hosted in Vancouver Island's capital city explores the world of wine with dinners, tastings and seminars.

**Edmonton Heritage Festival** (p179; heritagefest.ca; August) The world's largest three-day multicultural festival, celebrating global cuisine, art and entertainment.

**Okanagan Wine Festivals** (p135; thewinefestivals.com; June & October) Held twice yearly, these festivals showcase the best wines of the Okanagan Valley and beyond. Sample wine from Nk'Mip, North America's first Indigenous-owned winery.

Festival of the Grape, Oliver,

BOCHKAREV PHOTOGRAPHY/SHUTTERSTOCK ©

Crab legs

| GINGER BEEF | ALBERTA WAGYU BEEF | BC SPOT PRAWNS | FIDDLEHEADS | POUTINE |
|---|---|---|---|---|
| Canadian-Chinese dish made of beef, ginger and a sweet sauce. | Highly marbled top-quality beef for maximum taste and tenderness. | Peeled and sautéed or seared in garlic butter and herbs. | Furled fronds of fern boiled or steamed and served as a vegetable side dish. | Quebecois classic comprised of French fries topped with gravy and cheese curds. |

## Local Specialities

### Street Foods & Snacks

**Bannock** This Indigenous fry bread is made using various types of flour and using different cooking methods.

**Ketchup chips** These tangy ketchup flavored potato chips are a staple snack, commonly consumed by Canadians (and curious visitors).

**Poutine** This dish emerged in Quebec and is made of French fries topped with cheese curds and steaming hot gravy.

Poutine

### Sweet Treats

**Nanaimo bars** Hailing from the Vancouver Island city of the same name, these no-bake bars are made of three layers: a coconut crumb base, a custard center and a chocolate top.

**Beaver tails** Flat pieces of fried dough create a base shaped like the tail of a beaver. Dusted with sugar and cinnamon.

**Butter tarts** Small pastry shells filled with butter, sugar, syrup and egg, and crowned with a crispy top make up this Canadian-born dessert.

### Dinner & Drinks

**Alberta beef** An assortment of renowned, high-quality, grain-fed beef from the healthy cattle that graze the grasslands of Alberta's farms.

**Caesar cocktail** A classic Canadian cocktail made of vodka, clamato (combination of tomato and clam juice) and Worcestershire sauce, served in a salt-rimmed glass and garnished with celery.

**Wild salmon** Five species of salmon are caught on the West Coast: pink, sockeye, coho, chum and chinook.

### MEALS OF A LIFETIME

**Published on Main** (p73) Vancouver Michelin-star restaurant recognized for high-quality, creative fare and freshly foraged produce plucked from local farms.

**Gaucho Brazilian BBQ** (p42) Brazilian grilled meats make this churrascaria in Canmore, Alberta, a must-try.

**Tojo's** (p78) Dine on the chef-guided *omakase* at this upscale sushi spot in Vancouver, favored by celebrities and top chefs.

**Salmon n' Bannock** (p58) Vancouver's only Indigenous-owned restaurant takes the dining experience beyond the plate.

**Major Tom** (p174) Rooftop restaurant (40th floor) with sweeping views of Calgary, serving contemporary dishes and classic steakhouse fare.

**Richmond Dumpling Trail** (p81) A self-guided tasting tour through the best Asian food spots found in Richmond.

## THE YEAR IN FOOD

### SPRING

April brings the bloom of fiddleheads, which sprout from ostrich ferns in spring. Spot prawn season is big from May to June, kicking off with a festival focused on the sweet shellfish, held mid-May.

### SUMMER

August to September is the start of migration season for wild salmon, and BC's fresh berries peak during the summer months, with locally grown blueberries, cherries and raspberries ripened to perfection.

### AUTUMN

Harvest season is short in Alberta, with seasonal produce popping up at the end of summer. Pumpkins, carrots and brussels sprouts peak during the early fall months, between September and November.

### WINTER

Local grains and nuts, and some root vegetables, are available during the winter months. This is a great season for Alberta beef and freshly plucked potatoes, or warm up with a hearty bison stew.

43

Canadian caesar

MUMEMORIES/SHUTTERSTOCK ©

Camping, Peyto Lake (p221)

# THE OUTDOORS

Dive into the delightfully diverse landscapes found around this region, where there's so much to see and do, you'll never want to go indoors.

Whether you're looking for a calm, quiet stroll through the woods, or an action-packed, alpine adventure among mountain peaks, this region has something for everyone, with many outdoor activities available year-round. From slopeside skiing and glacier hikes during the cooler months to coastal kayaking and backcountry hiking when the weather warms up, there's no shortage of outdoor offerings to be explored here. And it's not just for the adults, you can bring the kids too.

## Hiking

For fresh air and soul-stirring scenery, look no further than BC and the Canadian Rockies, where an endless expanse of tree-lined trails await. You'll find hiking trails of all lengths and levels here, where you can take a taxing multi-day trek through some of the region's most challenging terrain, skip town for a short and scenic family-friendly hike, or tantalize all five senses with a tranquil forest bathing excursion through old-growth forests.

Try to avoid hitting the trails in July and August when you'll find larger crowds and hotter temps. Instead, aim for May to June, or September to October when the foot traffic is lighter but the weather remains mild.

**Adrenaline Sports**

**BEAR VIEWING**
Take a river float with **Great Bear Adventures** (p121) and watch as grizzlies and black bears snatch salmon from the water.

**GLACIER HIKING**
Clip on your crampons for a challenging glacier hike at **Columbia Icefield** (p223) at Jasper National Park.

**KAYAKING**
Watch for wildlife along Telegraph Cove on an excursion with **North Island Kayak Tours** (p106).

## FAMILY ADVENTURES

**Venture out on a family-friendly hike** found near Canmore that takes you to the beautiful **Grassi Lakes** (p152).

**Wobble** your way around **WildPlay Nanaimo** (p92) on Vancouver Island, where adventure courses, bungee jumping and a primal swing await.

**Float along** on a gentle two-hour rafting adventure best enjoyed by tube, paddleboard, kayak or canoe on the **River of Golden Dreams** (p117) in Whistler.

**Cycle the seawall** at Vancouver's **Stanley Park** (p62), a flat bike ride that takes you past water parks, an outdoor pool and restaurants.

**Descend** the **Malahat Skywalk** (p92) on a tube slide after strolling to the top of this scenic spiral tower.

**Walk through Stanley Park** on an Indigenous-led Talking Trees tour with Talaysay Tours (p63).

## Mountain Biking

Mountain biking is a massively popular sport in BC and the Canadian Rockies, where a vast network of varied trails can be found across the region. BC's breathtaking trails bring cyclists to the West Kootenays region, Vancouver's North Shore and Cumberland on Vancouver Island.

Mountain bikers from around the world flock to Whistler, home to one of the best mountain-bike parks on Earth, where 70 marked, lift-serviced trails wind through unparalleled terrain, with gnarly, gravity-defying vertical drops and speedy berms. This is also home to mountain biking's biggest festival.

In Alberta, the High Rockies Trail in Kananaskis offers epic rides with Rockies views, and the Minnewanka Trail in Banff National Park is Alberta's most popular cross-country mountain-biking trail.

## Skiing & Snowboarding

When it comes to snow sports, there are endless options in this region. If you're staying in Vancouver, you can hit the slopes of one of three local mountains in just 30 minutes, and Whistler-Blackcomb, North America's largest and best-equipped ski resort, is only 90 minutes by car from downtown. In BC's Kootenay Rockies region, you can cruise the 'Powder Highway,' passing eight amazing alpine ski resorts. And on Vancouver Island, you'll find the less-crowded Mt Washington. Banff National Park has three ski resorts to choose from, and Marmot Basin has the highest elevation of any Canadian ski resort.

**MOUNTAIN BIKING**
For mountain biking see p118 and p152

RAMON CLIFF/SHUTTERSTOCK ©

Bike trail, Kananaskis (p152)

**SURFING**
Hit the ocean swells in **Tofino** (p100) on Vancouver Island for thrilling cold-water surfing.

**WHITEWATER RAFTING**
For adrenaline-pumping river rafting, head to **Kananaskis** (p152), thought to be one of the best spots in the province.

**CLIMBING**
Scale Mt Logan located in **Kluane National Park** (p194), Canada's highest mountain and the second-highest in North America.

**SPELUNKING**
Rappel into the underground depths of **Horne Lake Caves** (p97) on Vancouver Island, recognized as the best spelunking in Canada.

# ACTION AREAS

Where to find British Columbia & the Canadian Rockies' best outdoor activities.

## National Parks

1. Pacific Rim National Park (p102)
2. Yoho National Park (p137)
3. Banff National Park (p210)
4. Jasper National Park (p224)
5. Waterton Lakes National Park (p160)
6. Kluane National Park (p195)

## Cycling

1. Stanley Park (p62)
2. Whistler Mountain Bike Park (p118)
3. Kettle Valley Rail Trail (p130)
4. Canmore Nordic Centre Provincial Park (p154)
5. Grey Mountain (p188)
6. Ridge Road Heritage Trail (p199)

## Walking/Hiking

1. Sooke Potholes Provincial Park (p88)
2. West Coast Trail (p194)
3. Tweedsmuir Park Lodge (p119)
4. Kananaskis (p152)
5. Crypt Lake Trail (p158)
6. Horseshoe Canyon (p165)
7. Bow River Pathway (p173)

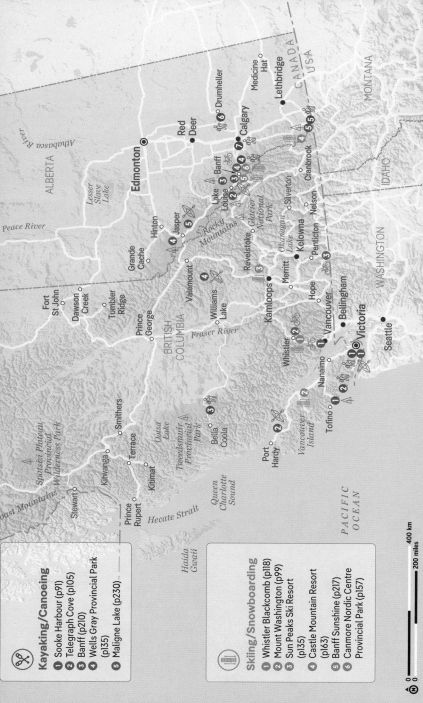

ALBERTA

Athabasca River

Peace River

Lesser Slave Lake

Edmonton

Red Deer

Hinton

Jasper

Grande Cache

Fort St John

Dawson Creek

Tumbler Ridge

Prince George

BRITISH COLUMBIA

Fraser River

Williams Lake

Valemount

Rocky Mountains

Revelstoke

Glacier National Park

Kamloops

Merritt

Hope

Okanagan Lake

Kelowna

Penticton

Silverton

Nelson

Cranbrook

Drumheller

Medicine Hat

Lethbridge

Calgary

Banff

Lake Louise

CANADA

USA

MONTANA

IDAHO

WASHINGTON

Whistler

Vancouver

Bellingham

Victoria

Nanaimo

Seattle

Tofino

Port Hardy

Vancouver Island

Smithers

Terrace

Kitwanga

Kitimat

Prince Rupert

Stewart

Spatsizi Plateau Provincial Wilderness Park

Ootsa Lake

Tweedsmuir Provincial Park

Bella Coola

Coast Mountains

Hecate Strait

Queen Charlotte Sound

Haida Gwaii

PACIFIC OCEAN

## Kayaking/Canoeing

1. Sooke Harbour (p91)
2. Telegraph Cove (p105)
3. Banff (p210)
4. Wells Gray Provincial Park (p135)
5. Maligne Lake (p230)

## Skiing/Snowboarding

1. Whistler Blackcomb (p118)
2. Mount Washington (p99)
3. Sun Peaks Ski Resort (p135)
4. Castle Mountain Resort (p163)
5. Banff Sunshine (p217)
6. Canmore Nordic Centre Provincial Park (p157)

0   200 miles
0   400 km

47

# THE GUIDE

Yukon
Territory
p180

Alberta
p146

British
Columbia
p108

Banff & Jasper
National Parks
p206

Vancouver
Island
p82

Vancouver
p50

Chapters in this section are organised by hubs
and their surrounding areas. We see the hub as
your base in the destination, where you'll find
unique experiences, local insights, insider tips
and expert recommendations. It's also your
gateway to the surrounding area, where you'll
see what and how much you can do from there.

**Vancouver Island (p83)**

TOMAS KULAJA/SHUTTERSTOCK ©

# Vancouver

## GREEN CITY BY THE SEA

Stunning seascapes, majestic mountains and towering trees frame this coastal city, where you can cycle, shop, ski and swim all in one day.

Like a layered landscape painting, the stunning skyline of Vancouver showcases a colorful foreground of sea and city, against a background of sierra and sky. The natural beauty is what draws people in, and the mild climate and friendly people are what make it hard to leave.

It's the combination of all of these qualities that lures long-term lodgers to the city, which is known as one of the world's most liveable. And beyond its layered beauty is a layered cultural landscape that greatly contributes to how Vancouver has evolved, and to what the city has become today.

Located on the traditional, ancestral and unceded territory of the Coast Salish peoples of the Sḵwx̱wú7mesh (Squamish), x<sup>w</sup>məθkʷəy̓əm (Musqueam) and səl̓ilwətaʔɬ (Tsleil-Waututh) Nations, the city that is now known as Vancouver has a history that long predates 1886, when Vancouver is said to have been founded. First Nations have occupied the land since time immemorial, and Vancouver (originally called K'emk'emeláy, which means 'a place of many maple trees') was once a thriving village site before the land was taken from its original inhabitants, and turned into a city.

From the significant Indigenous sites found around scenic Stanley Park to the modern museums and galleries that showcase the stories and works of Indigenous artists, the rich history of Vancouver shines through the stories and experiences shared by those who first called the land home.

Chinese-Canadian roots run deep here too, with a history that dates back to 1788 during the fur-trade settlements. The city is Canada's major Pacific port, and after WWII, it became the country's main hub for trade from Asia and the Pacific Rim, eventually attracting the largest population of Asian immigrants in North America.

Vancouver's natural surroundings and diverse cultural offerings put the city on the world stage in 2010 when it played host to the Olympic and Paralympic Winter Games, driving a huge boost in international tourism. Since then, Vancouver has been recognized as a top tourism destination and one of the most beautiful cities in the world.

ORGANIC DESIGN/SHUTTERSTOCK ©

## THE MAIN AREAS

| | | | |
|---|---|---|---|
| **DOWNTOWN & CHINATOWN** | **GRANVILLLE ISLAND & YALETOWN** | **MAIN STREET** | **FAIRVIEW & SOUTH GRANVILLE** |
| Gardens, galleries and green spaces. **p56** | Famed isle of the arts. **p64** | Vintage shopping and striking street art. **p70** | Stylish boutiques and casual cafes. **p75** |

**Above: Coal Harbour, Vancouver; left: Dr Sun-Yat Classical Chinese Gardens (p57)**

# Find Your Way

Vancouver's core is compact, so attractions are easily accessible. It's a walkable city with paved pathways linking to most activities, and if you venture further afield, you can get anywhere by bike, bus or boat.

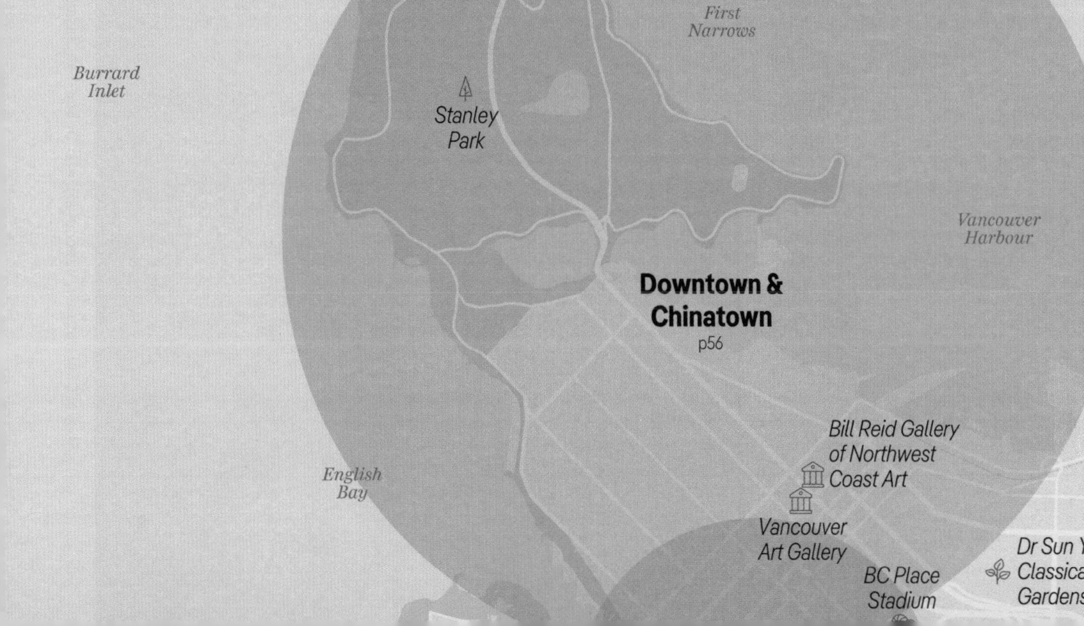

## BOAT

Vancouver's waterways make for easy transport between neighborhoods like Yaletown and Granville Island, which are just across the water from each other and are accessible by Aquabus – a rainbow-colored mini ferry (you can even bring a bike!).

*Burrard Inlet*

*First Narrows*

*Vancouver Harbour*

Stanley Park

*English Bay*

**Downtown & Chinatown**
p56

Bill Reid Gallery of Northwest Coast Art

Vancouver Art Gallery

BC Place Stadium

Dr Sun Yat-Sen Classical Chinese Gardens

1 mile
2 km

*Granville Island Public Market*

**Granville Island & Yaletown**
p64

*Engine 3/4 Pavilion*

*Olympic Village*

*Creekside Park*

*Science World*

**Main Street**
p70

*Kids Market*

*Stanley Theatre*

**Fairview & South Granville**
p75

*Bloedel Conservatory*

*VanDusen Botanical Gardens*

 *Richmond Night Market (6km)*

## FROM THE AIRPORT

Vancouver International Airport (YVR) is rated one of the best airports in North America and is the primary way to arrive from an international destination. Taxis, shuttles, ride-share services or public transportation takes you into the city in about 30 to 45 minutes.

## BIKE

Vancouver's mild climate makes it easy to access attractions by bike, with rental shops on most streets, dedicated bike lanes and trails weaving throughout the city. Mobi, a public bike-share system, offers an affordable way to get around.

## BUS

The public-transportation system in Vancouver is a safe and easy way to get around the city, with regular bus and SkyTrain services to get you anywhere you want to go.

53

# Plan Your Days

Not sure if you want to play outside, or peruse the city's museums and shops? With some planning, you can do it all in one day.

Stanley Park seawall (p63)

ALENA CHARYKOVA/SHUTTERSTOCK ©

## Day 1

### Morning
● Start with a morning stroll or cycle along the **Stanley Park seawall** (p63). Keep an eye out for Siwash Rock, and the Girl in a Wetsuit statue – seawall landmarks that you'll spot along the way.

### Afternoon
● Visit the **Vancouver Aquarium** (p60), a must-visit site in the center of Stanley Park, and then head to **Totem Park** (p62) for an Indigenous-led Talking Trees tour with **Talaysay Tours** (p63).

### Evening
● Finish your day with a visit to **Canada Place** (p60), where you can take a virtual flight with **FlyOver Canada** (p61), and then dine at one of the waterfront restaurants found nearby.

## You'll Also Want To...

Venture beyond Vancouver's city center for a pint, a hike, or just to smell the flowers and enjoy the views.

**CELEBRATE SCIENCE**

Get hands-on with engaging exhibits at the family-friendly **Science World** (p72), housed in the city's famous dome.

**GRAB A PINT**

Check out the craft-beer scene with a visit to **Brewery Creek** (p73), Vancouver's urban brewery district.

**SEE A SHOW**

For thespian pursuits, head to the **Stanley Theatre** (p76), Vancouver's famed art-deco heritage theater.

## Day 2

### Morning
● Begin with a browse through the **Vancouver Art Gallery** (57, and then head to the **Bill Reid Gallery of Northwest Coast Art** (p57), found just down the street.

### Afternoon
● Make your way to the **Chinatown Storytelling Centre** (p61) to learn about Vancouver's Chinese-Canadian roots. Then visit the **Dr Sun Yat-Sen Classical Chinese Gardens** (p57) for a tranquil walk and a complimentary cup of Chinese tea. Hungry for lunch? Pop into **Torafuku** (p61) for a 'Kickass Rice Bowl.'

### Evening
● Gallivant through **Granville Island** (p64), a foodie's paradise. Then pick a patio, such as **Tap & Barrel Bridges** (p67), and settle in for dinner with sunset views.

## Day 3

### Morning
● Grab a coffee and meander along **Main Street** (p70), spotting massive murals along the way as part of the **Vancouver Mural Festival** (p74).

### Afternoon
● Head to the **Brewery Creek** district (p73) and pop into Main Street Brewing for po'boys and pints, and then check out the vintage boutiques along the Main Street corridor, such as **Mintage Mall** (p72) and **Turnabout Luxury Resale** (p72).

### Evening
● Catch a SkyTrain to Richmond for an evening at the **Richmond Night Market** (p80), where you should choose from over 600 food dishes from around the world and take in a show before heading back downtown.

**CATCH A GAME**
Football fans flock to **BC Place** (p66), or hit **Nat Bailey Stadium** (p79) for a summer ball game.

**ENTERTAIN THE KIDS**
Granville Island's **Kids Market** (p66) is a wonderland for kids, with shops, snack spots, arcades and play spaces.

**SMELL THE FLOWERS**
The **VanDusen Botanical Gardens** (p76) are a garden lover's paradise, and the **Bloedel Conservatory** (p76) is a must-see.

**HIT THE WATER**
Hop on the **Aquabus** (p69), a mini pedestrian ferry, for scenic city views from a new perspective.

# Downtown & Chinatown

## GARDENS, GALLERIES AND GREEN SPACES

Vancouver's downtown core is an ocean-fringed peninsula easily divided into three parts: the grid-patterned city-center with shops, restaurants and glass towers fanning out from the intersection of Granville and West Georgia Sts; the well-maintained 1950s apartment blocks and residential side streets of the West End (home to Vancouver's gay district); and Stanley Park, Canada's finest urban green space and home to some of the city's best attractions

As the city's oldest downtown neighborhood, Gastown combines cobblestone streets and heritage buildings with modern galleries and trendy bars. The historic 12-block stretch is a hub for shopping and entertainment – best enjoyed on foot. Almost as old, neighboring Chinatown is one of Canada's largest, a vibrant community dotted with dim sum restaurants, traditional bakeries and food shops, and hip cocktail spots.

## TOP TIP

It's easy to go car-free here, as most parks, beaches, galleries and shops can be found within walking distance of Vancouver's downtown core. Don't feel like going by foot? Try Mobi, the city's public bike-share system. Buses also stop frequently throughout the area.

RUSS HEINL/SHUTTERSTOCK ©

**Stanley Park, Coal Harbor and Vancouver**

# Vancouver Art Gallery

### Urban visual-arts institution

Step into Western Canada's largest public art museum, where blockbuster international shows are combined with selections from its striking contemporary collection. The Vancouver Art Gallery (or VAG to locals) is a magnet for art fans. There are often three or four different exhibitions on its public levels, but save time for the top-floor Emily Carr paintings, showcasing swirling nature-themed works from BC's favorite historic artist. If you're on a budget, consider the by-donation entry after 5pm on Tuesdays, but arrive early and expect a line.

**Bill Reid Gallery of Northwest Coast Art**

**Vancouver Art Gallery**

## Bill Reid Gallery of Northwest Coast Art

### Contemporary Indigenous art by hailed Haida artist

Opened in 2008, the Bill Reid Gallery of Northwest Coast Art is Canada's only public art gallery dedicated to the contemporary Indigenous art of the Northwest Coast. Hailed Haida artist Bill Reid (1920–98) was known for building bridges between Indigenous and settler people through his work as an artist, broadcaster and community activist. The gallery was named in his honor and showcases some of his artwork, as well as contemporary works by other Indigenous artists. Look for the full-scale totem pole carved by James Hart of Haida Gwaii, and a bronze masterpiece called *Mythic Messengers*, created by Reid himself.

## Dr Sun Yat-Sen Classical Chinese Gardens

### Tranquil Chinese garden in the city

Opened in time for Vancouver's Expo '86, this delightful oasis was the first Chinese "scholars' garden" to be built outside Asia, and is one of the city's most-beloved ornamental green spaces. Wrapped with tile-topped walls and centered on a mirror-calm pond fringed by twisting trees, its covered walkways offer a tranquil respite from clamorous Chinatown.

The intimate 'garden of ease' reflects Taoist principles of balance and harmony. Entry includes an optional 45-minute guided tour, in which you'll learn about the symbolism behind the placement of the gnarled pine trees, winding covered pathways and ancient limestone formations. Look out for the colorful carp and lazy turtles in the water, and conclude your visit with a complimentary cup of traditional tea.

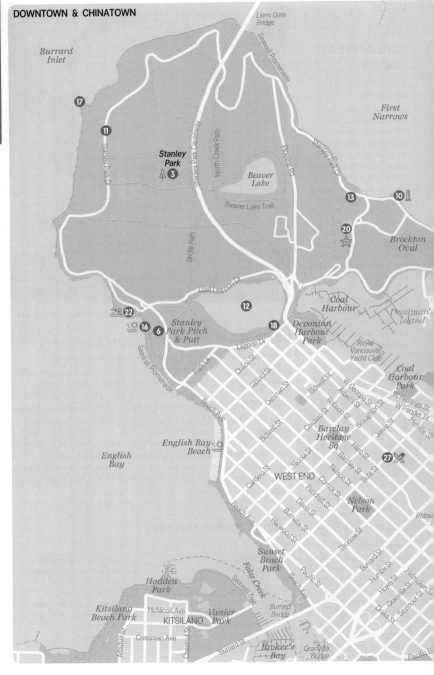

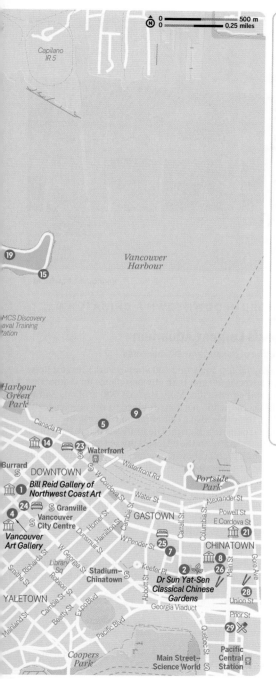

**HIGHLIGHTS**
1. Bill Reid Gallery of Northwest Coast Art
2. Dr Sun Yat-Sen Classical Chinese Gardens
3. Stanley Park
4. Vancouver Art Gallery

**SIGHTS**
5. Canada Place
6. Ceperley Meadows
7. Chinatown Millennium Gate
8. Chinatown Storytelling Centre
9. FlyOver Canada
10. Girl in a Wetsuit
11. Hollow Tree
12. Lost Lagoon
13. Lumberman's Arch
14. Marine Building
15. Nine O'Clock Gun
16. Second Beach
17. Siwash Rock
18. Stanley Park Nature House
19. Totem Poles
20. Vancouver Aquarium
21. Vancouver Police Museum & Archives

**ACTIVITIES, COURSES & TOURS**
22. Second Beach Pool

**SLEEPING**
23. Fairmont Waterfront
24. Rosewood Hotel Georgia
25. Skwachàys Lodge

**EATING**
26. Bao Bei
27. Breka Bakery & Cafe
28. Phnom Penh
29. Torafuku

## ART-DECO ARCHITECTURE

Vancouver's most exquisitely ornate tower block, and also its best art-deco building, the elegant 22-story Marine Building is a tribute to the city's maritime past. Opened in 1930, the building was once recognized as the tallest building in the British Empire. Now, its towering terra-cotta exterior is shaded by newer skyscrapers that dominate the skyline. Check out its elaborate shell of seahorses, lobsters and streamlined steamships, then nip into the lobby, which is like a walk-through artwork. Stained-glass panels and a polished floor inlaid with signs of the zodiac await, as does a working antique telephone (bring your coins).

**Vancouver Aquarium**

MORE IN DOWNTOWN & CHINATOWN

## Canada's Largest Aquarium
### A collection of coastal aquatic creatures

As Canada's largest aquarium and Stanley Park's biggest draw, the Vancouver Aquarium is an obvious choice for connecting with coastal aquatic life. More than 65,000 animals can be found here, and while it's a great place to get up-close with ocean life, the site is also a center for marine research, ocean literacy and climate activism. The fluffy sea otters have unofficial celebrity status in the city, and the sea lions (one weighing in at 860kg) are a show-stopping sight. Other highlights include the 4D Experience, a multi-sensory film that allows you to see, smell and feel the special effects; the Wet Lab, an educational space where kids learn about live invertebrates; and Clownfish Cove, an interactive play space.

## Fun Under Five Sails
### An iconic waterfront landmark

The area's original convention-center building, sail-shaped Canada Place, is a top sight. Stroll its pier-like outer prome-

 **BEST PLACES TO STAY**

**Skwachàys Lodge**
Canada's first Indigenous arts hotel with an on-site art gallery and immersive Indigenous experiences. **$$**

**Rosewood Hotel Georgia**
Historic hotel in the heart of downtown, where a roaring 20s vibe matches a more modern feel. **$$$**

**Fairmont Waterfront**
Adjacent to Canada Place with amazing waterfront views and a rooftop garden and apiary. **$$$**

nade and watch the floatplanes taking off from and landing on the water here. Take flight with FlyOver Canada, a thrilling flight-simulation ride that takes you on a virtual trip through some of Canada's most beautiful natural sights. Strap in and let your legs dangle as you watch lifelike landscapes splash across a spherical screen. Stroll along the Canadian Trail, a pathway of colored glass found along the west promenade that represents Canada's 13 regions (10 provinces and three territories). This is also home to the city's cruise-ship port, and the city's largest convention centers.

## Chinese-Canadian History Uncovered

**Vancouver's Asian community showcased**

At the Chinatown Storytelling Centre you'll find a showcase of Vancouver's Chinese-Canadian history, including a life-sized diorama of the first housing units built for the workers who arrived from China to work on the Canadian Pacific Railway in the 1880s, an interactive etiquette table and the Robert HN Ho Living Legacy Project, which highlights the personal stories of Vancouver's most prominent Chinese-Canadians from the 1880s to the present day. This is Canada's first permanent exhibit dedicated to the Chinese-Canadian journey, and the individual stories shared create a truly unique perspective on the Asian community in Vancouver. Stroll through solo, or book a guided tour (only available for groups of 10 or more).

## The City's Past Through a Blue Lens

**North America's oldest police museum**

Criminal cases, unsolved murder mysteries and forensic science are just some of the things you can discover at the Vancouver Police Museum & Archives, found on the edge of Chinatown. Housed in an authentic heritage building, the museum was first opened in 1986 by the Police Historical Society as a way to celebrate the centennial anniversary of the city's police department. Featured exhibits include True Crime, a deep-dive display of the city's most chilling criminal cases, highlighting real cases and real evidence; Behind the Lines: A Traffic Story, a behind-the-lens look at the history of Vancouver's evolving traffic scene – from carriages to riot control, to present-day road safety; and Morgue & Autopsy Suite, a peek into the morgue and autopsy suite where pathologists and coroners worked to uncover the city's most notable true crimes from 1932 until 1980.

**CHINATOWN MILLENNIUM GATE**

The triple archways that make up the grand entrance to Chinatown were only erected in 2002, but the Chinatown Millennium Gate is a fitting testament to the neighborhood's longevity. Crane your neck for the colorful upper-level decoration and don't miss the ground-level lion statues. Then stand well back, since the decoration is mostly on its lofty upper reaches, where you'll find an elaborately painted section topped with a terra-cotta-tiled roof. The characters inscribed on its eastern front implore you to 'Remember the past and look forward to the future.'

**BEST ASIAN CUISINE**

**Torafuku**
Exquisite Pan-Asian dishes and cocktails crafted with precision and creativity. Michelin recommended. **$$$**

**Phnom Penh**
Authentic Vietnamese-Cambodian haven where bold spices bring traditional recipes to life. Expect a wait. **$$**

**Bao Bei**
Casual space serving modern Chinese sharing plates, where dishes like the Sticky Rice Cakes satisfy. **$$$**

FELIX LIPOV / SHUTTERSTOCK ©

Scan this QR code for a full digital map of Stanley Park.

TOP SIGHT

# Stanley Park

One of North America's largest urban green spaces, Stanley Park is revered for its dramatic forest-and-mountain oceanfront views. But there's more to this 400-hectare woodland than looks. The park is studded with nature-hugging trails, family-friendly attractions, sunset-boasting beaches and tasty places to eat. There's also the occasional surprise sight to search for (besides the raccoons that call the place home).

**DON'T MISS**

Vancouver Aquarium

Totem Park

Nine O'Clock Gun

Lost Lagoon

Hollow Tree

Seawall Landmarks

Second Beach

## Vancouver Aquarium

Over 65,000 animals and 30 galleries and exhibits can be found here, and the site is also home to a center for marine research and the country's only marine mammal rescue center. From swimming otters to jubilant jellies, the Vancouver Aquarium is a must-visit site to see aquatic animals. It's found in the center of Stanley Park.

## Totem Park

Stanley Park showcases the history of the area through the totem poles that stand tall at the park's edge. Located on the traditional, unceded territories of the xʷməθkʷəy̓əm (Musqueam), Sḵwx̱wú7mesh (Squamish) and səlilwətaɬ (Tsleil-Waututh) Peoples, the totem poles tell the story of the park's roots through the creative methods and people behind the works of art, which have stood erect just steps from the city since 1920.

## Nine O'Clock Gun

Every night at 9pm, a cannon is fired from Brockton Point in Stanley Park, its blast heard from across the city. The Nine O'Clock Gun is a Vancouver tradition that has been seen and heard for over a century. Originally located at the Brockton Point Lighthouse and fired manually each night for people to set their timepieces, the tradition remains, now managed by the Parks Board. You can view the blast from its site, just be sure to wear ear plugs for the big boom!

## Lost Lagoon

Stanley Park's Lost Lagoon is loaded with local wildlife. On its perimeter pathway, keep your eyes peeled for blue herons, wrens, hummingbirds, chittering Douglas squirrels and wandering racoons. You might also come across a coyote or two; treat them with respect and give them a wide berth. For an introduction to the area's flora and fauna, start at the Stanley Park Nature House. You'll find friendly volunteers and exhibits on wildlife, history and ecology – ask about their well-priced guided walks.

## Hollow Tree

An old Western Red Cedar tree in Stanley Park has become one of the most visited sites in Vancouver, thanks to its huge hollow stump, which has become a desired photo spot for tourists. Known simply as the **Hollow Tree**, the remains of the nearly 1000-year-old tree feature an interior opening with a circumference of about 18m.

## Seawall Landmarks

As you make your way around the seawall, look out for the **Girl in Wetsuit** statue that sits on a rock in the water just off the north side of the park. The statue – which is often mistaken for a mermaid – was a gift from sculptor Elek Imredy in 1972 and represents Vancouver's dependence on the sea. **Siwash Rock** is another landmark to look out for, a famous rock with a tree on its tip. Over thousands of years, the water has separated the rock from the park, and it now sits on its own in the sea.

## Second Beach

If it's sandy beaches you're after, the park has several alluring options. Second Beach is a family-friendly area on the park's western side, with a grassy playground, an ice-cream-serving concession and a huge outdoor swimming pool. It's also close to **Ceperley Meadows**, where popular free outdoor movie screenings are staged in summer.

### TALKING TOTEMS TOUR

To gain a deeper understanding of Stanley Park and its significance, book a Talking Totems trek with **Talaysay Tours**, which takes you on an eye-opening journey through the towering totem poles that have stood erect in the park since 1920. Led by an Indigenous guide, you will be awed by the art of the totems that make the site a must-see stop.

### TOP TIPS

- Access is easy. Save on paid parking by opting to walk, bike, bus, scoot, rollerblade or take a horse-drawn carriage to your desired park destination.
- Stanley Park stuns in all seasons. Summer is best for beaches and pools, and during the fall you'll find colorful foliage and fewer crowds.
- Plan your route. The 5.5-mile paved seawall leads to most sites. You'll want to spend a full day here to see it all.
- Sidestep the Vancouver Aquarium's summer lines by making it your first stop of the day.
- Gather a great picnic and snag a grassy spot near Lumberman's Arch.

# Granville Island & Yaletown

**CITY CHIC MEETS ARTISAN HUB**

These coastal communities straddle tranquil False Creek. Yaletown, a revitalized warehouse district, has become one of the city's chicest, where cool boutiques and posh urban patios draw crowds. Yaletown's waterfront parks, including David Lam Park and George Wainborn Park, are connected by a seawall, and the expansive green spaces found only steps from the city streets invite grassy picnics with water views.

A short ride on a rainbow-colored mini pedestrian ferry will take you across the water to Granville Island, which combines industrial heritage with modern-day architecture. The area is lauded as Vancouver's artisan capital, home to Western Canada's biggest public market. The human-made peninsula (it's not actually an island) was once home to dozens of hard-toiling factories, and remnants from older times can be spotted throughout the area.

**TOP TIP**

Both areas can be reached by transit or car, but cycling is your best bet. Yaletown is connected by a paved seawall; however, you may want to park your bike if you venture inland to browse shops. Granville Island is also suitable for cycling and offers free, secure bike valet service.

DAN BRECKWOLDT/SHUTTERSTOCK ©

Yaletown, Vancouver

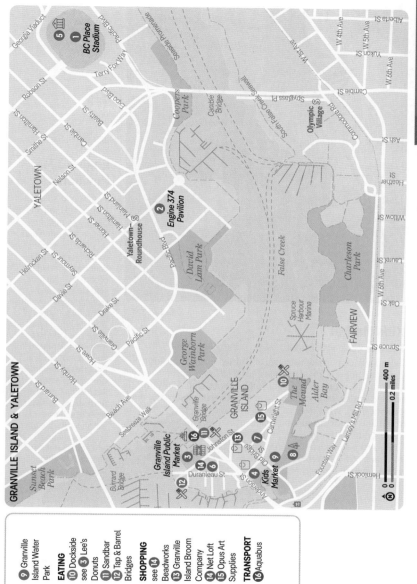

## GRANVILLE ISLAND & YALETOWN

**HIGHLIGHTS**
1 BC Place Stadium
2 Engine 374 Pavilion
3 Granville Island Public Market
4 Kids Market

**SIGHTS**
5 BC Sports Hall of Fame & Museum
6 Geza Burghardt Luthiery
7 Railspur Alley
8 Sutcliffe Park

**ACTIVITIES, COURSES & TOURS**
see 3 Bon Macaron Patisserie

9 Granville Island Water Park

**EATING**
10 Dockside
see 3 Lee's Donuts
11 Sandbar
12 Tap & Barrel Bridges

**SHOPPING**
see 4
13 Granville Beadworks
13 Granville Island Broom Company
14 Net Loft
15 Opus Art Supplies

**TRANSPORT**
16 Aquabus

65

**Engine 374**

## Engine 374 Pavilion

**Vancouver's first transcontinental train**

On May 23, 1887, CPR Engine 374 pulled the very first transcontinental passenger train into Vancouver, linking the country by train from coast to coast and kickstarting the eventual metropolis. Retired in 1945, the engine was, after many years of neglect, restored and placed in the splendid pavilion found at the Roundhouse Community Arts & Recreation Centre in the heart of the city. The friendly volunteers here will show you the best angle for snapping photos and at the same time share a few railroading stories from yesteryear.

## Kids Market

**Massive kid-centric mall**

Found adjacent to the entrance of Granville Island beside a picturesque pond, Kids Market is a three-story, warehouse-style shopping center aimed at kids. The yellow-hued building is topped with a rainbow sign, and invites youngsters to shop, eat and play, with over 25 shops and services on site. There you'll find handcrafted toys, locally owned boutiques and bookstores, interactive arcades, multi-level play spaces, and sweet and savory snack spots to fuel up after a day of play. Be sure to check out the website (kidsmarket.ca) for family-friendly events, which happen year-round.

## BC Place Stadium

**Sports lovers central**

Vancouver's main sports arena is home to two professional teams: the **BC Lions** Canadian Football League team and the **Vancouver Whitecaps** soccer team. Also used for international rugby tournaments, rock concerts and consumer shows, the stadium – with its huge, crown-like retractable roof – hosted the opening and closing ceremonies for the 2010 Olympic and Paralympic Winter Games.

Inside you'll find the BC Sports Hall of Fame & Museum, a showcase of BC's top athletes, both amateur and professional, with an intriguing array of galleries crammed with fascinating memorabilia. There are medals, trophies and sports uniforms from yesteryear on display, plus tons of hands-on activities. Don't miss the Indigenous Sport Gallery, covering everything from hockey to lacrosse to traditional Indigenous games.

# Isle of the Arts

### Artists in action

Granville Island is packed with creative curiosities for art enthusiasts of all types. Stroll through Railspur Alley and watch artists create masterpieces before your eyes. See glassblowers, jewelers, potters, painters, blacksmiths and carvers craft beautiful pieces live in-studio and listen as they share the inspiration behind their work. Head to the Granville Island Broom Company and watch two sisters handcraft Shaker-style woven brooms in their whimsical storefront, and visit the **Geza Burghardt Luthiery**, where you can watch as a Hungarian luthier builds, repairs and restores guitars, violins, cellos and other string instruments.

Then, get hands-on at **Beadworks**, where you can shop through an expansive collection of beads – from Swarovski crystals to bone beads – and then take a seat and create your own original piece of jewelry to take home. Satisfy your sweet tooth while mastering the art of macaron-making with a private class at **Bon Macaron Patisserie**, or sign up for an in-store painting class at **Opus Art Supplies**, a spacious store that has become a staple of the Vancouver art community.

# Water Park Play

### Spray, splash and slide

Granville Island is home to the largest free outdoor water park of its kind in North America, where fire hydrants, in-ground sprays, fountains and a twirly yellow slide make for the perfect summer cool down for kids. Slather

on the sunscreen and enjoy the splash pads, and then pick up some snacks from the Granville Island Public Market – a short walk from the park – and settle in on the expansive grassy green space of adjacent **Sutcliffe Park**.

**Granville Island Water Park**

**WHY I LOVE GRANVILLE ISLAND**

**Bianca Bujan**, Writer

I'm one of a rare group of local Vancouverites who grew up right in Granville Island. The area was my backyard, and even though it's been more than 30 years since I called it home, I visit regularly, witnessing first hand its slow transition from sleepy hideaway to major tourist draw. During Expo '86, I met Princess Diana and Prince Charles here, and I learned to ride a bike along the paved pathway that leads to **Kids Market** – my favorite childhood place to play. Today, the food here is the biggest draw, from the fresh meats and sweet treats found in the **Public Market** to the warm raspberry jelly donuts at **Lee's Donuts**.

## WHERE TO DINE ALFRESCO

**Tap & Barrel Bridges**
Sprawling, sun-drenched patio with waterfront Vancouver views, housed in a historic yellow building. $$

**Sandbar**
Seafood shines at this restaurant perched over the water, and under the Granville St bridge. $$

**Dockside**
Luxury dining with majestic marina views, found in a quieter corner of bustling Granville Island. $$

FIIPHOTO/SHUTTERSTOCK ©

Scan this QR code for a full list of retail and restaurant offerings.

TOP SIGHT

# Granville Island Public Market

One of North America's finest public markets – a foodie extravaganza specializing in deli treats and pyramids of shiny fruit and vegetables. It's ideal for whiling away an afternoon, snacking on goodies in the sun among the buskers outside or sheltering from the rain with a market tour. You'll also find side dishes of locally made arts and crafts here.

**DON'T MISS**

Foodie Tour

Lee's Donuts

Mini Ferries

The Net Loft

Boardwalk Buskers

Arts & Crafts

Food Court

## Foodie Tour

If you're looking for a local take on the food found around the famed market, a guided walk organized by **Vancouver Foodie Tours** is the way to go. This leisurely stomach-stuffer weaves around the vendors and includes several tasting stops that will quickly fill you up. It also caters to vegetarians if you mention it when you book. The company runs friendly tasting tours in other parts of the city too, if you're keen to keep eating.

## Lee's Donuts

This mom-and-pop donut shop is legendary – just ask local celebrities like Seth Rogan who frequent the joint when they're in town. Serving handmade donuts since 1979, Lee's offers a large variety of classics that are made daily from scratch (the sugar-topped raspberry jelly donut tops the list). Be sure to arrive early and expect a line – don't worry, though, the donuts are worth the wait.

## Mini Ferries

Found at the end of the boardwalk behind the market is a small dock where you can catch the Aquabus – a rainbow-colored mini pedestrian ferry. Take a short tour of the city by water, or use it as transport to get to some of the city's best waterfront spots. The Aquabus connects Granville Island to several locations found between downtown's Hornby St and Science World, with several scenic spots found along the way.

## The Net Loft

Found across the street, the Net Loft is sort of an extension of the main market's artsy offerings. There you'll find a cluster of craft shops that offer a variety of handcrafted keepsakes. At Beadworks, shop through an expansive collection of beads, from Swarovski crystals to bone beads, and make your own jewelry.

## Boardwalk Buskers

A park-bench picnic behind the market is a preferred pastime for Granville Island locals and tourists alike. Snack on treats collected during your stroll through the food stalls, and sit by the water, watching seagulls swoop (be sure to keep your food close or it might get snagged), while listening to talented buskers perform live music. In Granville Island, busking is done through a licensed program, allowing everyone from magicians to musicians to showcase their talents on-site. For updated schedules and locations check out granvilleislandbuskers.com.

## Arts & Crafts

There's a cool arts-and-crafts focus here, especially among the collection of day vendors that dot the market and change every week. Hand-knitted hats, hand-painted ceramics, framed art photography and quirky carvings will make for excellent one-of-a-kind keepsakes. Further artisan stands are added to the roster in the run-up to Christmas, if you happen to be here at that time. For an updated list of day vendors that appear at the market, visit granvilleisland.com/public-market.

## Food Court

In the unlikely event that you're still hungry after snacking your way through the market stalls, there's also a small international food court filled with varied offerings from around the world. Avoid off-peak dining if you want to snag a table and indulge in a good-value selection that runs from Mexican tacos to German sausages.

### FORGOTTEN PAST

The Public Market is one of Canada's most impressive urban-regeneration projects. Originally built as a factory district, the abandoned sheds attracted artists and theater groups by the 1970s. New theaters and studios were built and the Public Market became a popular anchor tenant. Now, only independent, one-of-a-kind businesses operate here.

### TOP TIPS

- Arrive early to sidestep the summer crowds.
- If driving, weekdays are the easiest times to find on-island parking.
- Arrive by bike and enjoy the complimentary bike-valet service in summer.
- The food court is the island's best-value dining. But tables are scarce at peak times.
- Early morning weekdays are best for shorter lines at the famous Lee's Donuts.
- Bird-watcher? Look for the cormorants nesting under the Granville Bridge.
- Venture to other neighborhoods via the mini-ferry, which docks behind the market's back patio.

# Main Street

**ALTERNATIVE AND MULTICULTURAL**

Deemed one of North America's coolest streets, this formerly faded and gritty neighborhood is now a hub for hipsters and home to numerous independent shops, global restaurants and hip bars, all found within a 20-block stretch. Unlike some of Vancouver's other shopping districts, you won't find any big-box stores here.

The area is developing rapidly, including the lower Olympic Village area – a waterfront neighborhood that's always adding new drinking and dining options. Along the village, you'll also find a collection of massive murals that color the city streets, part of the Vancouver Mural Festival. Some of the city's best restaurants can be found here too, including a handful of newly Michelin-recognized spots. The restaurant scene is culturally diverse, offering a mix of laid-back and high-end restaurants serving up everything from Malaysian to South Indian to Caribbean classics.

## TOP TIP

The Main Street neighborhood is easily accessible by bus – the number 3 runs the length of Main St in both directions. The SkyTrain connects to bus 3 services at the Main Street-Science World Station, and there's limited metered parking on Main St, with side-street parking the further south you drive.

ADAM MELNYK/SHUTTERSTOCK ©

**Olympic Village, Vancouver**

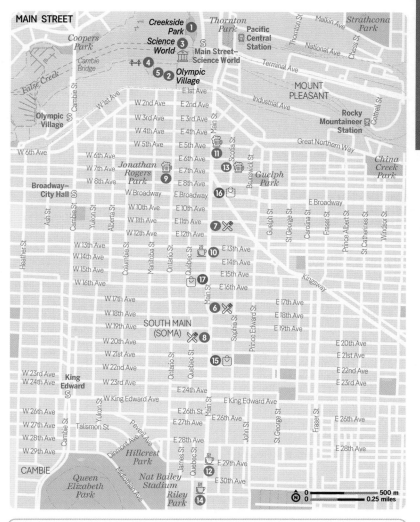

# MAIN STREET

## HIGHLIGHTS
1. Creekside Park
2. Olympic Village
3. Science World

## SIGHTS
4. Canoe Bridge

5. Sparrow Sculptures

## EATING
6. Anh & Chi
7. Burdock & Co
8. Published on Main

## DRINKING & NIGHTLIFE
9. 33 Acres Brewing
10. 49th Parallel Coffee Roasters
11. Brassneck Brewery
12. Breka Bakery & Cafe
13. Main Street Brewing
14. Matchstick

## SHOPPING
15. Front & Co
16. Mintage Mall
17. Turnabout Luxury Resale

*Science World*

## Creekside Park

### Vancouver's largest playground

A popular outdoor venue for summer events and festivals and the gateway to Science World, this accessible playground features a high-reaching wooden climbing tower, swings, giant tube and hill slides, musical instruments, water and sand play areas, and a play hut, all housed on a colorful rubberized surface. A zipline, perhaps the biggest draw, adds extra zest to the park's features. Surrounding shade trees provide cooler seating areas around the park's perimeter, perfect for picnics. And waterfront and skyline views attract park dwellers without kids too.

## Olympic Village

### Waterfront pubs, patios and parks

Originally built to house athletes for the 2010 Winter Olympic and Paralympic Games, Vancouver's Olympic Village has now evolved into a happening spot, packed with pubs, patios and parks on the waterfront. Look for a pair of giant **sparrow sculptures** created by local artist Myfanwy MacLeod – an artistic comment on the relationship between humans and birds, and the effects of urban development in a formerly natural space (standing at 18ft tall in the center of the square, the birds are hard to miss). Be sure to cross **Canoe Bridge** (a popular photo spot), which is especially beautiful when illuminated at night.

## Science World

### A family-friendly science showcase

One of the city's most photographed structures, the dome isn't just a shiny shoreline bauble. Found inside is a multi-level mashup of activities and exhibits that offer fun for all ages. There are two floors of educational play, from plasma balls to whisper dishes. Hands-on exhibits make learning fun, as do the live science demonstrations on the Centre Stage. Find live critters in the Sara Stern Gallery, behold the bodily functions exhibited in the BodyWorks area, then fly over a city on the virtual-reality Birdly ride ($8 extra). If the weather's fine, save time for the outdoor Ken Spencer Science Park. Focused on sustainable communities, it's a quirky collection of climbing frames, interactive games and stage demos, plus a coop full of beady-eyed chickens.

## 🛍 BEST VINTAGE SHOPS

**Mintage Mall**
Seven super-cool vintage vendors offering everything from 1970s outfits to antique taxidermy.

**Turnabout Luxury Resale**
Well-stocked shop stuffed with curated and consignment luxury fashions, footwear and finds.

**Front & Co**
New and vintage clothing, plus cool housewares and must-have gifts and accessories.

## Main Street's Michelin Meals

### Savor the flavors

At the end of 2022, Vancouver's very first Michelin guide was released – a long-awaited status symbol collating the city's best restaurants, many of which are located along the Main Street corridor. Eight spots in total received star recognition, and another 12 received bib gourmand designation. Several others were also added to the esteemed list of restaurants in the city. The dining options are definitely worth discovering, offering distinct dishes that showcase both the freshly plucked local ingredients found in the region (especially seafood), and the city's Asian influence, with many of the dishes found nowhere else outside Asia. Be sure to book your table well in advance.

Topping the list of must-try spots in the area is **Published on Main**, where executive chef Gus Stieffenhofer-Brandson and his team prepare picture-perfect dishes using ingredients foraged from local forests and farms. The food here is high-quality, and the presentation is equally impressive. The tender halibut with buttery broth is a crowd pleaser. **Anh & Chi** brings a modern, vibrant Vietnamese menu to life in Vancouver, backed by a brother-and-sister team who embrace their culinary roots, producing authentic Vietnamese dishes like *Khay Bánh Hỏi Lụi Nướng*, a DIY street-side platter served with a modern twist. **Burdock & Co** is another popular choice. With Andrea Carlson – the only female chef on Vancouver's Michelin list – at the helm, this spot is best known for its regional farm-to-table plates, which make up the ever-changing seasonal set-course menu here (open for dinner Mondays to Thursdays).

## Historic Brewery Creek

### Raise a glass in cheer

Beer lovers will want to pay a visit to Brewery Creek – a historic urban brewery district. The area was named after a fast-moving creek that once powered water wheels at several area breweries. But after decades of consolidation, the neighborhood's last brewery closed in the 1950s. That wasn't the end of the story, though. In recent years, Vancouver's latter-day craft-brewing renaissance has seen several new producers open in the area. Wondering where to start? Quench your thirst at local favorite Brassneck Brewery. For a self-guided tour of the best of the rest, be sure to follow the **BC Ale Trail**.

### SUMMER FAIR

An annual, family-friendly Vancouver event still going strong after more than a century, the Pacific National Exhibition (pne.ca) – known simply as the PNE by locals – launched in 1910, and is a summer tradition for generations of Vancouverites who flock to Hastings Park, a 15-minute drive east of Main St, for amusement park rides, concerts and cultural activities. The site is home to Playland Amusement Park (open May to September), and hosts high-profile, off-season events like the Halloween-themed Fright Nights in October, and the PNE Winter Fair in December.

Scan this QR code for the BC Ale trail.

### BEST COFFEE SPOTS

**49th Parallel Coffee Roasters**
Sustainably sourced and crafted coffee roasted locally, with an exceptional selection of donuts.

**Matchstick**
Community coffee shop with five locations around the city, where pastries are baked fresh on-site.

**Breka Bakery & Cafe**
Latest location of the family-owned chain of cafes, offering an array of sweet and savory treats.

THE GUIDE

MAIN STREET VANCOUVER

## MURAL MEANDER

Explore the city through an artistic lens with a self-guided tour of the Vancouver Mural Festival – a stunning showcase of over 300 outdoor murals and public art displays found in 11 neighborhoods throughout the city, created by local and international artists. Before you go, be sure to download the free VMF app, which includes a full list of murals, the stories behind the art and a mapping feature to help you plot out your stops.

Start with a stroll along the beautifully diverse murals of Main Street. The mural **1 Beauty in Post-Colonial Society** (700 Main St) features an ethnically ambiguous woman who does not submit to traditional beauty standards, yet her beauty prevails. It's part of the Black Strathcona Resurgence Project, which supports intercultural relations in the community. The **2 Free Yourself** (68 East 2nd Ave, in lane-

way) mural combines architecture and 3D anamorphism to invoke a moment of reflection while conveying a unique perspective on freedom and what it means to the viewer. A Vancouver-based street artist (who works under a moniker to protect his identity) offers social commentary with **3 Thirsty** (2015 Main St, in the alley), a stencil piece featuring a child posing for selfies while sipping on a juice box. Created collaboratively by three Vancouver-based First Nations artists, **4 Past & Presence** (240 East 5th Ave) is a visual celebration of the 30th anniversary of the Native Education College (NEC). Awareness of the present is the theme of **5 The Present Is a Gift** (2543 Main St, view from alley), a portrait piece that parallels two community residents: Paisley, of the Coast-Salish First Nations, and Dr Bob, optometrist for six decades.

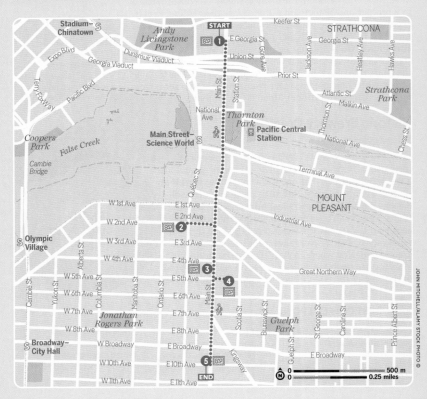

# Fairview & South Granville

**UPSCALE URBAN SHOPPING DISTRICT**

Combining the boutiques and restaurants of well-to-do South Granville with Fairview's busy Broadway thoroughfare and cozy Cambie Village, there's something for everyone in this area. South Granville is home to tree-lined residential streets, heritage buildings and casual cafes intermixed with modern boutiques and high-end eateries. A stretch of stylish shops and independent galleries make this vibrant, upscale shopping district worth the trek.

Massive murals add charm, and colorful open-air plazas invite a rest stop after an afternoon spent shopping and snacking. Art lovers will want to walk along 'Gallery Row' – a stretch of art galleries that line the lower South Granville corridor. Green-thumbed visitors should also save time for some top-notch park and garden attractions here.

**TOP TIP**

For art galleries, start from the Granville St bridge and work your way up to West 8th Ave. If you're looking to browse boutiques, the best are clustered between Broadway and West 16th Ave. You'll need to hop on a bus or drive to explore the expansive gardens in the area.

MAX LINDENTHALER/SHUTTERSTOCK ©

**False Creek, Fairview**

TOP LEFT: STEPHANIE BRACONNIER/SHUTTERSTOCK ©; BOTTOM RIGHT: STEPHANIE BRACONNIER/SHUTTERSTOCK ©

**Bloedel Conservatory**

## Bloedel Conservatory

**Tropical birds and plants in a domed paradise**

Housed at the highest point of picturesque Queen Elizabeth Park, this domed conservatory is a delightful destination on a rainy day. Here you'll find tropical trees and plants bristling with hundreds of free-flying, bright-plumaged birds. Listen for the noisy resident parrots, but also keep your eyes peeled for rainbow-hued Gouldian finches, shimmering African superb starlings and maybe even a dramatic Lady Amherst pheasant snaking through the undergrowth. Ask nicely and the attendants might even let you feed the smaller birds from a bowl. If the kids get antsy, ask for a free scavenger hunt sheet so they can track what they spot.

## Stanley Theatre

**Landmark heritage theater**

Officially called the Stanley Industrial Alliance Stage, but better known as 'The Stanley' to locals, this art-deco-style heritage theater is part of the Arts Club Theatre Company, Vancouver's biggest. The site originally opened in the 1930s as a movie cinema and vaudeville house, and has since become the flagship stage of Western Canada's largest theater company, showing everything from off-Broadway musicals to comedy shows to classic plays by up-and-coming actors. Unable to catch a show? The stunning exterior is worth a walk-by.

**VanDusen Botanical Gardens**

## VanDusen Botanical Gardens

**Outdoor oasis for garden lovers**

Opened in 1975, this 22-hectare (55-acre) green-thumbed wonderland is home to more than 250,000 plants representing some of the world's most distinct growing regions. You'll find trees, shrubs, flowers, succulents and more from across Canada, the Mediterranean, South Africa and the Himalayas, many of them identified with little plaques near their roots. It's not just humans that are hooked by this sparkling nature spot; this is also a wildlife haven. Look out for turtles, herons and a variety of ducks in and around the main lake. A stroll through the **Elizabethan Maze** is also a must. Grown from more than 3000 pyramidal cedars, VanDusen's giggle-triggering garden maze is the perfect spot to tire out your kids.

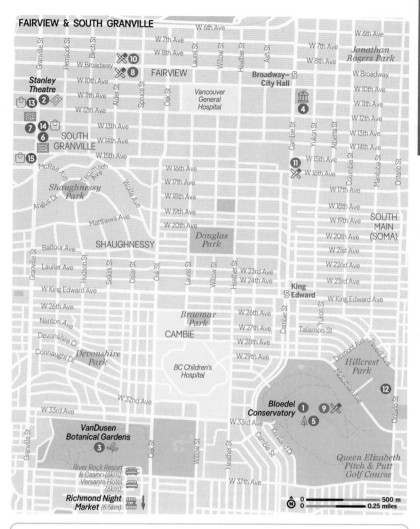

# FAIRVIEW & SOUTH GRANVILLE

**HIGHLIGHTS**
1 Bloedel Conservatory
2 Stanley Theatre
3 VanDusen Botanical Gardens

**SIGHTS**
4 City Hall
5 Queen Elizabeth Park

6 South Granville Plaza East
7 South Granville Plaza West

**EATING**
8 Salmon n' Bannock
9 Seasons in the Park
10 Tojo's
11 Vij's

**ENTERTAINMENT**
12 Nat Bailey Stadium

**SHOPPING**
13 Hill's Dry Goods
14 Latest Scoop
15 Turnabout Luxury Resale

## CITY HALL ART DECO

Despite the economic malaise of the 1930s, mayor Gerry McGeer spared no expense to build a new City Hall in 1936. Defended as a make-work project for the idled construction industry, the $1 million project (a huge sum for the time) was completed in just 12 months. Despite the controversy, the building is now one of Vancouver's most revered art-deco edifices, complete with a soaring, Gotham-style exterior and an interior of streamlined signs, cylindrical lanterns and embossed elevator doors. Before you leave, snap some photos of the statue of Captain George Vancouver outside, then check out the wooden heritage mansions on nearby Yukon St and W 12th Ave.

RONNIE CHUA/SHUTTERSTOCK ©

**Queen Elizabeth Park**

MORE IN FAIRVIEW & SOUTH GRANVILLE

# Relax in Queen Elizabeth Park

**Picturesque park at the city's highest point**

At 125m above sea level, Queen Elizabeth Park is the city's highest point, offering panoramic views of the mountain-framed downtown skyscrapers. A tree-lover's dream, this 130-acre park claims to house specimens of every tree native to Canada. Sports fields, manicured lawns and formal gardens keep the locals happy, and you'll probably also see wide-eyed couples posing for their wedding photos in particularly picturesque spots. This is a good place to view local birdlife: keep your eyes peeled for chickadees, hummingbirds and huge bald eagles whirling high overhead. This park is home to the domed **Bloedel Conservatory** and has a great fine-dining restaurant, **Seasons in the Park**, which is perched at the park's top. Picnics and pitch-and-putt are popular pastimes for locals here.

 **BEST GLOBAL CUISINE**

**Salmon n' Bannock**
The only Indigenous-owned restaurant in Vancouver, serving modern dishes made using traditional ingredients. **$$**

**Vij's**
Famed Indian fusion restaurant with celebrity chef Vikram Vij at the helm. **$$**

**Tojo's**
First-class Japanese cuisine lauded by the world's top CEOs, celebrities and chefs. **$$$**

ERIC BUERMEYER/SHUTTERSTOCK ©

**Nat Bailey Stadium**

## Grab a Game at Nat Bailey Stadium

### Take me out to the ball game

Catching a **Vancouver Canadians** minor-league baseball game at old-school **Nat Bailey Stadium** (known as 'The Nat' by locals) is a summer tradition for many Vancouverites. But for some, the experience isn't complete unless you also add a hot dog, peanuts and some ice-cold beers to the ball game. Non-traditional options are available too, like sushi. Be sure to check out the Wall of Fame exhibit while you're there, which highlights former Canadian players who have gone on to the majors. Enhancing the festivities are the non-baseball she-nanigans, ranging from kiss cams to mascot races. Arguably the most fun you can have at a Vancouver spectator sport, it's also one of the most budget-friendly options (depending on how many hot dogs you down).

**PUBLIC ART**

South Granville showcases an array of massive wall murals found on side streets lined with heritage homes, just steps from the main strip. The collection of colorful murals is always growing, and many provide a backdrop for open-air seating spaces that are perfect for picnicking during the warmer months. Look for the two main public plaza areas found at the center of the neighborhood: **South Granville Plaza West**, located at Granville St and West 13th Ave, and **South Granville Plaza East**, located at Granville St and West 14th Ave. These two community hubs combine creative seating structures with colorful murals to create inviting outdoor gathering areas, the perfect place to relax, connect and dine outdoors.

 **BEST FASHION SHOPS**

**Latest Scoop**
A lifestyle store offering lovely items for your closet and your home.

**Turnabout Luxury Resale**
Vancouver's westside location of Canada's largest luxury consignment retail shop.

**Hill's Dry Goods**
Find high-end fashion, jewelry, accessories and an apothecary under one roof.

ABERUGO/SHUTTERSTOCK ©

Scan this QR code for hours and updated event details.

TOP SIGHT

# Richmond Night Market

Home to the Vancouver International Airport (YVR), Richmond is best known for its hyper-diverse population. The city has the largest number of Chinese residents found outside Asia, and the night market – the largest of its kind in North America – reflects Richmond's roots through its cultural and culinary offerings, with over 110 food stalls serving up over 600 different dishes from around the world.

**DID YOU KNOW?**
Richmond Night Market began in 2000 as a tented pop-up in a parking lot. Entrepreneur Raymond Cheung foresaw an event that nodded to the Asian night markets found in Hong Kong. Now, the market draws over a million visitors a year.

## Live Entertainment

Each year the decor reveals a special theme (previous years have included 'Summer Chill Party' and 'Magic Rainbow') with on-theme attractions to suit the mood. A 15m live performance stage brings nightly entertainment such as musical acts, martial arts displays, dance showcases and more.

## Global Food Stalls

The night market isn't just a showcase for Asian cuisine – you can dine around the world here. Churros and butter beer are new additions to the tasty roster, along with foods from Indonesia and Turkey. Tornado potatoes, or 'rotatoes,' are a classic hit, and *takoyaki* (Japanese octopus balls), Bajan jambalaya and deep-fried *bao* buns add to the list of savory options. For sweet-toothed snackers, there's plenty of treats too! Mochido donuts, handcrafted rolled gelato and the quintessentially Canadian beaver tails top the list. There are always new offerings, so be sure to check the posted list of the 10 most popular vendors of the month on a supersized sign that you'll pass upon entry.

## Colorful Keepsakes

Pack your wallet because you'll also want to browse the vendor stalls found throughout the site, where you can shop for toys, handmade goods, clothing and accessories, phone gadgets and quirky keepsakes. From samurai swords to cute Korean socks, you're sure to find something for everyone on your vacation gift list.

## For the Kids

New in 2023, a larger-than-life, 18m-tall bouncy castle provides a fun place for kids to jump the night away after stuffing their faces with sweet treats. A games area, a candy-colored forest and oversized prop chairs will also lure the little ones. Marvel at the moving velociraptors, triceratops and TRex in the **Magical Dino Park**, and take a peek at the pooches in the dog play area, where four-legged friends can join in on the fun – as long as they stay away from the food.

## Nearby Stays

Make a night of your visit to Richmond with a stay at one of the nearby hotels, where you can enjoy post-event drinks before drifting off to sleep. The **River Rock Resort & Casino** is only minutes away by foot, where you'll find an on-site casino (one of the largest in the province), a heated indoor pool with a waterslide and a soothing spa. **Versante Hotel**, about a seven-minute walk from the market, is Richmond's only boutique hotel. There you'll find **Bruno** – likely the best brunch spot in the area.

### RICHMOND DUMPLING TRAIL

Take your admiration for Asian eats beyond the market with a tasting tour through town. On the self-guided Dumpling Trail tour (dumplingtrail.ca) through Richmond, foodies can slurp on steaming hot wonton soup, nibble on crunchy, deep-fried dumplings, or gobble up a mouthful of pork-stuffed pouches at the over 20 eateries listed on the pre-planned route.

### TOP TIPS

- Parking is extremely limited, so consider public transit instead. The market is only one block away from the Bridgeport Station of the Canada Line SkyTrain – Richmond's elevated subway system that takes you directly to the site from several locations between downtown Vancouver and the YVR airport.

- Before you head in, be sure to browse the top 10 vendors of the month posted near the entry gates. This will help you decide where to start in a sea of food stalls.
- Skip the long-stretching lines with a Zoom Pass, which gives you priority entry, access to shorter lines, and cost savings once you're inside.

**Above: Salmon River estuary; right: Little Huson Caves**

# Vancouver Island

## CHARMING COMMUNITIES & WILDERNESS WONDERS

Outdoor adventure meets laid-back lifestyle on this archipelago on the Pacific Coast, where sprawling beaches, snug inlets and rugged wilderness are speckled with cosmopolitan centers.

Vancouver Island is a vast archipelago with varied landscapes, spanning nearly 500km long and 100km wide. It's the largest populated landmass between western North America and New Zealand, and is packed with attractions and activities that distinctly differ from those offered on the more bustling mainland of Vancouver.

The region that we now know as Vancouver Island sits on the traditional ancestral and unceded territories of the Kwakwaka'wakw, Nuu-chah-nulth, and Coast Salish. Many are familiar with its crown jewel on the coast – BC's capital city of Victoria – which is the island's main entry point and a hub for historic sites, but there's so much more to see and do beyond "Canada's garden city".

From the Swartz Bay ferry terminal (the primary arrival point), up through the Saanich Peninsula, the South Island region features clusters of charming communities, pretty parks and scenic sights and attractions. Nanaimo (the secondary arrival point by ferry) introduces you to the Central Island region, where sandy beaches, underground caves and tree-lined trails invite adventure outdoors. Things slow down and the wilderness opens up as you head toward North Island, where remote stretches of wildness allow you to witness wildlife and explore Indigenous cultures in the unspoilt, raw beauty of Western Canada's last stop. Ecoadventures await those who are looking for truly off-the-beaten-path experiences.

## THE MAIN AREAS

**GREATER VICTORIA**
Garden city and brunch capital. p86

**CENTRAL ISLAND**
Relaxed coastal communities. p95

**PACIFIC RIM**
Surfers' paradise. p100

**NORTH ISLAND**
Rugged wilderness. p105

# Find Your Way

If you're looking to enjoy a shorter stay in BC's capital city, it's possible to go car-free, but you'll need a vehicle if you plan on exploring beyond Victoria, as the island is vast.

## Central Island, p95

Find colorful coastal communities surrounded by nature, with forested trails, far-reaching beaches, and Canada's tallest waterfall.

## Greater Victoria, p86

This is home to Canada's first Chinatown, and Butchart Gardens, one of Canada's National Historic Sites.

## Pacific Rim, p100

This region is home to Canada's surf town, and the wilderness invites endless adventure outdoors.

## North Island, p105

Go off grid for untouched landscapes, wildlife sightings and eco adventures in the rugged West Coast.

## FERRY

From Vancouver (Tsawwassen), a car/passenger ferry will take you across the water to Victoria (Swartz Bay) or Nanaimo (Duke Point) via BC Ferries.

## SEAPLANE

If you're planning on going car-free, seaplane service from Vancouver (downtown) or Richmond (YVR) will take you directly to downtown Victoria, Nanaimo and Tofino via Harbour Air.

0 100 km
0 50 miles

N

WASHINGTON (USA)

BRITISH COLUMBIA

Queen Charlotte Sound

Cape Scott Provincial Park

Queen Charlotte Strait

Port Hardy
Port McNeill
Malcolm Island
Telegraph Cove

Winter Harbour

Quatsino Sound

Port Alice

Woss

Zeballos

Sayward

Johnstone Strait

Seymour Narrows

Schoen Lake Provincial Park

Brooks Bay

Brooks Peninsula

Kyuquot

Fair Harbour

Kanuquot Sound

Esperanza Inlet

Nootka Island

Yuquot
Nootka

Nootka Sound

Hot Springs Cove

Flores Island
Ahousat

PACIFIC OCEAN

Tofino
Cox Bay Beach

Pacific Rim National Park Reserve

Ucluelet

Gold River

Mt Golden Hinde

Strathcona Provincial Park

Vancouver Island Mountains

Kildonan

Bamfield

Port Renfrew

Sooke

Heriot

Campbell River

Comox
Courtenay

Buckley Bay

Port Alberni

Alberni Inlet

Lake Cowichan

Cowichan Lake

Port Alberni

Horne Lake Caves

Qualicum Beach
Parksville
Coombs

Nanaimo

Duncan
Cowichan Bay

Malahat Skywalk

Victoria

Strait of Juan de Fuca

Seymour Narrows

Bute Inlet

Toba Inlet

Powell Lake

Saltery Bay

Powell River

Texada Island

Jervis Inlet

Egmont
Earls Cove

Sechelt

Langdale

Squamish

Horseshoe Bay

Gibsons

Vancouver

Tsawwassen

Strait of Georgia

Gulf Islands

Swartz Bay
Sidney
Butchart Gardens

Chemainus

Puget Sound

POEMNIST/SHUTTERSTOCK ©

**Old Country Market**

# Plan Your Time

Vancouver Island is huge, so be sure to save enough time to either dive deeper into a single region or drive further and see a bit of it all.

## Weekend by the Water

Take a day to discover downtown **Victoria** (p86), starting with brunch by the water (p90), then cruise by foot through historic **Chinatown** (p86). Head to Inner Harbour for a stroll, shop and snack along **Fisherman's Wharf** (p87). Sneak away to **Sooke** (p91) for a scenic hike along the Sooke River at **Potholes Provincial Park** (p91) and cool off with a dip at Crescent Beach.

## 7 Days to Explore

Start with a night in **Nanaimo** (p95) and pick up some treats along the **Nanaimo Bar Trail** (p98), then take a few days to play in **Parksville** (p97), where you can spelunk through **Horne Lake Caves** (p97) before grabbing ice cream at **Goats on a Roof** (p97). Drive cross-island to **Ucluelet** (p101), and wrap up your stay with a few nights in **Tofino** (p100).

## Seasonal Highlights

| SPRING | SUMMER | AUTUMN | WINTER |
|---|---|---|---|
| Flora flourishes. For the best blooms, check out Butchart Gardens (p90), which reaches its peak season mid-April. | The biggest crowds as locals and visitors head to the beaches and out for hiking, biking, boating and swimming. | Fall leaves add color to outdoor adventures, and smaller crowds mean you'll mostly have the trails to yourself. | Storm-watching season, best enjoyed in Tofino (p100), and snowy Mount Washington (p99) welcomes skiers. |

# Greater Victoria & Inner Harbour

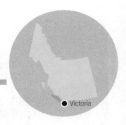

● Victoria

GARDEN CITY AND BRUNCH CAPITAL

Greater Victoria is a coastal city rich in natural beauty and cultural gems. When it comes to achieving accolades, BC's capital city takes the top spot. Founded in 1858, Victoria's Chinatown was the first in Canada. One of its most notable streets, Fan Tan Alley, is recognized as the narrowest street in Canada, and in Victoria's Beacon Hill Park, you'll find the world's tallest free-standing totem pole, which reaches a height of 39 meters tall.

Victoria has the mildest climate in the country (it's located in a sub-Mediterranean zone) providing the perfect garden growing conditions, which is why the city is known as 'Canada's Garden City', with Butchart Gardens, a designated Natural Historic Site of Canada, garnering international recognition. Victoria is also known as the "brunch capital of Canada" with a wide roster of restaurants worthy of a stop, and a visit wouldn't be complete without partaking in a traditional afternoon tea.

### ☑ TOP TIP

Victoria has a vibrant scene with 100+ festivals. Check out the Indigenous Cultural Festival (Jul) to learn about Indigenous heritage, or sniff, swirl, and sip your way through the Victoria International Wine Festival (Sep). Foodies favor Dine Around and Stay in Town, the city's top culinary fest (Jan-Feb).

## Explore Chinese Canadian Culture

Canada's oldest Chinatown

In 1858, BC's port cities saw an influx of Asian immigrants arriving to work on the Canadian Pacific Railway. Since then, Victoria's **Chinatown** (Canada's oldest) has remained a historical gateway to the country's Chinese Canadian past and present.

Located right in the heart of downtown and only blocks away from the waterfront, Chinatown is easily walkable. As you enter the three-block stretch that makes up Chinatown, be sure to stop and admire the **Gate of Harmonious Interest**. The *paifang* (traditional Chinese archway) was built in 1981 to commemorate Chinatown's revitalization, and is adorned in ornate red and gold symbols.

Continue towards the center of Chinatown and take a turn down **Fan Tan Alley**, Canada's narrowest street (less than 3ft wide at its narrowest point). The alley entrance can be found

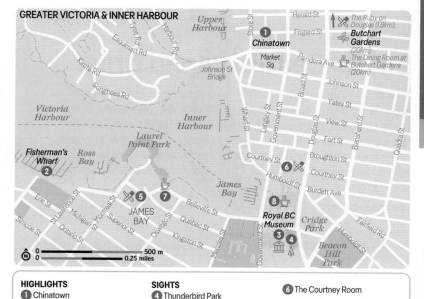

**GREATER VICTORIA & INNER HARBOUR**

0 — 500 m
0 — 0.25 miles

**HIGHLIGHTS**
1. Chinatown
2. Fisherman's Wharf
3. Royal BC Museum

**SIGHTS**
4. Thunderbird Park

**EATING**
5. Nourish Kitchen & Cafe

6. The Courtney Room

**DRINKING & NIGHTLIFE**
7. Pendray Inn & Tea House
8. Tea at the Empress

---

halfway down Fisgard St and the street stretches toward Pandora Ave. Browse the locally owned shops and then be sure to duck in for dumplings at one of the many traditional Chinese dining spots found along the way.

## Wander the Wharf

*Fish 'n' chips and floating homes*

Around the corner from Victoria's Inner Harbour is **Fisherman's Wharf**, a quaint community of colorful floating houses, where you can stroll, shop, eat and play by the water. This is an ideal destination to pick up fresh fish (which you can buy right off the boat). The docks are also home to a selection of takeaway food stalls, where you can dine on pizza, tacos, fish 'n' chips, ice cream and sweet treats while taking in the bustling boatside surroundings. Pick up some locally made crafts at one of the shops, and watch quietly for aquatic wildlife to swim by.

### TIME FOR TEA

Inherited from the city's early tea-swigging British settlers, a devout love for afternoon tea still remains in Victoria. The cathedral of afternoon tea in Victoria is the Empress Hotel, where a spread of sandwiches and sweets with tea will cost you $95 per person, or $142 with champagne.

 **BEST BRUNCH SPOTS**

**The Courtney Room**
Centrally located in a boutique hotel downtown, serving fancy (and hearty) brunch feasts. $$

**Nourish Kitchen & Cafe**
Charming eatery serving farm-fresh, veggie-forward food in the cozy dining room of a heritage home. $$

**The Ruby on Douglas**
Rainbow-hued, retro-style eatery serving up everything from savory waffles to quinoa porridge. $$

DRIVING TOUR

# South-Central Island Drive

This action-packed, one-way road trip begins with must-see architectural and cultural sites in the city. A cruise along the coast leads to colorful towns with exciting outdoor adventures found along the way. Further up the road, a cute country market with goats grazing on its roof makes for a tasty rest stop. Then, the drive is wrapped up with a riveting spelunking tour through Vancouver Island's renowned underground caves.

## 1 Beacon Hill Park

Start at Beacon Hill Park, just minutes from Downtown Victoria. This 200-acre parkland was once home to the Lekwungen People, now known as Esquimalt Nation and Songhees Nation. The park houses the world's tallest free-standing totem pole, the Story Pole, which was erected in 1956 and reaches 39 meters high. Meander along manicured pathways and look for The Moss Lady, a moss-covered statue that appears to be sleeping on the soil.

**The Drive:** A 50-minute cruise along the southern coast of Vancouver Island will take you to the town of Sooke.

## 2 Sooke Potholes Provincial Park

See Sooke River, where clear pools of water puddle in the crevices of naturally-carved bedrock, creating splash-worthy swimming holes (potholes). Walk along weaving tree-lined trails and discover a waterfall, or creep up steeper slopes and stand above the rock pools for a different perspective. There are several spots around the park that are per-

**Mary Vine Falls at Sooke Potholes Provincial Park**

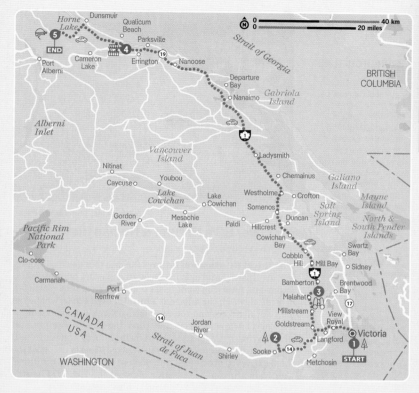

fect for a picnic so bring snacks, bring snacks to enjoy while there.

**The Drive:** It will take 45 minutes to drive from Sooke up to Malahat, where a sky-high adventure reveals far-off views.

### 3 Malahat Skywalk

Found just off the Malahat Highway amongst the lush landscape of the Cowichan Valley, the Malahat Skywalk takes you 250 meters above sea level for a truly unique bird's eye view. Start with a short trek along the elevated TreeWalk. Then wind your way to the top of the tower and brave the winding slide back down.

**The Drive:** A smooth highway drive will get you to Coombs in about an hour and a half, where you'll want to leave plenty of time to shop and dine at the country market.

### 4 Coombs Old Country Market

Known famously as Goats on a Roof due to the goats grazing on the sod roof (May

to October), this charming country market is more than a grocery store. Cool trinkets and keepsakes crowd the shelves of the shop, and on the grounds, a delicious doughnut shop, an Italian eatery, an ice cream stand and a Taqueria Cantina offer a range of snacks and treats.

**The Drive:** A mere 30-minute drive along the highway and along a forested road that wraps around Horne Lake will take you to an underground adventure like no other.

### 5 Horne Lake Caves

The collection of caves found at Horne Lake Caves Provincial Park offers subterranean spelunking adventures for visitors of all ages and skills. Explore the untouched underworld on the more spacious Riverbend Cave Tour (best for beginners) or, for serious spelunkers, the five-hour Max Depth Adventure Tour involves rappels, crawlways and climbs into the deepest chambers of the cave.

**BRUNCH CULTURE**

Declared the "brunch capital of Canada" by *You Gotta Eat Here!* host John Catucci back in 2016 due the high volume of restaurants in the area, Victoria still lives up to its name – the city is brimming with brunch spots that serve up bennies and bacon and eggs during that sweet spot between breakfast and lunch. Fueled by fare sourced from the 1000+ farms in the area, the food is fresh, delivering high-quality eggs, fruit and produce.

Because brunch is so popular here, you can expect long lines, if possible book in advance – and not just on weekends. With so many options, the biggest challenge is deciding where to eat.

CANADASTOCK/SHUTTERSTOCK ©

Totem poles, Thunderbird Park

## Discover BC's Natural & Human History

Prominent cultural institution

The **Royal BC Museum** features the province's shared stories, nature, history and culture through engaging permanent exhibits and revolving world-class temporary exhibits. Start with a stroll through the adjacent **Thunderbird Park**, where you can admire towering totem poles by Kwakwaka'wakw master carver Mungo Martin and other Indigenous carvers, and the Northwest Coast style Wawaditła (Mungo Martin House) where earlier totem carvings took place. Guests can visit the house to learn about past and present Indigenous traditions. Add value to your visit with a show at the **IMAX Theatre** where you can watch BC's largest film screen.

## Smell the Flowers

Garden City's best blooms

Home to over a million blooms, the **Butchart Gardens** became a designated National Historic Site of Canada in 2004. Jennie Butchart transformed her former limestone quarry backyard into a 55-acre, five-garden site, attracting visitors from around the world for generations.

See the original **Sunken Garden**, including the green-covered walls of the quarry. The **Japanese Garden** is a serene space surrounded by maple and beech trees. Enjoy a cone of gelato as you step through the Italian Garden. Exotic international plants are showcased in the **Mediterranean Garden**, and 280 varieties of roses are revealed in the **Rose Garden**. Kids (and kids at heart) love taking a spin on the **Rose Carousel**.

 **BEST AFTERNOON TEA ROOMS** ────

**Tea at the Empress**
World-famous afternoon tea in a château-style site where famed royals and celebrities have supped. **$$$**

**Butchart Gardens**
Traditional tea with gorgeous garden views at the Butchart family's former residence. **$$**

**Pendray Inn & Tea House**
Afternoon tea served in the decorative dining room of a historic home near Victoria's waterfront. **$$**

# Beyond Greater Victoria & Inner Harbour

Venture beyond Victoria's downtown core and discover scenic seascapes and forested frolics.

Spread along the southwestern coast of Vancouver Island, the town of Sooke is the gateway to outdoor adventure, where you can paddle, hike or bike through some of the area's most beautiful landscapes. Head to the harbor and kayak along the coast, or dip in the cool waters of the potholes that pool in the river's bedrocks. Take a trek along the world-famous 75km trail, and look for wildlife while you work your way through the woods. If you'd rather wander through nature while staying closer to the crowds, climb the winding tower that gives you a beautiful bird's eye view of the forest floor below. Beyond the city, there's so much more to discover.

**Places**
**Sooke** p91
**West Coast Trail** p94

**TOP TIP**

Rent a car and cruise along the coast, where windswept beaches, birdwatching spots and hiking trails invite adventure beyond the city.

## Sooke

See Sooke's river potholes

Running adjacent to the Sooke River, **Sooke Potholes Provincial Park** is a forested find favored by hikers, especially during the summer months. Located 40 minutes by car from downtown Victoria, this expansive park features a unique collection of naturally formed rock pools and potholes that brim the river's bedrock. The crystal-clear waters of these pools invite a refreshing dip after a day spent strolling the scenic park trails where waterfalls delight, and the remaining ruins of an abandoned resort invite curious questions from passersby.

For hikers, several shorter trails run along the river and into the forest, while more advanced adventurers use this site as the start or end point of a longer hike or bike along the **Galloping Goose Trail**, a rail trail that runs 55km between Victoria and northern Sooke. Many choose to make it a multiday trip, camping or stopping for a stay in smaller communities found along the way.

Sooke Harbour by water

Water adventures await at **Sooke Marina**, where you can rent (and buy) Vancouver Island's only Hobie kayaks (pedestrian pedal-powered kayaks) and Hobie Eclipse pedalboards (a souped-up version of the stand-up paddleboard) through **West Coast Outdoor Adventure** (westcoastoutdoor.com). Guided tours will take you along the coast of Sooke Harbour,

MR NIKON/SHUTTERSTOCK ©

Scan this QR code for prices, hours, and special events.

TOP SIGHT

# Malahat Skywalk

Take a casual corkscrew climb to a platform above the trees. Reaching 250m above sea level, this stunning 10-story spiral structure is the first of its kind in BC. Situated on the traditional territory of the Malahat Nation, the Skywalk offers views of Finlayson Arm, Saanich Inlet, Saanich Peninsula, Gulf Islands, San Juan Islands and the Coast Mountain range.

**DON'T MISS**

TreeWalk

Spiral Tower

Spiral Slide

Adventure Net

Art in Nature

Tower Plaza

Retro Food Carts

## Spiral Tower

It takes about 10 minutes before you get near the soaring **Spiral Tower**, which reveals itself as you emerge from the trees. As you ascend the 10-story sloped walkway, various views appear before you – from the woods that sit below, to the waters that reach far along the horizon. At the top, 360º panoramic views are revealed. And once you've explored from above, an adventurous exit route provides a fun way down.

## Spiral Slide

Instead of strolling back down, take a zip down the speedy spiral tube slide that runs 65ft down to the base (sliders must be at least five years of age and 42in tall, and everyone must slide solo).

## Adventure Net

At the top of the tower, thrillseekers can take a walk/bounce along a suspended cargo net, which provides an above-ground view of the forest floor below. Those afraid of heights may want to avoid this one though.

### MALAHAT NATION

The Malahat SkyWalk is located on the traditional territory of the Malahat Nation of the WSÁNEĆ peoples and their Indigenous stories are embedded throughout the experience. The site was developed as part of an economic and cultural partnership between the Malahat Nation and Malahat Skywalk Corp.

### Tower Top Yoga

Wellness enthusiasts can partake in yoga sessions, hosted at the top of the tower on Sundays and Wednesdays between June and September. It's a great way to find your "om" outdoors.

## Art in Nature

Wooden sculptures by Indigenous artists can be spotted throughout your journey, as well as a new addition to the art offerings: a series of one-of-a-kind, large-scale AI art installations created by two local Vancouver Island artists have been erected along the TreeWalk, in collaboration with the Riopelle Foundation and The Department of Canadian Heritage and Culture Pour Tous. The art pieces showcase reimagined, modern works of famed Canadian painter Jean Paul Riopelle. While this is a temporary exhibit, more works of art will follow.

## Tower Plaza

A newly updated plaza can be found adjacent to the base of the tower, where a nature-inspired climbing structure provides a place for kids to play, and colorful chairs offer a welcome resting place to sit and enjoy the views while sipping on drinks and noshing on snacks.

### Retro Food Carts

Grab a slice from Bicycle Pizza, where hand-stretched, oven-baked pizzas are made with local ingredients and served out of a vintage Airstream trailer. Then cool off with a cone from Softys, made fresh on Vancouver Island.

### Summer SkyWalk Music Series

During the summer months, live music creates a fun atmosphere on the plaza, where local bands and artists hit the outdoor stage during the afternoon/evenings from July until September.

### TOP TIPS

- Avoid long lines and larger crowds by visiting during off-season dates (summer is busiest) and, if possible, plan for a weekday visit as weekends can be busier.
- Keep your eye on the weather (clear days are best) and be sure to book well in advance.
- Wear comfortable walking shoes as the area is explored by foot.
- The SkyWalk is fully accessible, so wheelchairs and strollers can enjoy the experience too.
- The top of the tower can be breezy at times, so be sure to bring an extra layer.
- Parking is free and there's plenty of space for RVs and motorhomes.

ADRIANA MARGARITA LARIOS ARELLANO/SHUTTERSTOCK ©

**West Coast Trail**

where you can weave through the beams of the wooden board-walk, glide through the crystal-clear waters of the Sooke Basin and, if you're lucky, spot wildlife along the way, such as seals, otters, jellyfish and orcas. For a more extensive wildlife viewing experience, consider taking a whale watching tour (there are several on offer in the area).

## West Coast Trail

Take a multiday outing

Sooke is the starting point for the world-famous **West Coast Trail**: a challenging 75km, multiday hike that takes experienced hikers through muddy landscapes, fast-flowing river waters and up more than 100 steep ladders. This is no stroll through the woods; the West Coast Trail is rigorous, known to bring even the most advanced adventurers to their knees. Reservations must be made in advance, as camping spots should be secured for overnight stays. The backcountry trek takes approximately six to eight days to complete or, for those looking for a shorter (but equally as difficult) version, there's a midway entry point at Nitinaht Village. The trail was once used byIndigenous Peoples for travel and trade routes through the West Coast.

 **BEST BEGINNER HIKES IN SOOKE**

**Ed MacGregor Park**
A Sooke boardwalk stroll shifts into a switchback wooden walkway through the woods.

**Whiffen Spit Trail**
Gravel pathway along a skinny slice of land with views of the Juan de Fuca Strait.

**Ross Cove Regional Park Loop**
Ocean views and old-growth cedar trees delight on this wander through the rainforest.

# Central Island

RELAXED COASTAL COMMUNITIES

Victoria

Calm coastal communities speckle this stretch of the island, where sprawling sandy beaches and meandering mountain trails offer outdoor adventures for all ages and skill levels. Find natural feats and sweet treats in Nanaimo, Vancouver Island's 'second city' and home to the island's legendary Nanaimo Bar dessert. Comb the expansive beaches at low tide and creep through the underground caves that lure thrillseekers to Parksville, nature's playground. Add country markets fueled by local farms and up-close encounters with local wildlife wildlife, and visitors to Qualicum Beach are in for a laid back stay by the water. Veer inland for a peek at the Canada's tallest waterfall, near Port Alberni. And just west of Courtenay, you'll find a surprising spot for snow lovers: the island's best (and only) ski hill.

## Forested Fun in Nanaimo

Teeter above the trees

Found just south of the city of Nanaimo, **WildPlay Nanaimo** takes tree climbing to the next level with aerial adventure courses that challenge climbers of all ages. Cross wobbly bridges, crawl over cargo nets, grip rope swings and zoom across ziplines as you traverse along multi-level platforms set in the trees. Take your treetop thrills to the next level with a bungy jump off a sky-high steel bridge, or make like Tarzan and tackle the Primal Swing, where you drop to the river at speeds of up to 140km/hour. Not gung-ho about heights? The scenic walkways are pleasant here too.

## Nanaimo Culture

History and heritage

Located downtown, the **Nanaimo Museum** showcases the city's Indigenous origins and architectural highlights. Start with the Snuneymuxw exhibit and learn about the rich living culture of the Snuneymuxw First Nation. Other highlights include the heritage Miner's Cottage; the restored Steam Locomotive, originally built in 1889; The Bastion, the last remaining wooden Hudson's Bay Company bastion built in 1853; and the Sports Hall of Fame.

---

☑ **TOP TIP**

If you're visiting the area from Vancouver, consider taking the car ferry from Horseshoe Bay in West Vancouver to Departure Bay in Nanaimo instead of the more popular Tsawwassen to Victoria route. This will cut down on driving time once you reach the other side.

---

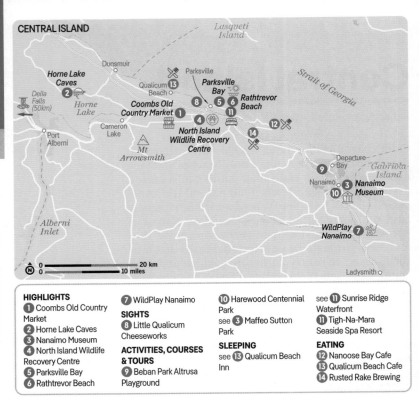

**HIGHLIGHTS**
1. Coombs Old Country Market
2. Horne Lake Caves
3. Nanaimo Museum
4. North Island Wildlife Recovery Centre
5. Parksville Bay
6. Rathtrevor Beach

7. WildPlay Nanaimo

**SIGHTS**
8. Little Qualicum Cheeseworks

**ACTIVITIES, COURSES & TOURS**
9. Beban Park Altrusa Playground

10. Harewood Centennial Park
see 3 Maffeo Sutton Park

**SLEEPING**
see 13 Qualicum Beach Inn

see 11 Sunrise Ridge Waterfront
11. Tigh-Na-Mara Seaside Spa Resort

**EATING**
12. Nanoose Bay Cafe
13. Qualicum Beach Cafe
14. Rusted Rake Brewing

## Nanaimo's Popular Pathway

Hiking and biking

Park the car and take the **E&N Trail** (named after its origins as the Esquimalt to Nanaimo Railway back in the day) through the city instead. This multi-purpose paved pathway connects Nanaimo's waterfront with the Parkway Trail, offering over 8km for walking, biking or blading through the area, passing the city's schools, shops and recreational sites along the way.

## Parksville's Underworld Adventures

Creep through caves

Vancouver Island is home to the highest concentration of caves in North America, yet many are unaware of the spelunking

 **BEST BITES IN QUALICUM BEACH**

**Qualicum Beach Cafe**
West Coast–inspired fare with Italian influences enjoyed in a spacious dining room or patio with sweeping ocean views.$$

**Nanoose Bay Cafe**
Modern dining room with marina views serving fresh, seafood-packed meals with Asian influences.$$

**Rusted Rake Brewing**
Gourmet eatery and delightful farm-to-tap craft brewery set on a scenic farmstead in Nanoose Bay.$

sites that are hidden in (or under) their own backyard. Found just over 30 minutes from Parksville, **Horne Lake Caves** offers caving tours for all skill levels. Get your toes wet (literally) with a shorter, multi-cave tour fit for beginners. Choose a more action-packed option where you crawl, climb, slide and squeeze through the crevices of the deeper depths of the caves, or go all in with an extreme, max-depth adventure that involves a challenging rappel descent and up to six hours of cave touring through the deepest underground tunnels.

## Parksville by the Beach

Low-tide beach play

Best known for its breathtaking beaches, Parksville is a place packed with seaside fun. Unsurpassed in size, Rathtrevor Beach has 2kms of shoreline, with far-reaching low tides that invite treks along the sandy shores in search of seashells and sand dollars. The beach at Parksville Bay has a beach party atmosphere, where rounds of beach volleyball create a buzzing vibe. Paddleboarding and swimming are also popular here. The Waterfront Walkway is also a favorite place for locals to get moving outdoors. In July, be sure to check out the Parksville Beach Festival, a five-week festival best known for the sand sculpting competition where master sculptors from around the world compete for the top title.

## Goats on a Roof in Coombs

More than a market

Since 1973, the **Coombs Old Country Market**, found about 10 minutes by car from Parksville, has drawn crowds for its very unique feature: a sod roof topped with grazing goats. Inspired by their Norwegian heritage, the original owners built the market with a grass roof, later deciding to add goats to keep the grass mowed, and to add entertainment for passing cars. Today, the roof-roaming goats are a top attraction, likely the most famous sod roof in the world. Not just a spot to gaze at goats, the massive indoor market houses some great gifts and international foods. The site is also home to a delicious doughnut shop, an ice cream stand, an authentic Italian restaurant and a Taqueria Cantina food truck.

## Wildlife Encounters

Eagles, owls and bears

Sitting on 8 acres of meticulously manicured land, **North Island Wildlife Recovery Centre**, only five minutes from

**CANADA'S TALLEST WATERFALL**

**Della Falls**, located in Strathcona Provincial Park in the Central Vancouver Island region, is Canada's tallest waterfall and the 16th highest in the world. Plunging 440m into Great Central Lake, these raging rapids are a sight to behold – if you can get to them. It takes a challenging multiday, high-elevation hike along the 29km (out and back) Della Falls Trail to see them. But first, you'll have to cross Great Central Lake to get to the trailhead, as it's only accessible by water.

A 55-minute water taxi is available during the summer months for $200 per person round trip. Be sure to do your research before you go.

 **WHERE TO STAY IN PARKSVILLE QUALICUM BEACH**

| **Tigh-Na-Mara Seaside Spa Resort** | **Sunrise Ridge Waterfront Resort** | **Qualicum Beach Inn** |
|---|---|---|
| Spacious rooms with forested ocean views, a grotto spa, an indoor pool and beach access. | Suites with seasonal pool and hot tub, plus access to a sandy stretch of beach. | Seaside boutique hotel with indoor pool and stunning sunset views. |

Sweet-toothed travelers haven't completed a visit to Nanaimo without a taste-testing tour of the tasty tri-layered, no-bake bars that were born here. A wafer crumb base with a creamy custard center, topped with a layer of chocolate ganache – locals may roll their eyes (they've likely had one too many), but these treats are definitely worth a try. Start your tour at **1 La Isla Cafe**, where a selection of baked goods (including Nanaimo Bars) are made fresh on site. A mere three-minute walk away, **2 A Wee Cupcakery** serves up the classic bars too, as well as a cupcake take which is equally as tasty. Walk it off and stretch your legs on a five-minute stroll to **3 Red's Bakery**, which offers a variety, including a peanut butter version of the classic bar, and even a Nanaimo Bar cheesecake. Don't eat too much though, cause there are plenty more places to try. **4 Serious Coffee**

is only steps away. It has several locations around Vancouver Island (and on the mainland too), and for good reason. Serious Coffee may be best known for its high-quality coffee beans, but its baked goods are tasty too. **5 Vault Cafe** is close by, and housed in a pretty pink building – it's easy to spot. There you'll find eclectic decor, green-hued walls, and a packed pastry case with the classic bars on display. And round out your tasting tour with a final stop at **6 BOCCA Cafe**, found in the Old City Quarter, serving up a gluten-free, dairy-free version of Nanaimo Bars for those with dietary restrictions. These are only a few stops on the extensive Nanaimo Bar Trail, which includes over 30 spots around the region.

See the full list of Nanaimo Bar Trail stops at the QR code

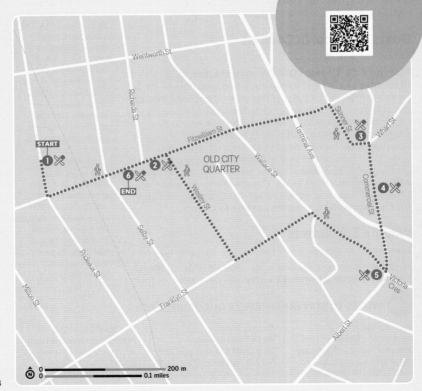

RUSS HEINL/SHUTTERSTOCK ©

Plan your ultimate mountain adventure on the Mt Washington website via the QR code

**Ski station, Mount Washington**

Parksville, is a haven for rescued wildlife. The nonprofit association cares for and rehabilitates local wildlife in need. See a rescued eaglet that was found with a broken wing, or a great grey owl (the tallest owl breed in BC). A large outdoor bear den houses a trio of motherless black bear cubs, and there's a super rare white raven that's unable to survive in the wild. A glistening pond is encircled by a gravel pathway, where you can stroll and spot tons of turtles and ducks, and if you time it just right, a public animal release ceremony is a must.

## Central Island Skiing

Snow play

Visitors to Vancouver are very familiar with the trifecta of ski hills found on the North Shore mountains, but many don't realize that Vancouver Island offers slopeside fun too. **Mount Washington**, located 30 minutes north of the Comox Valley, has over 1700 acres of alpine terrain, where skiing, snowshoeing trails and a tube park offer snow play. During the warmer seasons, mountain biking, hiking and wildlife viewing are big here too. Music lovers should be sure to check out the **Music in the Mountains** concert series during the summer months, where musical acts are paired with samplings of local beer, wine and ciders on Sundays.

### FAMOUS FARMSTEAD

Cheese lovers will want to make time for a stop at **Little Qualicum Cheeseworks**, a family-run farm that produces Swiss-style, handcrafted artisan cheeses found in shops throughout BC. The farm is home to Canada's first-ever milk on tap dispenser, where locals can bring in their own reusable bottles and fill them with fresh milk for a small fee. Pet calves, sheep and goats as you roam the farmstead, learn about milking and even take a peek at the cheese production plant. Guided tours are also available if you want to learn more about the farm life and get a behind-the-scenes tour of how it all works.

## BEST PLAYGROUNDS IN NANAIMO

**Maffeo Sutton Park**
Playground with harbor views featuring climbing structures, slides, a zipline and custom-carved canoe.

**Harewood Centennial Park**
Community park with accessible swings, a merry-go-round, water park and mountain bike park.

**Beban Park Altrusa Playground**
Recreation complex complete with slides, swings and a racing track for toddlers on trikes.

# Pacific Rim

SURFERS' PARADISE

● ◉ Victoria

BC's raw west coast wilderness, sandy surf beaches and charming coastal communities collide in the Pacific Rim region of Vancouver Island. This area consists of a trifecta of small towns: Tofino, Canada's surf town; Ucluelet, a harbor hub for angler adventures; and Bamfield, an off-the-beaten-path inlet offering rugged outdoor fun.

The Pacific Rim National Park Reserve lies along the west coast of the area, on the traditional territories of the Nuu-chah-nulth First Nations, and is renowned for its backcountry hiking trails, cold water surfing swells and authentic Indigenous cultural sites. On its northern tip, the Unesco-designated Clayoquot Sound Biosphere Reserve is renowned for its diverse range of ecosystems, most notably the temperate rainforest and coastal shores, and the population of around 5000 people of the Nuu-chah-nulth First Nations, whose traditional territories encompass the entire biosphere reserve.

☑ **TOP TIP**

Fuel up and get an early start to your day, as the drive from Victoria to the Pacific Rim National Park Reserve can take nearly five hours (excluding stops). Check for updates and road closures before you go.

## Surfing in Tofino

Canada's surf capital

Year-round swells lure surf bums of all skill levels to Tofino for unparalleled cold-water surfing along Vancouver Island's west coast. For lessons at all levels, check out **Surf Sisters**, originally aimed at encouraging more women to try the sport, and now a top surf school for anyone who wants to try. **Cox Bay Beach** is Tofino's main surfing destination, where most surf competitions are held and the surf is most consistent. **Long Beach** has a long history in surf culture and is best for summer swells. **Chesterman Beach** is known for having some of the best breaks for beginners, with three different sections (north, south and middle); South Chesterman Beach is the best place to start. And finally, the calm waters of **Mackenzie Beach** provide a quieter spot for beginner lessons, where stand-up paddleboarders also prefer to go as the tidal rocks provide protection from the winds here.

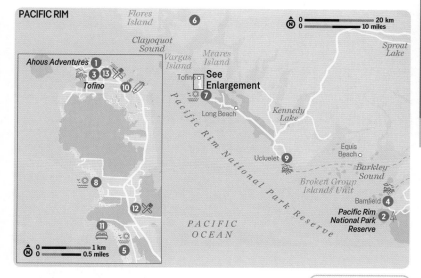

# Tofino Through an Indigenous Lens

**Eco and cultural tours**

Owned and operated by the Ahousaht Nation, **Ahous Adventures** offers authentic Indigenous tours throughout the Pacific Rim region, shared through the lens of the people who have lived on the lands and waters of the area since time immemorial. Explore the natural hot springs found at Hot Springs Cove, search for gray and humpback whales along the wild waters of Tofino on a whale watching tour or observe black bears in their natural habitat along the coast of Clayoquot Sound, all while learning about the history, culture, storytelling and the experiences of the Ahousaht Nation.

# Ucluelet Sea Life

**Tide pools and touch tanks**

One of Ucluelet's most popular local attractions, the **Ucluelet Aquarium** is a great family-friendly site and Canada's first catch-and-release aquarium that focuses on showcasing the marine critters found in the region's local waters of Barkley and Clayoquot Sounds. You can see everything from the

**HIGHLIGHTS**
1 Ahous Adventures
2 Pacific Rim National Park Reserve
3 Tofino

**SIGHTS**
4 Bamfield
5 Chesterman Beach
6 Clayoquot Sound Biosphere Reserve
7 Cox Bay Beach
8 Mackenzie Beach
9 Ucluelet
**see** 9 Ucluelet Aquarium

**ACTIVITIES, COURSES & TOURS**
10 Surf Sister Surf School

**SLEEPING**
11 Wickaninnish Inn

**EATING**
**see** 9 Pluvio
12 Tacofino
13 Wolf in the Fog

 **BEST PLACES TO STAY IN TOFINO**

**Hotel Zed**
Step into the '70s with a stay at this retro-chic hotel, complete with mini disco and hidden arcade. **$$**

**Pacific Sands Resort**
Surf-in, surf-out beach houses and spacious suites situated right on the ocean. **$$**

**Wickaninnish Inn**
Storm-watching central, where luxury accommodations offer sweeping water views from an historic landmark. **$$$**

DANITA DELIMONT/SHUTTERSTOCK ©

For more info and to plan your visit, scan this QR code

TOP SIGHT

# Pacific Rim National Park Reserve

Natural wonders, cultural history and outdoor adventures amaze in this national park. Located on the traditional territories of the Nuu-chah-nulth people, the park consists of the surf beaches of Long Beach, the calm waters of Broken Group Islands, and the tree-lined paths of the West Coast Trail. The protected coast of Clayoquot Sound is a Unesco-designated site, recognized for its natural and cultural characteristics.

**DON'T MISS**

Clayoquot Sound

Long Beach

ʔapsčiik ťašii pathway

Nuu-chah-nulth Trail

West Coast Trail

Broken Group Islands

## Long Beach

Tofino is Canada's surf town and **Long Beach** has the swells to satisfy. It's the largest and longest beach found in the **Pacific Rim National Park Reserve**, stretching 16km along the coastline between Tofino and Ucluelet. Keep an eye out for passing gray and humpback whales while beachcombing, swimming, surfing or just sunbathing on its warm, sandy shores.

## ʔapsčiik ťašii Pathway

Also found in the Long Beach area of the Pacific Rim National Park Reserve is ʔapsčiik ťašii (pronounced ups-cheek ta-shee, meaning "going the right direction on the path" in

Nuu-chah-nulth dialects). This paved, multi-use pathway runs 25km along the coast, connecting Tofino and Ucluelet, making the region more accessible for those who are car-free. The path invites visitors to cycle or stroll, exploring the beauty of the reserve while respecting and honoring the Indigenous land and communities of the area.

## Nuu-chah-nulth Trail

Formerly known as the Wickaninnish Trail, Nuu-chah-nulth Trail is the longest hiking trail in the park, connecting Long Beach to Florencia Beach. Beginning along the South Beach Trail, hikers go on a 3.8km journey through dense rainforest and raised wooden boardwalks. Along the way, look for remnants of the rich history of the land, such as old logs that run under the more modern wooden boardwalks, remaining sections of a trail that was originally used by the Nuu-chah-nulth, and later covered by logs by settlers for easy access.

## West Coast Trail

A bucket-list trek for the most experienced hikers, this 75km backcountry trail consists of challenging and technical terrain, taking you up a series of ladders, through muddy bogs, and along washed-out walkways. Along the trail, **Tsusiat Falls** is a hike highlight, with scenic, wide-spanning falls, a swimming beach and one of the more popular campsites found along the trail. The hike takes six to eight days to complete from end-to-end, with campgrounds along the way.

## Broken Group Islands

A collection of over 100 tiny islands and outcrops found along calm, sheltered coastlines, Broken Group Islands has become a paradise for backcountry campers and kayakers. **Gibraltar Island** is a popular starting point for paddlers who make their way along the water weaving through the islets and camping along the way, with sites found on Gilbert, Clarke, Turret, Willis and Hand Islands. Many guided kayak tours through the islands are offered, which is a great way to get around without getting lost if it's your first go.

**NATIONAL PARKS PASS**

All visitors to the Pacific Rim National Park Reserve are required to purchase a National Parks Entry Pass (youths 17 and under are the exception and gain free access to all of Canada's national parks). Adults can purchase daily passes ($10.50), annual passes ($52.25), or walk passes for select beaches ($6.50). For info visit parks.canada.ca.

**TOP TIPS**

- For beginner surfers, visit June–August when the water is warmer and the swells are smaller.
- For first-time surfers, skip Long Beach and consider South Chesterman Beach instead; this is where most surf schools offer starter lessons.

- Visit the Parks Canada website (parks.canada.ca) and download the preparation guide before you tackle overnight hikes.
- When hiking overnight, be prepared to pack out everything you bring with you – follow the Leave No Trace guidelines.

- Check for sites with food poles and storage boxes when camping in the backcountry.
- When camping around Broken Group Islands, keep campfires below tide lines.

### TACO THE TOWN

From slinging tacos from a truck in a surf shop parking lot back in 2009, to becoming an iconic West Coast brand, **Tacofino** is now a staple around Vancouver Island and the Lower Mainland, serving up the best tacos in town. Here, you'll find fresh, California- and Mexico-inspired fare, like the famous fish tacos made of tempura lingcod or the seared albacore tuna taco, best enjoyed with a side of loaded tater tots. Hit the original orange truck, which still stands in a parking lot in Tofino, or opt for a sit down at one of the 11 locations that have popped up around Vancouver, Victoria and Tofino – just be prepared to wait in line!

alien-like sea cucumbers to squirming Pacific octopus in a fun and engaging setting on the waterfront. Touch tanks even let little ones get hands-on with the critters of the sea. The enthusiastic staff sets this place apart, educating visitors on issues of conservation in a way that's easy for kids to understand. Expect to walk away with renewed excitement about the wonders of ocean wildlife.

# Hiking in Ucluelet

Wild wilderness walk

Take a trek along the **Wild Pacific Trail** in Ucluelet, where the temperate rainforest meets the ocean. The residents of "Ukee" have built the magnificent 10km trail that can be equally spectacular in both the sun and stormy weather. The hike starts with a 2.6km loop that winds around a 1915 Amphitrite lighthouse and progresses northwest as far as the Ancient Cedars loop and the Rocky Bluffs beyond. The trail is well signposted with a well-marked map. To complete the whole 10km, you'll need to take a couple of interconnecting pathways along quiet roads that link to several attractive beaches on the way. Various info boards provide background on the area's history and nature, and the path is dotted with benches, lookouts and artist's loops equipped with viewing platforms that are perfect for inspired artists looking to take painting stops along the way.

# Storm Watching

Get out in the wild weather

Along the exposed coast of Tofino, winter weather brings moody skies, wild winds and torrential downpours – conditions that would normally repel visitors during the cooler months. In 1996, after years of witnessing dramatic storms along **Chesterman Beach**, the McDiarmid family opened the **Wickaninnish Inn** hoping others would enjoy storm watching too. Now winter storm watching is one of Tofino's biggest draws, bringing visitors from around the world to try to get a glimpse of the winter weather phenomenon.

Scan here to book book a storm-watcher's stay.

### BEST PLACES TO EAT IN TOFINO

**Wolf in the Fog**
Award-winning, seafood-centric food with a rustic, beach-in-the-wilderness vibe. **$$**

**Tacofino**
West Coast flavors meet Mexican staples at this street-food-style chain that started as a food truck in Tofino. **$**

**Pluvio**
Ucluelet's newest restaurant, serving sophisticated multicourse tasting menus in a warm and casual setting. **$$$**

# North Island

RUGGED WILDERNESS

Go way off grid as you move further up to the North Island region of Vancouver Island, where wildlife such as eagles, whales and bears roam free among untouched landscapes, and Kwakwaka'wakw First Nations traditions, art and living culture surround you.

In this remote region of outstanding natural beauty, the infrastructure is rudimentary. Like anything north of Campbell River, it's what islanders call the 'real north.' With its tiny population, wild coastline and temperamental seas, the area is faintly reminiscent of the Scottish Highlands, but with more trees. In fact, several local landmarks are named after Scots, including the most northwesterly point, Cape Scott. Find colorful buildings set on stilts along the coast of Telegraph Cove, once a fishing village and now the launch point for ecotourism in the region. Kayak with orcas in Johnstone Strait, or immerse yourself in Kwakwaka'wakw culture here.

---

☑ **TOP TIP**

The north of Vancouver Island is most easily reached by car. The main Hwy 19 (aka Island Hwy) runs from Nanaimo through to Port Hardy (approx. four hours). Charter flights are available from Vancouver to Port Hardy, but you'll want to rent a car for most North Island spots.

---

## Telegraph Cove

Colorful community

Named after its beginnings as a one-shack telegraph station, **Telegraph Cove** evolved into a fishing village and cannery in its earlier days, and has since grown into what is now recognized as the kickoff point for ecotourism to the more remote northern regions of the island. Around 20 people call this tiny town home, but during the summer months the crowds swell, as the town floods with daytrippers looking for off-grid adventures in the wild. This town is where BC's first whale watching company launched in 1980, and it's still famed for its aquatic adventures. The snug cove houses a series of colorful shacks that sit on stilts, creating a charming, picture-perfect harbor town.

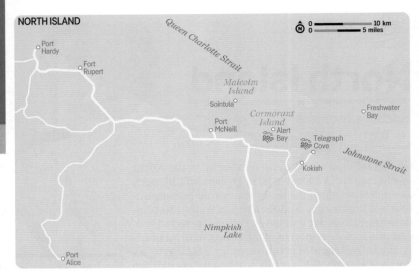

NORTH ISLAND

Queen Charlotte Strait

Port Hardy

Fort Rupert

Malcolm Island

Sointula

Port McNeill

Cormorant Island

Alert Bay

Telegraph Cove

Freshwater Bay

Johnstone Strait

Kokish

Nimpkish Lake

Port Alice

0   10 km
0   5 miles

# North Island Waterways

## Kayakers' paradise

Launching from Telegraph Cove, **North Island Kayak Tours**, the largest kayaking tour operator in the area, offers wildlife watching and sea-kayak trips with guides from June to September. These range from two-hour family excursions along the coast to eight-day basecamp expeditions, all in search of humpback whales, sea lions and Indigenous cultural sites.

# Cultural Experiences

## Aboriginal history at Alert Bay

Learn about the heritage of the Kwakwaka'wakw people at the U'mista Cultural Centre in Alert Bay, a longhouse-like facility that houses culturally significant artifacts, including an exhibit showcasing the history and treasured masks and traditional paraphernalia of the "potlatch," a traditional dance ceremony that was banned during the late 1800s. Summer programs include book readings and cedar-bark-weaving demonstrations, while the on-site gift shop brims with ethically sourced Kwakwaka'wakw art.

 **BEST NORTH ISLAND WILDLIFE TOURS**

**North Island Kayak Tours**
Go whale watching by sea kayak and see orcas and other whales swimming right alongside your boat.

**Great Bear Nature Tours**
Grizzly bear–viewing tours from Port Hardy to the river valley of the Great Bear Rainforest.

**k'awat'si Tours**
View wildlife from the water and roam remote beaches while listening to stories from an Indigenous guide.

Orcas, Telegraph Cove (p105)

# British Columbia

## AWE-INSPIRING MOUNTAINS SCULPTED BY TIME

From lush rainforests to soaring mountains and pristine coastlines, British Columbia is a province that celebrates its diversity in landscapes and Indigenous cultures.

From millions of years ago to the present time, glaciers have carved the terrain into the British Columbia we know today. They've shaped the valleys, peaks and rivers into a landscape that wildlife roam, salmon use for spawning, Indigenous Peoples use for hunting and trade, and European explorers used to find their way, and also shaped the roads, waterways and trails along which you'll travel on your trip. Canada's westernmost province offers adventures for all abilities, with more kilometers of ski runs and hiking and biking trails than some countries have in roads, and so many lakes that you'll surely find one that's just right.

JIRI KULISEK/SHUTTERSTOCK ©

While some might think of British Columbia as a 'new' province in a 'new' country, its history reaches far beyond the date of confederation in 1871. Evidence of Indigenous civilization dating back more than 13,000 years was recently discovered in Haida Gwaii and in the Great Bear Rainforest. These are the ancestral roots of the present-day Indigenous Peoples with whom you can learn and explore on one of the many transformational Indigenous experiences in British Columbia. The gold rush of the late 19th century is one reason British Columbia is not part of the United States (p128), and the province as we know it today has plenty of stories to tell from those who have been here since time immemorial.

## THE MAIN AREAS

### COAST MOUNTAINS & GREAT BEAR RAINFOREST
Wildlife, culture and remote temperate rainforests. p114

### CARIBOO CHILCOTIN
Paddling paradise, biking and cowboy culture. p124

### THOMPSON OKANAGAN
Wineries, waterfalls, lakes and superb skiing. p130

IGOR KYRYLIUK/SHUTTERSTOCK ©

**Above: Snowpatch Spire, Bugaboo Provincial Park; left: Glacier National Park**

**KOOTENAY
ROCKIES**
Groovy towns and
majestic mountain
parks. **p137**

**HAIDA GWAII
& THE NORTH**
Engaging Indigenous
history and vast
wilderness. **p143**

## CAR

Renting or buying a vehicle is the ultimate way to explore the province. All-wheel-drive or 4WDs are recommended for winter driving and most highways require vehicles to have M+S (mud and snow) tires from October to April. Request M+S tires before renting a car.

## BUS

Rider Express has a daily service between Vancouver and Calgary, with stops at major towns on the Trans-Canada Hwy. Kootenay Charters, Kootenay Gateway Shuttle Service and Mountain Man Mike's Bus service the Kootenay Rockies. Daily buses between Vancouver, Squamish and Whistler are also available.

## AIR

A short flight can save days of driving. Pacific Coastal Airlines flies to some of the most remote parts of the province. Lynx Airlines connects you to the rest of Canada affordably, and Air Canada and WestJet are still the biggest airlines in the country.

### Haida Gwaii & the North, p143

Find time-honored totem poles and petroglyphs alongside Indigenous storytellers who connect it all in British Columbia's northernmost archipelago.

### Coast Mountains & Great Bear Rainforest, p114

Famous for Whistler Blackcomb Resort, the Coast Mountains give way to the lush, misty Great Bear Rainforest.

### Thompson Okanagan, p130

Venture from world-class wineries to rushing waterfalls. Also offers bike-friendly wine touring, water sports and North America's largest canoe-only lake.

# Find Your Way

Explore Canada's most mountainous province through transformative Indigenous experiences and four seasons of epic adventures. Like the grapes of BC's wine regions, we've hand-picked the best ways to see the most interesting places.

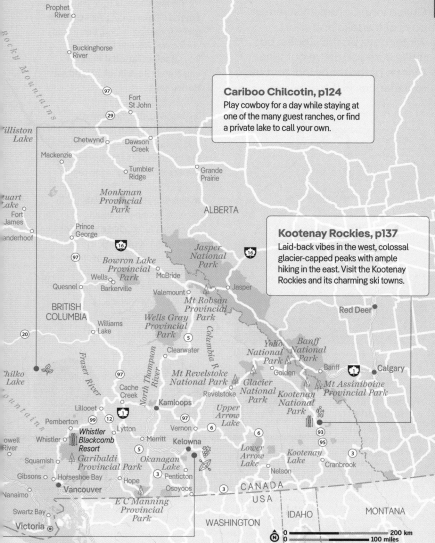

**Cariboo Chilcotin, p124**
Play cowboy for a day while staying at one of the many guest ranches, or find a private lake to call your own.

**Kootenay Rockies, p137**
Laid-back vibes in the west, colossal glacier-capped peaks with ample hiking in the east. Visit the Kootenay Rockies and its charming ski towns.

NORTHWEST TERRITORIES

Fort Nelson

Prophet River

Buckinghorse River

Rocky Mountains

Williston Lake

Chetwynd

Mackenzie

Fort St John

Dawson Creek

Tumbler Ridge

Grande Prairie

Monkman Provincial Park

ALBERTA

Stuart Lake

Fort James

Vanderhoof

Prince George

Bowron Lake Provincial Park

Wells

Quesnel

Barkerville

McBride

Valemount

Jasper National Park

Jasper

Mt Robson Provincial Park

Red Deer

BRITISH COLUMBIA

Williams Lake

Wells Gray Provincial Park

Columbia R.

Clearwater

Yoho National Park

Banff National Park

Chilko Lake

Fraser River

Cache Creek

North Thompson River

Mt Revelstoke National Park

Revelstoke

Glacier National Park

Golden

Banff

Calgary

Kamloops

Upper Arrow Lake

Kootenay National Park

Mt Assiniboine Provincial Park

Lillooet

Pemberton

Whistler

Lytton

Merritt

Vernon

Kelowna

Lower Arrow Lake

Kootenay Lake

Cranbrook

Whistler Blackcomb Resort

Squamish

Garibaldi Provincial Park

Okanagan Lake

Penticton

Nelson

Gibsons

Horseshoe Bay

Hope

Vancouver

Osoyoos

CANADA USA

Powell River

Nanaimo

Swartz Bay

Victoria

E C Manning Provincial Park

WASHINGTON

IDAHO

MONTANA

0    200 km
0    100 miles

# Plan Your Time

Chase long Canadian summer days at the lake and short winter days on the slopes, but make sure you carve out time for one of the many Indigenous experiences in the province.

## Three Days to Travel Around

● Drive from Banff to Vancouver along Hwy 1/Trans-Canada Hwy. Stop at **Yoho National Park** (p137) for **Takakkaw Falls** (p137) and **Emerald Lake** (p137). Visit **Golden** (p137) for skiing, hiking, biking and via ferrata. Ascend Rogers Pass into **Glacier National Park** (p160) and **Mount Revelstoke National Park** (p140).

● Descend into the town of **Revelstoke** (p140) for summer and winter activities at Revelstoke Mountain Resort and continue into the Thompson Okanagan region.

● Head south to **Kelowna** (p135) for wine country or west to Kamloops for its **three wineries** (p134). From Kamloops, ascend into the Coquihalla Canyon via the Coquihalla Hwy and then down into the Fraser Valley before arriving in Vancouver.

EB ADVENTURE PHOTOGRAPHY/SHUTTERSTOCK ©

Chairlift, Whistler (p116)

## Seasonal Highlights

For those looking for wildlife, hiking and the late-setting summer sun, May–September is for you. Autumn is beautiful, although short but sweet, and the best snow usually falls between January and March.

### FEBRUARY
Winter is in full swing! Hit the deep ski hill bases, shred the backcountry, take to the air for heli-skiing, or go skating and ice fishing.

### APRIL
April is for **aprés!** Ski resorts across the province celebrate spring skiing with tons of outdoor concerts and events.

### JUNE
Celebrate heritage, culture and resilience of Indigenous Peoples on National Indigenous Peoples Day on June 21.

EB ADVENTURE PHOTOGRAPHY/SHUTTERSTOCK ©, VIEW APART/SHUTTERSTOCK ©, JOI54/SHUTTERSTOCK ©

## Another Three Days to Travel Around

● Drive up the **Sea-to-Sky Hwy** (p116) to spend a night or two in **Whistler** (p116) before continuing east to **Pemberton** (p119).

● Take the **Duffey Lake Road** (p118) to **Joffre Lakes Provincial Park** (p118), pre-book your time. Visit **Fort Berens Estate Winery** (p125) and join **Xwisten** (Hoyshten, p127) in Lillooet for lunch and an Indigenous tour.

● Head south towards Lytton down Hwy 12 to Hwy 1 and either drive through to Vancouver or stay at **Kumsheen Rafting** (p127) in a glamping tent. Explore the **Gold Rush Trail** (p128) at your leisure as you circle back to Vancouver.

## 10 or More Days to Explore

● To loop through the Great Bear Rainforest, catch BC Ferries' Coastal Sea Wolf from Port Hardy on Vancouver Island to **Bella Coola** (p119) and the world's largest coastal temperate rainforest while navigating alongside passing whales through dramatic fjords.

● After exploring the Bella Coola area, drive east towards **Nimpo Lake** (p121) in the Chilcotin. Here you can choose a **floatplane-accessible adventures** (p121) to remote lodges, glaciers, lakes and waterfalls.

● Enjoy **lakeside living** (p127) and **cowboy culture** (p127) as you head south through the **Cariboo** (p124) and then through **Lillooet** (p127), **Pemberton** (p119) and **Whistler** (p116) before returning to Vancouver via the **Sea-to-Sky Hwy** (p116).

**JULY**
Find Canada Day celebrations throughout the province on July 1 of each year.

**AUGUST**
Don't stray too far from the many swimming opportunities during what is usually the hottest month of the year.

**SEPTEMBER**
In autumn, the salmon leap and bears feast. Book a tour in the **Great Bear Rainforest** (p114) and witness nature's fierce beauty.

**OCTOBER**
Celebrate the bounties of the crops at fall harvest festivals such as the **Okanagan Wine Festival** (p136) in Penticton.

# Coast Mountains & Great Bear Rainforest

Vancouver ●

**WILDLIFE, CULTURE AND REMOTE RAINFORESTS**

### GETTING AROUND

Traveling to this region requires a flight or lengthy drive. Pacific Coastal Airlines connects Powell River, Bella Coola and Bella Bella to Vancouver, while WestJet and Air Canada service Prince Rupert and Terrace. The Sunshine Coast, near Vancouver, is accessible via an exciting seaplane journey or a serene BC Ferries voyage from Horseshoe Bay terminal. To truly experience the entirety of this region, a vehicle is essential.

### ☑ TOP TIP

Avoid visiting Whistler on holidays and weekends, when it's inundated. Don't have a car? Buses frequently run between Whistler and downtown Vancouver and Vancouver International Airport. Unless you're heliskiing, the Great Bear Rainforest is only accessible April–October.

Rising from the shores of the Pacific Ocean are the rugged and glacier-capped granite peaks of British Columbia's Coast Mountains and Great Bear Rainforest. Few places can match their pristine and remote wilderness, which is packed with alpine adventures, old-growth forests, wildlife and annual snowfall. The Great Bear Rainforest is where the rarest bear in the world makes its home, and where many Pacific salmon begin their spawning journey in what is one of the most important animal migrations in the Pacific Northwest. Ninety minutes north of Vancouver, Whistler Blackcomb claims fame as North America's largest ski resort and one of the world's best. The charming town of Whistler and its abundance of four-season adventures are the reason some come for a season and stay for a lifetime.

## Working up a Sweat in Squamish & Garibaldi

### Basecamp to adventure

Sandwiched between dramatic granite mountains and the turquoise bay, Squamish is a hiking-biking-rock climbing adventure-junkie mecca. Even though it's hardcore, this town's wholesome charm, great restaurants and abundance of trails, such as the **Stawamus Chief** hike, make it worthy of an overnight, and it's also a more affordable basecamp for Whistler.

While you're here, lace up your hiking boots. In addition to the Stawamus Chief trail, you can explore the waterfall at **Brandywine Falls Provincial Park** (a five-minute walk from the parking lot), between Squamish and Whistler. The 70m-tall waterfall cascades over volcanic rocks into the deep canyon below.

For the hardcore hikers, make the 25-minute drive to **Garibaldi Provincial Park**, where trailblazers will love hiking to ancient volcanic peaks and the glacially fed turquoise waters of Garibaldi Lake. This is one of the best parks near Vancouver for hiking and backcountry camping with several trails of note like Panorama Ridge, Elfin Lakes and Cheakamus Lake. Some parking lots like Cheakamus and Elfin Lakes (via Diamond Head trailhead) require a free day-use pass.

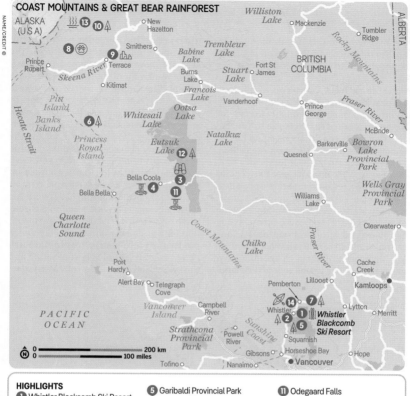

**HIGHLIGHTS**
1. Whistler Blackcomb Ski Resort

**SIGHTS**
2. Brandywine Falls Provincial Park
3. Burnt Bridge & Valley Viewpoint
4. Clayton Falls
5. Garibaldi Provincial Park
6. Great Bear Rainforest
7. Joffre Lakes Provincial Park
8. Khutzeymateen Grizzly Bear Sanctuary
9. Kitselas Canyon
10. Nisga'a Memorial Lava Bed Park
11. Odegaard Falls
12. Tweedsmuir Provincial Park

**ACTIVITIES, COURSES & TOURS**
13. Hlgu Isgwit Hot Springs
14. River of Golden Dreams

## Squamish Lil'wat Cultural Centre

### Honoring Indigenous cultures

Whistler occupies the unceded and ancestral territory of the Squamish and Lil'wat Nations, and just before the 2010 Winter Olympics, this facility was opened to celebrate both cultures and their history. No trip is complete without a visit here to learn about the people who have been here since time immemorial in an environment that exquisitely

 **PLACES TO EAT & DRINK IN SQUAMISH**

**Peak Provisions**
Dynamic community hub offering crafted bites, beverages and locally sourced grocery items.

**Backcountry Brewing**
Cozy taproom for enjoying top-notch craft beers, delicious local food and stunning nature views.

**Cliffside Cider**
Locally born craft cidery offering with a warm atmosphere and superb patio.

# DRIVING THE SEA-TO-SKY HIGHWAY

From Vancouver, this breathtaking drive up North America's southernmost fjord connects you to Whistler via several scenic roadside pullouts. After crossing Lions Gate Bridge from Vancouver, you'll pass **1 Horseshoe Bay**. This charming seaside community is most commonly known for the ferry terminal that gets you to Vancouver Island, the Sunshine Coast and Bowen Island but is a beautiful stop regardless. Further north stretch your legs with a walk or a swim at **2 Porteau Cove Provincial Park**, a waterfront recreation area. Ideal for picnics or overnight camping, it's one of the only places on the Sea-to-Sky to swim or paddle before leaving the ocean behind as you ascend into the mountains. Climb into a mining rail car and venture deep into the mountain through an immersive, multi-sensory live-action tour at **3 Britan-**nia Beach Mine Museum**, where you can learn about the geology and history of the area and how mining shaped BC's past. Far beyond a mere sightseeing lift, the **4 Sea-to-Sky Gondola** swiftly transports you to a world of alpine adventure. Once at the top, choose from several hikes, a walk across the suspension bridge, or the via ferrata. The views over Howe Sound and the surrounding peaks are unbeatable, and so is the mountaintop craft beer and food. With year-round accessibility, each season offers its own unique charm and array of activities to explore. From here, continue to the adventure-junkie town of **5 Squamish**, famous for kiteboarding and mountain biking. Thirty minutes past Squamish is **6 Brandywine Falls Provincial Park** before reaching final Sea-to-Sky stop and the bucket-list destination of **7 Whistler**.

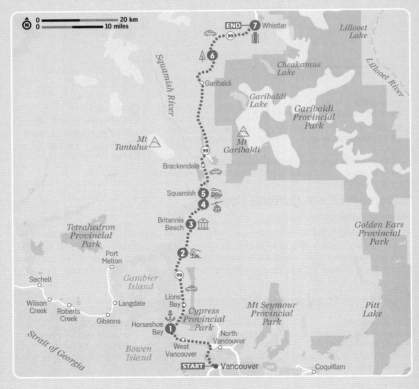

honors their presence. Daily tours that start with the beating of a drum and chanting of ancestral songs run on the hour and are included with admission. Local Indigenous guides present ancient history and show how both cultures have adapted to thrive by blending Indigenous heritage with 21st-century innovations. Enjoy local carvers working on-site and Indigenous cuisine at the **bistro** as well.

# Whistler Village Adventures

### Four seasons of mountain fun

Not a skier? Not a problem. Simply walking around, dining and shopping in the quaint upper village is enough to get lost in the enchantment of Whistler's Narnia-like experience. But for those after winter adventure without chairlifts, try a snowmobiling tour with the **Adventure Group**, cross-country skiing or snowshoeing at **Whistler Olympic Park**, or a heart-pounding dance with gravity while bobsledding at the **Whistler Sliding Centre**.

When winter's mantle recedes, it reveals a tableau ripe for exploration and adventure in the warmer months. After working up a sweat hiking regional trails such as **Crater Rim** or **Train Wreck Trails,** find your zen on a floatie in **Alta** or **Lost Lake**. **Green Lake** is glacially fed (from which it gets its color and name) and is better to look at than swim in. For a more adventurous float, hit the water on the **River of Golden Dreams**, which, yes, is as good as the name makes it sound. Connecting Alta Lake and Green Lake, the river is short (8.5km), narrow and perfect for floating down. The blissful navigation is incredibly scenic as snowcapped peaks and Whistler Wetlands pass by. Be aware, though, that the float is sometimes technical, especially in high water. Novice canoeists and unprepared dinghy sailors often find themselves popped or capsized in frigid waters. To avoid this, take a guided excursion with **Backroads Whistler** or **Whistler Eco-Tours**.

Out here, adrenaline is the local currency, and Whistler's rich in ways to spend it. Fancy playing Tarzan in the Great White North? Strap into a harness and soar across mountains and valleys with **Ziptrek**. Choose from several runs, including a year-round aerial ballet between Whistler and Blackcomb mountains.

Two wheels are your passport to the very best Whistler has to offer! Rent a bike for a day or more to conquer the town or trails. And when your muscles start singing the blues from your daring exploits, soothe them into serenity at the **Scandinave Spa** – your oasis of blissful wellness.

## SUNSHINE COAST

The sleepy, grassroots and groovy Sunshine Coast is made up of 139km of stunning coastline, charming communities, some island attitude (despite being on the mainland) and a lot of retirees. Only accessible via ferry from Horseshoe Bay or Comox on Vancouver Island, it's home to some great hut-to-hut hikes, kayaking, biking, and galleries. It's a verdant muse for all creative mediums and teeming with artists, top-tier galleries, studios and music events, rivaling any global art hub. From Gibsons to Powell River, find boutique hotels, breweries, quaint B&Bs and camping aplenty.

## EATING IN WHISTLER VILLAGE

**Rim Rock Café**
Renowned Canadian game and seafood in Whistler's Creekside area. $$$

**Bar Oso**
In Whistler's Upper Village, this chic spot elevates tapas, complemented by their signature cocktails. $$

**Crystal Hut**
Legendary Blackcomb Mountain hut serving waffles. By night, snowmobile up for fondue dinners. $$

## DUFFEY LAKE ROAD

Venture to Lillooet and the Cariboo Chilcotin via the Duffy's thrilling, steep and winding route, offering breathtaking vistas and a whiff of hardworking brakes. Visit the gem-hued lakes and imposing glacier of **Joffre Lakes Provincial Park** by reserving a mandatory day pass at bcparks. ca/reservations. Remember, Pemberton is your last chance for cell service, so book ahead. Find several campgrounds, the Marriott Basin Trailhead to **Wendy Thompson Hut** (reservations required), breathtaking views of the Coast Mountains at **Duffey Lake** and an idyllic picnic and swimming day-use park at **Seton Lake**.

Lost Lake, Whistler Blackcomb

# Whistler Blackcomb Ski Resort

### Year-round peak adventures

Host of the 2010 Winter Olympic and Paralympic Games and the obvious main attraction to Whistler is North America's largest (and arguably one of the best) ski resorts, Whistler Blackcomb. Skiers and snowboarders etch their artistry on the snowy canvas of the **duel-mountain ski resort** from November to May (purchase lift tickets ahead of time to save money). Come spring, the ski runs transform into dusty trails where mountain bikers embrace gravity's pull as they ride, glide, and fly like eagles– hopefully landing as gracefully as well. With 70 gravity-defying trails, the **Whistler Mountain Bike Park** is world-renowned.

Bridging the majestic Whistler and Blackcomb mountains is the colossal **Peak 2 Peak gondola** which offers thrilling adventures all year round, serving as a gateway to unparalleled views. Summertime unveils a network of **hiking paths** and access to the new **Cloudraker Skybridge** and **Raven's Eye viewing platform**, both accessible via the **Peak Chair**. From here, lift-serviced trails and sweeping panoramas of glacial grandeur are endless. Make sure to plan ahead if you're hitting the trails.

## FESTIVALS IN WHISTLER

**Whistler Pride & Ski**
Every January end, the town transforms into a vibrant canvas of rainbows and celebrations with skis and stilettos.

**Crankworx**
High-octane, gravity-defying mountain-biking extravaganza uniting thrill-seekers annually in July.

**Whistler World Ski & Snowboard Festival**
In April, adrenaline rushes on the slopes meet art, live music, revelry and unbeatable aprés.

## Learn about the Nuxalk People in Bella Coola Valley

### Indigenous heritage echoes amidst cultural experiences

Nestled in the heart of the Great Bear Rainforest, on the traditional territory of the Nuxalk (Nu-hawk) Peoples, lies the remote destination of the Bella Coola Valley. Known as the 'gateway to the Great Bear Rainforest', the wildlife-viewing and adventure destination is a six-hour drive west of Williams Lake or a 1½-hour flight from Vancouver. It's a place of fragility and sacredness, where Indigenous storytelling thrives and bears and eagles feast on salmon.

To truly understand the spiritual land and water of this valley, embark on a seasonal cultural tour led by a Nuxalk guide with **Copper Sun Journeys** or **Petroglyph Tours by Snuxta**. These tours use ancient cedars, totem poles, and over 5000-year-old petroglyphs as a living book, illustrating how the Nuxalk People live in harmony with Mother Earth. The Bella Coola Valley is not just a place of natural beauty, but also a testament to the enduring relationship between the land and its Indigenous inhabitants.

## Getting Active in Bella Coola

### Burn off calories in Bella Coola

The best glaciers, lakes and waterfalls in **Tweedsmuir Provincial Park** are accessed from the Chilcotin and Nimpo Lake (p121) side of the park – but in the Bella Coola Valley section, **Burnt Bridge & Valley Viewpoint** is a great short hike that includes a small suspension bridge that is accessed via a pullout before 'the hill' on Hwy 20. **Odegaard Falls** is a must-see behemoth and can be accessed via gravel forestry road, then an easy-to-moderate trail, while **Clayton Falls** is an easy walk from the car. There are several viewpoint hikes in the area, but note that some are 4WD access only. For off-road adventures that go to alpine trailheads and unbeatable views up into the mountains, check out **Over the Top Adventures**.

If you want to use your hands as well as your feet, you can climb above the valley on the only **via ferrata** in the Great Bear Rainforest through a network of metal rungs, ladders and wires, with no mountain-climbing experience necessary. This is available only through **Tweedsmuir Park Lodge**; the lodge also has heli-sightseeing and other guided tours available for both guests and non-guests, and all of these are best enjoyed from May to mid-October. We would be remiss not to

### PEMBERTON VALLEY

In the shadows of Mt Currie and its neighboring dramatic peaks, the Pemberton Valley is on Hwy 99 between Whistler and Lillooet. Its lower elevation and fertile soil mean summers are warm and abundant in edible and drinkable bounties like those found at **Beer Farmers**, **Black Bird Bakery** and **North Arm Farm**. Pemberton is the gateway to a hiker's dream with gems like **Nairn Falls** and **Semaphore Lakes**, and serves as the roadmap to camping heavens like **Birkenhead Lake** and the therapeutic waters of **Sloquet Hot Springs**.

 **BEST PLACES TO STAY**

**Bella Coola Grizzly Tours Resort**
Live your log-home dream in these gorgeous fully equipped chalets and cabins. **$$**

**Bella Coola Mountain Lodge**
Cozy family-run lodge with sociable mountain vibes and a homey atmosphere. **$$**

**Firvale Wilderness Resort**
Package chic glamping, cabins and wellness amenities with adventures at this all-inclusive sanctuary. **$$$**

## DRIVING TO & AROUND BELLA COOLA

Accessing the Bella Coola Valley in the Great Bear Rainforest requires time and careful planning. Rent a car in Vancouver and follow the 10-day itinerary (p113) with a loop trip that includes a scenic, pre-booked 10-hour **BC Ferries' Northern Sea Wolf** journey from Port Hardy, Vancouver Island to Bella Coola. Alternatively, **Pacific Coastal Airlines** offers daily flights from Vancouver, and **Bella Coola Vehicle Rentals** provides the only local vehicle rental service. If driving, prepare for 'The Hill,' a steep 1500m gravel road with switchbacks descending from the Chilcotin Plateau into the valley. Always check DriveBC for road conditions.

BYRON LAYTON/SHUTTERSTOCK ©

**Clayton Falls, Bella Coola**

mention the bucket-list heli-skiing available in this region in the winter. **Bella Coola Heli Skiing** is an award-winning operator that services several lodges and world-class mountains.

For information on wildlife safety and hiking and mountain biking in Bella Coola, check out bellacoola.ca.

## Hot Springs & Sailing

### Get in (and on) the water

In order to truly experience the Bella Coola Valley, you must get out into the **Bella Coola fjords**. Sail away with a guided tour, and find marine life such as Pacific white-sided dolphins on the water and bears flipping over rocks looking for seafood on the shores while en route to a rugged yet private oceanside hot spring. Nestled amid lush rainforest vegetation, thermal waters collect in wild pools with waves gently lapping their walls and shores. These thermal waters combined with runoff from glacier-capped mountains gives these fjords their distinct turquoise color, giving the Norwegian fjords a run for their money. Many tours include a hike to the **Big Cedar Tree** – a tree so big even loggers couldn't get it out, and so they left it behind. It's a standing symbol of a resilient ecosystem that has significant meaning and purpose for Indigenous Peoples.

## PLACES TO STAY IN PRINCE RUPERT

**Cassiar Cannery**
Colorful waterfront cottages with activities at the mouth of the Skeena River near Prince Rupert. $$

**Crest Hotel**
This Gitxaala Nation–owned property offers stunning harbor and mountain views in town. $$

**Cow Bay Pioneer Guest House**
Cozy hotel rooms and hostel in the center of town. $

Let the winds carry you away with **Great Bear Sailing Adventures**. It's the only licensed sailing experience in Bella Coola and offers customized single- or multi-day excursions to places as far afield as Bella Bella on the outer coast of the Great Bear Rainforest. **Inner Coast Inlet Tours** and **Bella Coola Grizzly Tours and Adventure Resort** offer one-day excursions.

## Bear Necessities

### Grin and bear it

Out here in the Great Bear Rainforest, salmon are everything, and each fall the bears come to feed. As the lifeblood of the Pacific ecosystem, the salmon migrate up the rivers to spawn and bears come to feed as they prepare for hibernation. For the ultimate in bear viewing, choose a river float in Bella Coola with **Kynoch Adventures** or **Great Bear Adventures** and pass enormous grizzly bears as they snatch, dive and bite fish out of the river.

The Great Bear Rainforest is home to the rarest bear in the world, the Kermode bear, also known as the Spirit Bear. Their white fur is due to a recessive gene found in black bears and can only be seen in the most remote parts of the Great Bear Rainforest. While it's not possible to spot them near Bella Coola, the best chance to see a Spirit Bear is by flying into Bella Bella to stay at the exclusive Indigenous-owned and operated **Spirit Bear Lodge** or joining a small ship expedition with **Maple Leaf Adventures**.

## Tweedsmuir Provincial Park

### A protected playground

One of British Columbia's largest provincial parks is home to the freefalling **Hunlen Falls** (one of the highest in Canada), alpine lakes, glaciers, hikes and a canoe circuit. The park is located five hours west of Williams Lake, or two hours east of Bella Coola, and has hikes ranging from one day up to multi-day circuits. Guided hiking can be found in the region through various operators most commonly based on the Bella Coola side but extending into the Chilcotin. Short on time? **Tweedsmuir Air** at Stewart's Lodge operates floatplanes from **Nimpo Lake**, which will take days off your hiking trip by flying you over Hunlen Falls and towering glaciers with viewpoint hikes along the way. Their flights can be booked months or days in advance and can drop you off for a few hours or a few days if a backcountry camping trip sounds appealing. Alternatively, if

### KHUTZEYMATEEN GRIZZLY SANCTUARY

In 1994, 45,000 hectares of pristine wilderness in the traditional territory of the Tsimshian Peoples were dedicated to grizzly-bear conservation. At the time, hunting grizzlies was still legal, but thankfully in 2017 grizzly-bear hunting became illegal in British Columbia. It's Canada's only protected area for grizzly bears and is co-managed by the BC government and the Tsimshian Nation. See the bears for yourself with Prince Rupert Adventure Tours or during a stay at **Khutzeymateen Wilderness Lodge**.

## INDIGENOUS GALLERIES & MUSEUMS

**Museum of Northern British Columbia, Prince Rupert**
This waterfront longhouse hosts Indigenous collections of 10,000 years of local history.

**Sammy Robinson Gallery, Kitamaat Village**
This carver's gallery showcases intricate wood, silver and gold art narrating Haisla history.

**Blackfish Gallery, Kitamaat Village**
Indigenous art-focused gallery providing diverse woodwork and accessory masterpieces.

**WHY I LOVE COAST MOUNTAINS & GREAT BEAR RAINFOREST**

**Jonny Bierman,**
Lonely Planet writer

As someone who is fascinated with Indigenous culture and a lover of adventure in all seasons, I've found no better home than this region. Here, ancient rainforests meet the sea, creating thriving ecosystems for BC's most iconic and rarest wildlife, while Indigenous history ties its significance together. While our furry friends hibernate, we British Columbians answer the call of the snow gods and chase some of the finest powder in the world – and best après beers. Out here, the countless glaciers, hot springs and alpine lakes beckon, teasing me to explore their icy depths, emerald colors and thermal waters. On a quest to ski, soak, and hike them all, I love exploring the region's boundless terrain to my heart's content.

camping is not to your taste, take a floatplane from Nimpo Lake to **Nuk Tessli Lodge** (open June to September). The lodge nestles in remote wilderness on the shore of an alpine lake in the Coast Mountains. It has traditional log cabins, a wood-burning hot tub and delicious home-cooked meals. If you're coming from Bella Coola, the Bella Coola Valley Visitor Information Booth will also have park information. It's open seasonally from mid-June until the end of September (bellacoola.ca).

## Coastal Adventures & Hidden Hot Springs
### Truly off the beaten path

Northern BC's three westernmost communities, Terrace, Kitimat and Prince Rupert, are accessed via Hwy 16 in the north and haven't typically been places of note for tourists, until now.

Based in the town of Terrace, **Northern BC Jet Boat Tours** showcases some of northwest BC's most scenic rivers, waterways and ocean inlets. Organize a tour, ranging from one hour to a full day, to encounter waterfalls, remote hot springs, grizzlies, whales and even ghost towns. Just outside Terrace is **Kitselas Canyon**, on the traditional territory of the Kitselas (Git-sel-as) First Nation, where guided and self-guided tours are available through the archaeological research areas and hikes through the Skeena River canyons. Northwest of Terrace, on the **Nisga'a (Nis-gah) Lands**, find peace in the healing waters of **Hlgu Isgwit Hot Springs** (reservations mandatory; call 250-633-3038), the ancient **Anhluut'ukwsim Laxmihl Angwinga'asanskwhl** (Nisga'a Memorial Lava Bed Park), and the four communities of Gitlaxt'aamiks, Laxgalts'ap (Lak-al-zap), Gitwinksihlkw (Git-win-k-shisq) and Gingolx. Guided tours, self-guided maps for vehicle tours, and other info can be found at discovernisgaa.com.

Home to the Haisla people, the community of Kitimat has several totem poles, trails and wildlife-viewing opportunities to take in. **Kitimat Lodge** offers private boat-access-only hot-springs tours to rugged natural springs pools in the Douglas Channel as well as whale watching and kayaking trips.

**Prince Rupert** is the departure point to Vancouver Island and Haida Gwaii via BC Ferries. Often dubbed a budget cruise, the scenery and wildlife along the journey are spectacular. In the city, check out the **Museum of Northern British Columbia** and the **North Pacific Cannery** for a look into Northern BC's past, for scenic ocean and wildlife tours, including Khutzeymateen grizzlies (p121), check in with **Prince Rupert Adventure Tours**.

**Black bear**

# Cariboo Chilcotin

Vancouver

**PADDLING PARADISE, BIKING AND COWBOY CULTURE**

Defined by mighty rivers that have shaped people, place and culture for millennia, the Cariboo Chilcotin region borders the Coast Mountains from north to south and is most easily accessed by driving four hours north from Vancouver. Rugged adventure, cowboy culture, gold-rush history and unique Indigenous experiences bring a distinctive energy that draws visitors from all over the world, but particularly from Europe. The Cariboo Gold Rush Trail is more than gold-rush history, it's the melding of experiences that ignites curiosity and exploration with you as the prospector on a quest for your own version of the treasured element. In what could be described as BC's last frontier, the Chilcotin Mountains are where you'll find vehicle and floatplane-accessed hiking and mountain biking that take you eye-to-eye with stunning glaciers and lakes. Move aside Rocky Mountains! These lesser-known ranges are equally stunning, but uncrowded.

## ☑ TOP TIP

Many historic sites and seasonal lodges open their doors in May and close in early October. Like much of British Columbia, this region does not have great cell-phone coverage, so be sure to download your maps ahead of time.

## Indigenous Experiences on the Fraser River

### How a river shaped culture

The Fraser River has been the lifeblood of Indigenous communities for millennia. Here and in many parts of BC, salmon is life. This especially rings true on the Fraser, one of the most important waterways for salmon migrations. There are various Indigenous experiences to be had here that connect culture and history to manifestations of the natural world.

 **PLACES TO STAY IN THE CARIBOO**

**Fawn Lake Resort**
Located on its own lake off Hwy 24. Its log cabins provide a quintessentially Canadian experience. **$**

**Peaceful Cove Resort**
On the shores of Lac Des Roches are the campsites and cottages of this tranquil vacation spot. **$**

**Bowron Lake Lodge**
Conveniently on the famous Bowron Lake Canoe circuit, these cabins are also close to Wells and Barkerville. **$**

# DRIVING THE GOLD RUSH TRAIL

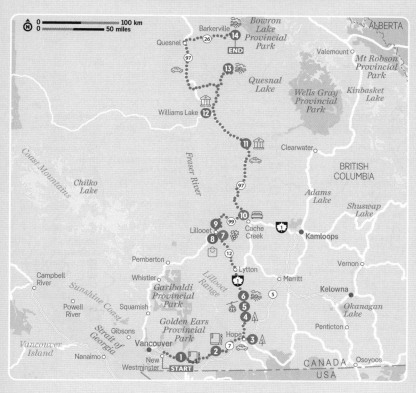

Start the Gold Rush Trail (goldrushtrail.ca) at New Westminster near Vancouver. Stop at the former Hudson's Bay trading post of **1 Fort Langley National Historic Site** for an introduction to BC's founding history through colonial-era displays and on-site Indigenous interpreters. In the Fraser Valley, follow the smell of fresh pies to **2 Kilby Historic Site** for lunch and riverside camping in a natural setting with a 19th-century historical spin. Near the town of Hope, **3 Othello Tunnels Provincial Park** hiking trails walk a former rail line chiseled through dramatic granite mountains alongside a roaring river. Next, venture into the Fraser Canyon and snap some photos on a former 95-year-old gold-rush wagon road bridge at **4 Alexandra Bridge Provincial Park**, and overlook the Fraser River from **5 Hells Gate Airtram**.

The town of Boston Bar is next, home to **6 Tuckkwiowhum (Tuck-we-ohm) Heritage Village** (p127). At Lytton, take Hwy 12 to Lillooet and have lunch at **7 Fort Berens Estate Winery**, overlooking fields of vineyards and epic mountainscapes. Pick up some Indigenous-made provisions at **8 Splitrock Environmental** and then learn about St'at'imc (Stat-lee-m) culture on a tour with **9 Xwisten** (Hoysh-ten) (p127). Find refuge in accommodations consisting of wagons and prospector tents at **10 Historic Hat Creek** and then continue up to **11 108 Mile Heritage Site**, and **12 Museum of the Cariboo Chilcotin** (which also serves as an information center). Ghostly photo-ops can be found at the abandoned mining town of **13 Quesnelle Forks** before you finish at **14 Barkerville Historic Town and Park**.

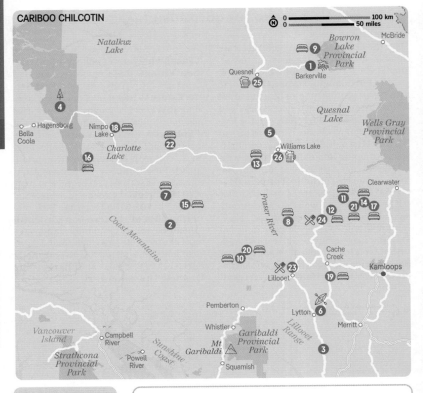

CARIBOO CHILCOTIN

## BC'S HIDDEN ADVENTURE SPOT

**Tyax Adventures** has float-plane-accessed cabins, glamping, mountain biking and hiking trips in South Chilcotin Mountains Provincial Park. Down the shore on the same lake is **Tyax Lodge** which offers heli-skiing in winter and lakeside adventures in summer, while nearby **Chilcotin Holidays** offers a sustainable guest-ranch experience.

### SIGHTS
1 Barkerville
2 Chilko Lake
see 23 Fort Berens Estate Winery
3 Tuckkwiowhum Heritage Village
4 Garibaldi Provincial Park
5 Xat'sull Heritage Site

### ACTIVITIES, COURSES & TOURS
6 Kumsheen Rafting Resort

### SLEEPING
7 Bear Camp
8 Big Bar Guest Ranch
9 Bowron Lake Lodge
10 Chilcotin Holidays
see 7 Chilko Experience
11 Fawn Lake Resort
12 Flying U Ranch
13 Historic Chilcotin Lodge
14 Lac Des Roches Resort
15 Nemiah Valley Lodge
16 Nuk Tessli Lodge
17 Peaceful Cove Resort
18 Retreat Wilderness Inn
19 Sundance Guest Ranch
see 7 Tsylos Park Lodge & Adventures
20 Tyax Lodge
21 Wettstone Guest Ranch
22 Woodlands Fishin Resort

### EATING
23 Abundance Artisan Bakery
24 Sugar Shack

### DRINKING & NIGHTLIFE
25 Barkerville Brewing
26 Fox Mountain Brewing
see 23 Lillooet Brewing

In the town of Boston Bar, **Tuckkwiowhum (Tuck-we-ohm) Heritage Village** brings local Nlaka'pamux (Ingla-kap-ma) traditions, culture and history to life through engaging tours, workshops, art and storytelling. The property features stunning Indigenous carvings, a pit house, a long house, a teepee village and beautifully manicured gardens. Call (604-860-9286) or email tuckkwiowhum@gmail.com ahead of time to ensure it's open or to book a workshop, such as making soapberry ice cream, salmon preparation or making drums. Tuckkwiowhum also operates a campground.

At the confluence of the Bridge and Fraser Rivers in the town of Lillooet are **Xwisten (Hoysh-ten) Experience Tours** and **Bearfoot Grill**. Tours focus on St'at'imc (Stat-lee-m) traditions such as the ancient and still-practiced art of dip-netting for salmon from the traditional fishing rocks, an ancient site once home to several pit houses, a pit-house replica and salmon-drying demonstrations. Grab a bannock burger or fresh salmon at the on-site Bearfoot Grill before or after a tour.

At **Xat'sull Heritage Site (Hat-sull)**, near Williams Lake, the traditional knowledge from local elders and the significance of flora and fauna native to the area are interpreted by local Secwepemc (shi-huep-muh-k) guides. Teepees, a pit house and traditional tools reveal how this community once lived.

Each of these Indigenous experiences, though dotted along the same river, tells a different story.

## Rafting & Glamping
**Combine white water with wellness**

Some of the best whitewater rafting in the world is found here in BC, and the Fraser is no exception. Families will love **Kumsheen Rafting Resort**, just outside Lytton, for its teepee accommodations, pool and one-of-a-kind motor-powered rafts where the only thing guests have to do is hold on as they charge through rapids. The property sits atop the Fraser Canyon with breathtaking mountain and river views. Two rail lines snake their way along the river, and rafting offers a very unique perspective of these engineering marvels built in the late 1800s.

## Guest Ranches & Cowboy Culture
**A relaxing home on the range**

The Wild West is alive and well in BC's Cariboo region, and if you've ever fancied living your best cowboy life, this is where to do it. Horseback ride, hike, swim or paddle under

**BC'S LAND OF HIDDEN WATERS**

BC's Land of Hidden Waters is a region between 70 Mile House and Kamloops (north of Clearwater) which is home to some of the province's best freshwater secrets. Combine thundering waterfall adventures, hiking and wildlife-viewing in **Wells Gray Provincial Park** (p135). Find places to stay and things to do online at landofhidden waters.com.

 **PLACES TO STAY IN THE CHILCOTIN**

**Historic Chilcotin Lodge** Close to the stunning Farwell Canyon, this quaint family-owned lodge has excellent fresh baking. $

**Retreat Wilderness Inn** Break up the trip to Bella Coola or explore the Chilcotins from this lakeside lodge in Nimpo Lake. $

**Woodlands Fishin Resort** Affordable cabins and campground on Punzi Lake with adventure fuel at the restaurant and bakery. $

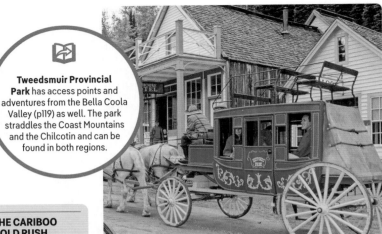

ALL CANADA PHOTOS/ALAMY STOCK PHOTO ©

**Tweedsmuir Provincial Park** has access points and adventures from the Bella Coola Valley (p119) as well. The park straddles the Coast Mountains and the Chilcotin and can be found in both regions.

**Stage coach, Barkerville Historic Town**

## THE CARIBOO GOLD RUSH

In 1857 gold was discovered on the Fraser River. Governor of Vancouver Island Sir James Douglas sent 800oz to the San Francisco Mint, knowing it would trigger a gold rush. Thousands of international prospectors made the journey up the Fraser River searching for gold. To avoid losing more territory to the Americans, Douglas petitioned Queen Victoria to establish a Colonial Government, and he later became its governor. The Cariboo gold rush shaped British Columbia's history and is one of the reasons it's not part of America today.

the summer sun, and fuel up with hardy, home-cooked meals that are often included in the package. **Flying U Ranch** on Green Lake is one of the oldest guest ranches in North America. It operates several rustic log cabins overlooking the lake, while horses roam freely on the property. The experience is all-inclusive of activities such as boat rides and tubing, trail rides, live entertainment, workshops, meals and more. Don't forget to check out the Wild West–style saloon and spend some time with the staff by the campfire. Also located on its own lake with a uniquely western experience is **Wettstone Guest Ranch** on BC's Fishing Hwy 24. The lodge and cabins are fully equipped and activities include horseback riding, canoeing and hiking.

## Barkerville Historic Town & Park

### Gold-rush-era boom town

Founded in 1862 during the Cariboo Gold Rush, Barkerville quickly became the largest city west of Chicago and north of San Francisco. Now a National Historic Site, this living history museum near the town of Wells and Bowron Lake Provincial Park is brought to life through whimsical characters

 **PLACES TO STAY**

**Big Bar Guest Ranch**
An Indigenous-owned experience with comfortable cabins and great food. $$

**Sundance Guest Ranch**
You'll meet other travelers over family-style cuisine, horse riding and wilderness adventures. $$

**Lac Des Roches Resort**
Rustic lakeside cottages and campsites with water activities and an Italian restaurant. $

that dress and act as if they were in the gold-rush era. Actors will never deviate from their role, but they will add a comedic 21st-century twist while giving you a real-life look at BC's beginnings as a British colony and then a province of Canada. The performance of the actors perfectly complements the 125 historic buildings that visitors can explore and the stagecoach transportation down the dirt street. Be sure to find the Indigenous interpreters who present an often untold and overlooked side of British Columbia's history. This marks the end of BC's Gold Rush Trail, and if you haven't found the yellow metal yet, you'll surely find it in the hands of a Barkerville character. If you're looking for a place to rest your head, there are several accommodation options to choose from in Barkerville as well.

## Getting High at Chilko Lake

**North America's largest high-elevation lake**

If the aquamarine colors of Chilko Lake in the heart of the Chilcotin Mountains aren't enough to make you change the GPS coordinates, perhaps the wildlife-viewing opportunities will. At the head of the Chilko River on the Chilcotin Plateau, the lake is surrounded by the highest volcanic mountains in British Columbia and offers world-class bear viewing in the fall. If you have your own paddling vessel, explore the area on the water or by foot from Ts'il?os (sigh-loss) Provincial Park, where two vehicle-accessed campgrounds and several back-country campsites can be reached. Guided adventures can be booked with **Tsylos Park Lodge & Adventures**, which provides lavish accommodations that include wildlife viewing. At the iconic **Bear Camp**, luxury glamping tents are perched over the water as bears meander below, while **Chilko Experience** is a luxury lakeside lodge. Both offer paddle sports, fishing, bear viewing, hiking and more.

### A NEW PATH FORWARD FOR THE TSILHQOT'IN PEOPLES

In 1864 unrest between colonizers and Tsilhqot'in (Tsill-coat-ten) Peoples led to the Chilcotin War of 1864 and ultimately the wrongful hanging of six Tsilhqot'in chiefs in New Westminster. This sparked outrage and long-term tensions around the same time land titles were stripped away during colonization. In 2014 the Supreme Court of Canada granted the Tsilhqot'in Peoples the declaration of Indigenous title to 1700 sq km, confirming the land belongs to the Tsilhqot'in Peoples. This was the first time an Indigenous title had been confirmed outside of a First Nations reservation in Canada. Today you can stay at the new Indigenous-owned **Nemiah Valley Lodge** between Chilko Lake and Hanceville off Hwy 20 where Tsilhqot'in experiences, culture and stories are shared.

## WHERE TO EAT & DRINK

**Fort Berens Estate Winery**
A locally sourced Lillooet culinary experience paired with fine wines and breathtaking views. $

**Lillooet Brewing**
This brewery empowers Canadian farmers with local ingredients and sits on 3 acres by the Fraser River. $

**Sugar Shack**
Its sign says, 'The best poutine west of Quebec,' maple syrup, and delicious smoked-meat sandwiches. $

# Thompson Okanagan

Vancouver

**WINERIES, WATERFALLS, LAKES AND SUPERB SKIING**

Raise a glass – or many – in the sun-kissed vineyards of BC's bountiful fruit-bearing wine region. Fertile land and idyllic hot weather mean the day's most difficult decision will be whether to cool off with a glass of renowned crisp white or in one of the many lakes and waterfalls. Why not both? In the south of the region, between Osoyoos and Kelowna, upscale wineries (and modest ones too) are dotted along a string of lakes that Canadians have long enjoyed for recreation. In the north, the region extends past Kamloops into the Lower North Thompson and into one of the most underrated parks in the province: Wells Gray Provincial Park. With ample opportunities for sipping, sightseeing and swimming, it's best to just go with the flow. And in the winter, copious amounts of champagne powder blanket the slopes of several hills that attract skiers and snowboarders from around the world.

## Wine & Culture at Nk'Mip

### Indigenous winery with cultural tours

**Nk'Mip Cellars** (In-ka-meep) became North America's first Indigenous-owned and operated winery when it opened its doors in Osoyoos. Located on Osoyoos Indian Band land overlooking the vineyard and Osoyoos Lake, the property hosts tastings in the cellar and Indigenous cultural tours from the new **Nk'Mip Desert Cultural Centre** (separate fees apply). Its onsite restaurants, Nk'Mip RV Park and Spirit Ridge by Nk'Mip Hotel have great views from its location up on the mountain making for an ideal place to stay for lunch or for a night.

## Cycling the South Okanagan

### Scenic riding through wine country

Whether you're a wino biking your way from vineyard to vineyard, a mountain biker keen to hit the trails or an e-biker looking to get after the gentle grade of the **Kettle Valley Rail Trail**

---

☑ **TOP TIP**

While the summer crowds (and prices!) of Kelowna can be a bit much, there's always a quiet and affordable corner of the Thompson Okanagan to call your own. BC's wine region also includes the Kamloops area, where there are even more lakes to camp at or find a cabin to rent.

# VINEYARD DRIVE FROM OSOYOOS TO PENTICTON

This road trip starts with one of the sunniest and hottest places in the country – **1 Osoyoos**. The town is small but popular, so if you're after a quieter countryside stay by a winery or lake, look further north. The Indigenous winery and cultural center of **2 Nk'Mip** (In-ka-meep) blends multigenerational knowledge with winemaking and cultural experiences. The **3 Osoyoos Desert Centre** provides a knowledgeable introduction to local ecology before delving into the many surrounding wineries. **4 Burrowing Owl** is an upscale winery and its restaurant has views that can't be beat. The metaphorically creative **5 Rust Wine Co** is just up the road, as is the idyllic **6 Rainmaker Wines** is just up the road, as are and a BC favorite, **7 Road 13**. Just before the town of Oliver is **8 Tinhorn Creek**, which is a sustainability-focused winery that hosts a summer concert series and has a delicious adjoining restaurant. The **9 District Wine Village** north of Oliver is a convenient boutique marketplace home to 12 wineries, a brewery, a distillery and a restaurant. **10 Liquidity Winery** gets its name from the properties' springs and has an on-site bistro. The beachside city of **11 Penticton** has mellow vibes. Find excellent hiking, mountain biking, beaches and unique places to stay here. The adjoining Naramata Bench region has over 40 wineries and is conveniently connected by a section of the Kettle Valley Rail Trail, a former rail line transformed into a mellow gravel biking path that winds through never-ending vineyards and unbeatable views of mountains and lakes. If there was ever a place to ditch the car and rent some bikes, this is it.

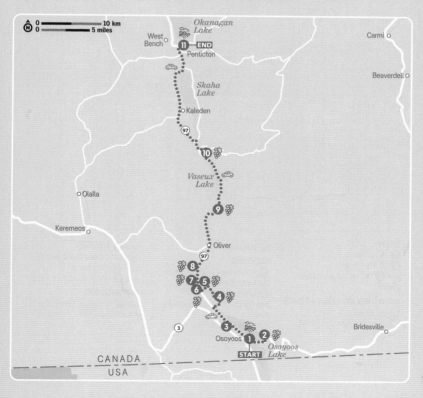

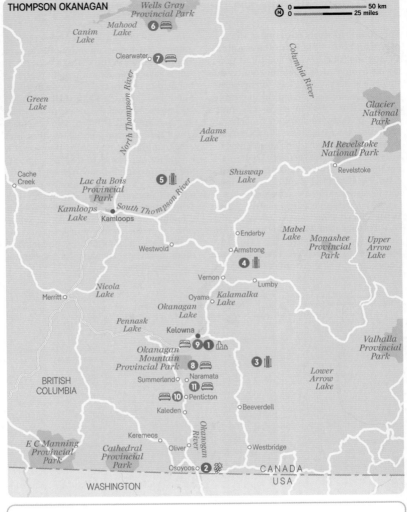

**THOMPSON OKANAGAN**

**SIGHTS**
1 Myra Canyon
2 Nk'Mip Cellars
see 2 Nk'Mip Desert Cultural Centre

**ACTIVITIES, COURSES & TOURS**
3 Big White
4 SilverStar Mountain Resort
5 Sun Peaks

**SLEEPING**
6 Across the Creek Cabins
7 Cedar Haven Resort
8 Chute Lake Lodge
see 7 Dutch Lake Resort & RV Park
9 Hotel Eldorado

see 9 Hotel Zed
10 Kettle Valley Beach Resort
11 Naramata Inn
see 2 Watermark Beach Resort

**INFORMATION**
see 7 Wells Gray Park Visitor Information Center

**Kettle Valley Rail Trail**

## PENTICTON ALE TRAIL

BC loves its craft beer, and Penticton is no exception. While wine may have made its debut first, beer has now entered the ring. The Penticton Ale Trail is a collection of eight craft breweries in and around the city: Yellow Dog Brewing Penticton, Neighbourhood Brewing, Highway 97 Brewery, Barley Mill Brew Pub & Bistro, Slackwater Brewing, Abandoned Rail Brewing Co, Tin Whistle Brewing and Cannery Brewing. Much like the wine of this region, its beer is also award-winning with the latter three of those fine establishments being gold-medal winners at the BC Beer Awards. Find the Penticton Ale Trail and others at the QR code.

(**KVR**), the Okanagan has a bike, trail and accompanying *après* stop for all abilities. Mountain bikers will want to drop into Penticton's flowy cross-country trails of Three Blind Mice, Campbell Mountain, and Skaha Bluffs. Winos should follow the verdant vineyards of **Naramata's 40+ wineries** via the KVR where it's possible to bike from winery to winery. Guided wine safaris and other tours via e-bike can be booked with **South Okanagan E-Bike Safaris**. The KVR is a former railway-turned-bike path that spans about 660km with the most developed sections being between Penticton and south of Kelowna. The Naramata Bench and Myra Canyon sections are the most popular. And while **Myra Canyon** may not have any wineries or watering holes, it does have 18 trestle bridges, two steel bridges, two tunnels and stunning views from high on the mountain. For those really up for an adventure, bike the KVR's most spectacular section on an 80km ride from Myra Canyon to Penticton. Myra Canyon has on-site bike rentals and Penticton has many e-bike rentals with delivery options, cruisers and mountain bikes downtown.

## PLACES TO STAY – PENTICTON & OSOYOOS

**Kettle Valley Beach Resort**
Newly reimagined beachside resort in Penticton with garden loungers and outdoor fireplaces. **$$$**

**Naramata Inn**
This heritage inn has over a dozen wineries near its front door and an insanely good restaurant. **$$$**

**Watermark Beach Resort**
Upscale resort on the quiet shores of Osoyoos Lake. Within walking distance of Osoyoos essentials. **$$$**

Whether it's wineries, lakes, waterfalls or the complete list, this journey from Kamloops to Wells Gray Provincial Park has it all. In **1 Kamloops** visit one (or more) of its three wineries. There's Monte Creek Ranch Winery, with its picturesque patio overlooking the Thompson River; Sagewood Winery, a small and casual boutique winery (reserve tastings online); and Privato Vineyard & Winery and Woodward Cider Co just north of the city on Hwy 5. From Kamloops, drive north to **2 Little Fort** for insider tips on lakes and fishing holes at Little Fort Fly and Tackle. After some classic milkshakes and diner food at High Five Diner, venture along **3 Fishing Hwy 24**, with its countless lakes and reely great fishing spots. Continue north to the town of **4 Clearwater**. Check in here with the Wells Gray Park Visitor Information Center for maps and trail conditions before a cooling dip in **5 Dutch Lake**. After you've dried off, take Clearwater Valley Rd north into Wells Gray to the hike-in three-layered **6 Triple Decker Falls**. Next, **7 Spahats Falls** and its adjacent old-growth forests are vehicle accessed and easier to see. Hike to and behind **8 Moul Falls** and then go back to the car and head north to **9 Green Mountain Viewing Tower**, a former fire lookout that gives views of a dormant volcano, Pyramid Mountain. Impressive **10 Dawson Falls** is nicknamed 'mini Niagara' at 107m wide and 20m tall, but no waterfall is more famous than the pièce de résistance, the star of the show, **11 Helmcken Falls**. The freefalling 141m single-drop waterfall is the fourth largest in Canada and an awe-inspiring sight in both summer and winter.

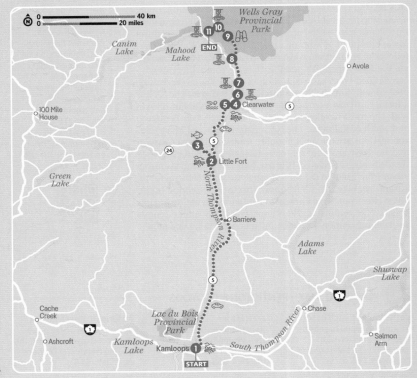

Big White Ski Resort

## Skiing & Winter Activities

**Snow ghosts and champagne powder**

Despite being in a desert region, the Okanagan receives world-famous snow due to the valley being surrounded by mountains that trap cold air. The result? Lots of dry snow (unlike the wet heavier snow the coast is known for) and milder temperatures (unlike what the Rockies are known for). Low-lying fog and clouds are also common, and they create ice on trees, to which snow sticks. This results in solid-white ghostly statues known as 'snow ghosts.' Perhaps the most renowned ski hill in the Okanagan is **Big White** near Kelowna. Near Vernon is **SilverStar Mountain Resort** and by Kamloops is **Sun Peaks Ski Resort**. Each has a quaint village, plenty of accommodation options, and non-ski winter activities such as snowshoeing, skating and ice fishing. In summer, mountain biking can be found at all three resorts as well.

## Explore Wells Gray Provincial Park

**Waterfall mecca born from volcanoes**

Rising from the ashes of dormant volcanoes in this once-geothermally active region, Wells Gray's hardened lava flows have

**OKANAGAN WINE TOURING**

Choosing which wine to buy in the store is overwhelming enough, let alone deciding which of the 100+ wineries you should visit. With the added complication of needing to drive, going on a guided wine tour might be your best and safest bet. Outfitters are knowledgeable about the region, have relationships with the wineries (and a great sense of humor!) and reserved tastings, so you'll roll up and get straight to the glass. **OK Wine Shuttle** in Osoyoos and **Grape Savvy Trolly Co** in Penticton offer hop-on-hop-off services, while dozens of other companies provide wine tours for all pallets.

Scan this QR code for tour options in the Kelowna area.

 **PLACES TO STAY IN & AROUND KELOWNA**

**Hotel Zed**
Step back into the '70s at Kelowna's funkiest hotel, located downtown and by the water. **$$**

**Hotel Eldorado**
Lakeside resort in Kelowna with old-world charm and modern amenities. **$$$**

**Chute Lake Lodge**
Rustic mountain lodge located in the wilderness but still close to Kelowna and Penticton. **$**

**Glacier Lake, Yoho National Park**

## MOUNT ROBSON PROVINCIAL PARK

Banff and Jasper get a lot of hype (and for good reason!), but if you look a little further west from Jasper and north of Wells Gray, you'll find the tallest mountain in the Canadian Rockies: **Mt Robson**. While you can still view its colossal glacier-capped peak, flooding in 2021 whipped out trail infrastructure to the famous **Berg Lake**. At the time of writing, the first 7km of the trail and Kinney Lake were open and the plan is to fully open Berg Lake by 2025.

been perfectly carved by its 40 named waterfalls, the Clearwater River and glaciers. Vehicle access and backcountry camping sites are dotted around the park, and the **Wells Gray Information Center** in Clearwater has all the up-to-date information you need. For safety in numbers (and locals), join a guided adventure with **Wells Gray Adventures**.

For self-guided canoe trips, look no further than Murtle Lake, North America's largest canoe-only lake. It's perfectly lined with beaches akin to Hawaii and absolute wilderness bliss. A multi-day canoe trip on Murtle Lake will bring about some of the most Canadian scenes ever. Rentals can be booked with **Murtle Canoes**. The Clearwater River's idyllic views while rafting its turbulent and sometimes tame flows are worth a trip on their own as well.

Whitewater rafting can be booked in Clearwater with **Riverside Adventures**, **Interior Whitewater Expeditions** and **Liquid Lifestyles**. Pro tip: book a trip that includes a short hike to Candle Creek Falls! Budget permitting you could also get above Wells Gray and fly over the dormant volcanos, or land on the snowcapped peak of Trophy Mountain on a flightseeing tour with **Yellowhead Helicopters**. Alternatively, take a more human-powered approach and glide over the scenery with **Xsky Paragliding**.

## PLACES TO STAY AROUND WELLS GREY

**Cedar Haven Resort**
Chic glamping tents and cabins with euphoric forest vibes and a sauna. $

**Across the Creek Cabins**
Cozy cabins on 10 acres of land directly off the road to Wells Gray's finest attractions. $

**Dutch Lake Resort & RV Park**
Lakeside paradise near all the amenities of Clearwater and at the gateway to the park. $

# Kootenay Rockies

Vancouver

**GROOVY TOWNS AND MAJESTIC MOUNTAIN PARKS**

There are mountain towns that are orchestrated tourist destinations like Banff and Whistler, and then there are Kootenay Rockies mountain towns, which are chill, have zero attitude and are a little bit weird. Many of them – like Fernie, Golden, Revelstoke, Nelson, Rossland and Kimberley – are reimagined industry towns that turned trendy with ski resorts and the rise of outdoor recreation. Elevating the Kootenay Rockies' cool factor are Yoho, Kootenay, Glacier (the Canadian one) and Mount Revelstoke National Parks, not to mention neighboring Banff National Park. Despite being cool, the region is also *hot*, with thermal springs galore. And with two of BC's main highways – Hwy 1 and Hwy 3 – running right through the Kootenay Rockies, you have no excuse not to stop to soak or ski, or just to spend time in some of BC's grooviest mountain towns.

## Yoho National Park & Golden

### Takakkaw Falls from above or below

From the end of June until mid-October, drive an hour northwest of Banff to Canada's second-highest waterfall, **Takakkaw Falls**, in Yoho National Park. See the waterfall from below at the parking lot or from high above on the **Iceline Trail**, one of the best hikes in the Rockies. The 20km loop takes you by the rustic **Stanley Mitchell Hut**, managed by the Alpine Club of Canada. Reserve in advance for an overnight stay or as a basecamp to uncover the region's magnificent glaciers, hidden azure lakes and striking vistas

Accessible by car and only a short drive from Takakkaw Falls, **Emerald Lake** rivals lakes found in Banff and Jasper, is open year-round, and has both camping and upscale accommodations at **Emerald Lake Lodge**. Take to the water on a canoe rental or splurge on a night at **Emerald Lake Lodge**, open year-round and equally enchanting in winter.

Just west of Yoho is the town of Golden, famous for **Kicking Horse Mountain Resort** and its Eagles Eye Restaurant, the

**GETTING AROUND**

The Kootenay Rockies are best traveled by car. In the winter, Kootenay Pass on Hwy 3 and Rogers Pass on Hwy 1 can get hairy and often close due to avalanches. Calgary International Airport and Kelowna International Airport are the best ways to access the region before onward travel by a rental car. Kootenay Charters, Kootenay Gateway Shuttle Service and Mountain Man Mike's Bus Service are reliable bus and charter services.

---

### ☑ TOP TIP

Didn't get that iconic paddle on Lake Louise? Don't worry, Emerald Lake in Yoho is even bigger and much quieter. In the winter and early spring, avalanches are frequent, so drivers should check DriveBC before venturing out.

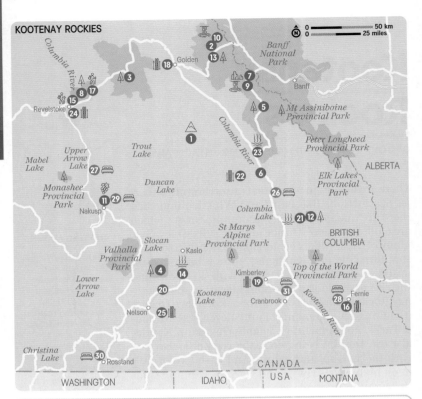

0       50 km
0       25 miles

**SIGHTS**
1 Bugaboo Mountains
2 Emerald Lake
3 Glacier National Park
4 Kokanee Glacier Provincial Park
5 Kootenay National Park
6 Lake Windermere
7 Marble Canyon
8 Mount Revelstoke National Park
9 Numa Falls

see 7 Stanley Glacier
10 Takakkaw Falls
11 Valley of the Springs
12 Whiteswan Provincial Park
13 Yoho National Park

**ACTIVITIES, COURSES & TOURS**
14 Ainsworth Hot Springs
15 Balsam Lake
16 Fernie Alpine Resort

17 Giant Cedars Boardwalk
18 Kicking Horse Mountain Resort
19 Kimberley Alpine Resort
20 Kokanee Mountain Zipline
21 Lussier Hot Springs
22 Panorama Mountain Resort
23 Radium Hot Springs

24 Revelstoke Mountain Resort
25 Whitewater Ski Resort

**SLEEPING**
26 Fairmont Hot Springs Resort
27 Halcyon Hot Springs Resort
28 Island Lake Lodge
29 Nakusp Hot Springs
30 Red Mountain Resort
31 St Eugene

highest restaurant in Canada. With some of the steepest terrain and toughest runs in the Rockies, beginner skiers may want to steer clear of Kicking Horse. In the summer, defy vertigo at the resort's **via ferrata.** On the other side of town at the new **Golden Skybridge**, the Railrider Mountain Coaster, Sky Zipline, Canyon Edge Challenge Course, ax throwing, a climbing wall and suspension bridge provide an active way to take in this part of the Rockies.

# Ancient Ice at Kootenay National Park
### Paleolithic ice and hot springs

Access this park from Hwy 93, halfway between Banff and Lake Louise. A moderately short hike to **Stanley Glacier** will get you close to ancient ice without a huge trek. Shaped by millennia of relentless water activity, bridges open year-round weave their way over Marble Canyon, dramatically revealing nature's formidable power. Experience the same raw power of glacial waters on a grander scale at **Numa Falls**. From the vantage point of a bridge, enjoy a close-up view of the water's vibrant blue hue, creating a stark contrast against the backdrop of black rocks. Hwy 93 unveils a dramatic tableau of nature's resilience and endurance, juxtaposing fire-scarred mountainsides, now teeming with vibrant new growth, against ageless glaciers. To complete this sensory journey, a rejuvenating soak in the therapeutic waters of **Radium Hot Springs** is a necessity. It's the most beautiful and least-crowded hot springs of any of the national parks and is right on Hwy 93.

# Lake Windermere & Panorama
### Skating, skiing or soaking

Drive nearly two hours south of Banff to skate on Lake Windermere – the world's longest naturally frozen skating trail in the winter – or frolic in its warm waters in the summer. Located just 20km east of the lake, **Panorama Mountain Resort** harmoniously combines family-oriented skiing with ski-in ski-out lodging, while also offering cross-country skiing, fat biking and cat skiing. Its strategic location makes it an excellent midway skiing option for those journeying towards Fernie or Kimberley. South of the lake on Hwy 93, **Fairmont Hot Springs Resort** is also a go-to family option, but it moves at a quieter pace and is great for beginners. Nearby, **Lussier Hot Springs** has natural riverside pools up a rough gravel logging road. Adjacent to Lussier is **Whiteswan Lake Provincial Park**, where there's lakeside camping, which, contrary to the name, you'll more likely be sharing with a pair of loons (the Canadian national bird) than swans.

# Hiking the Bugaboo Mountains
### Granite and glaciers

Nicknamed 'The Bugs,' these striking granite spires lined with glaciers are located in the Purcell Mountain Range, northwest of Radium. Services are very limited, but alpine scenery is the

**GIVING BANFF & JASPER A RUN FOR THEIR MONEY**

Although dwarfed by Banff and Jasper, Yoho, Kootenay, Glacier and Mount Revelstoke National Parks pack a very big punch with far fewer tourists. Find equally stunning lakes, gigantic glaciers and waterfalls, and mind-blowing hikes. Surrounding the parks are charming mountain towns, countless hot springs, lakes, provincial parks and prime camping spots.

Scan this QR code to learn more about this region.

## WHERE TO EAT IN THE KOOTENAYS

**Pitchfork Eatery**
This fine farm-to-table Nelson establishment has entertaining live music, craft cocktails, and a divine patio. **$$**

**Ktunaxa (Tun-ah-hah) Grill**
Indigenous-inspired menu at Ainsworth Hot Springs, with local ingredients, Indigenous wines and lake views. **$$**

**Velvet Restaurant & Lounge**
Elegant Rossland spot with modern flair and a symphony of mouth-watering cocktails and dishes on Red Mountain. **$$$**

opposite. Most that come here either backcountry camp at Applebee Dome campsite (pre-booking is necessary), car camp and hike, or stay in the **Conrad Kain Hut** (pre-book with the Alpine Club of Canada). For those looking to go all-out, **CMH Heli-Skiing** operates its glamorous lodge for summer and winter activities. Access the trailheads via Bugaboo Creek Forest Service Rd (a gravel road with no cell service or rest stops), Brisco Rd and Hwy 95, which takes you from Radium to Golden.

## Small-Town Skiing at Kimberley

### Switzerland in the Rockies

Kimberley, 120km south of Lake Windermere, is remarkably reminiscent of a Swiss mountain town – it even has a giant cuckoo clock! That quirk aside, most visitors come here for **Kimberley Alpine Resort** and its beginner-friendly slopes, small-town vibes and affordability. It also has far less attitude than the larger resorts. The center of town is not far from the resort and has lively bars and restaurants with a welcoming small-town atmosphere.

Nearby, **St Eugene** is an Indigenous-owned hotel, golf resort and casino dedicated to reclaiming history and culture through Indigenous culinary, guided tours, an interpretive center and recreation.

## Hitting the Slopes at Fernie

### Bowls of adventure

Known for huge bowls and lots of snow, **Fernie Alpine Resort** is a favorite among Albertans and eastern BC residents. The Town of Fernie, 120km southeast of Kimberley, is a year-round adventure destination, with lift-accessed downhill biking, trail riding and hiking. **Island Lake Lodge** has vibrant alpine hikes in the summer and world-class cat skiing in the winter.

## Revelstoke, Glacier & Mt Revelstoke National Parks

### Huts, hiking and unparalleled skiing

Historically, Revelstoke was established to provide service to the Canadian Pacific Railway, a story that can be thoroughly explored at the **Revelstoke Railway Museum**. Today, this quaint town, affectionately known as 'Revy' by British Columbians, is renowned as a ski destination, boasting the legendary powder at the relatively recent **Revelstoke Mountain Resort**. During summer, the resort transforms into a hub for outdoor activities, offering hiking, mountain biking,

### THE CONTINENTAL DIVIDE

Separating Kootenay and Yoho National Parks in BC with Banff National Park in Alberta is a continental divide known as the Great Divide, and it's also the border between BC and Alberta (hence the jagged imaginary line). This means that all water in BC flows to the Pacific Ocean, and all water from Alberta eventually flows to the Arctic and Atlantic Oceans. The nexus of where water parts three ways is called a 'triple divide,' and Canada's only one is at the Columbia Icefield (p223), which borders BC and Alberta but is most easily accessed from the Columbia Icefield Glacier Discovery Centre.

## 🛢 CRAFT BREWERIES IN THE EAST KOOTENAYS

**Mt Begbie Brewing**
A Revelstoke joint that's mastered the art of brewing and laid-back ski-bum vibes.

**Fernie Brewing**
Brewing craft beer since before it was cool, Fernie Brewing is an alchemy of tradition and innovation.

**Grist & Mash Brewery**
Located in Kimberley, Grist has Bavarian food and brews brilliant beers.

**Halcyon Hot Springs (p142)**

and even a mountain coaster. Revy also serves as an excellent starting point for those venturing south to Nakusp via the Upper Arrow Lake ferry.

Similarly to Yoho and Kootenay National Parks, these parks are often overlooked but offer big rewards to adventurous hikers. Both are accessed via Hwy 1, the Trans-Canada Hwy, which winds up the scenic **Rogers Pass**. In the summer, book ahead of time with the Alpine Club of Canada to stay at **AO Wheeler Hut** (accessible by road) or the mountaintop **Asulkan Hut,** accessed via the Asulkan Valley Trail from the Illecillewaet Campground. Ski touring to both is also available in the winter for those who are experienced and have avalanche training. Although the hike is steep and challenging, the tiny-house-like Asulkan Hut near the summit is in a league (and alpine paradise) of its own. **Giant Cedars Board Walk** and **Balsam Lake** are easier hikes to check off if you're just passing through.

## West Kootenay Mountain Towns

### A trio of mountain communities

Travelers park their cars in **Nakusp** to soothe their car-stiff muscles in the hot springs. Find both developed and natural springs in the area. Perched above Upper Arrow Lake is

## CRAFT BREWERIES IN THE WEST KOOTENAYS

**Rossland Beer Co**
This local hangout is a taproom of beer brilliance and insider tips on the best trails in town.

**Torchlight Brewing Co**
Mouthwatering pub grub and beer in Nelson at Torchlight.

**Angry Men Brewing**
Women-founded and mostly women-run brewery with delicious eats in the heart of Kaslo

### HOT SPRINGS CIRCLE ROUTE

This steamy circle route has over a dozen hot springs for you to soak in. Circling Cranbrook in the south and Revelstoke in the north, the views (and possibly sulfur) will take your breath away. Particularly notable is Ainsworth Hot Springs, an Indigenous-owned hot springs resort that's unique to BC and has a natural thermal water cave system.

Scan this QR code to map our your trip.

## THE POWDER HIGHWAY

Attention ski enthusiasts! This snow-laden route loops through the heart of BC's rugged mountains, connecting some of the best and most renowned ski resorts in the world. It loops from Fernie Alpine Resort in the south up to Kicking Horse Mountain Resort in Golden via Kimberley Alpine Resort, Fairmont Hot Springs Resort and Panorama Mountain Resort. From Golden, it continues west to Revelstoke Mountain Resort, then turns south to Red Mountain Resort and Whitewater Ski Resort. Finally, it heads east to close the loop at Fernie. Purchase an IKON Pass online to save money at some of these resorts and nearby attractions.

Scan this QR code for more Powder Hwy information.

**Halcyon Hot Springs Resort** with its chic cabins and classy restaurant. In town, **Nakusp Hot Springs** has a more rustic experience but is equally relaxing. Prior to your spa experience, pick up a bottle of wine from **Valley of the Springs Winery**.

Once Nakusp has soaked away your travel weariness, drive two hours south to **Nelson**, BC's funkiest mountain town. This town has modern hippy vibes and a history full of draft dodgers and the marijuana industry (before it was legal). While a little bit offbeat, Nelson's progressive ideologies have shaped it into a modern mountain destination with restaurants that source everything locally. After you've explored the town, it's time for some adventure. Shred at **Whitewater Ski Resort** in winter, get high (not that kind) at **Kokanee Mountain Ziplines** and explore the trails of **Kokanee Glacier Provincial Park**. For a change of pace, head back into town and take a ride on the old-fashioned tram at the **Nelson Streetcar**.

**Rossland**, an hour southwest of Nelson, is one of only a few Kootenay towns you don't just pass through. The reason most people stop is **Red Mountain Resort**. It's known for abundant and reliable dry powder and is hands-down the best skiing in the West Kootenays. Rossland itself is a quaint mountain community and is quickly becoming a mountain-biking center. Nearby, **Endless Adventure** does guided whitewater-rafting trips on the Slocan River and has kayak and SUP rentals.

## Festivals in the Kootenay Rockies
### Cultural, celebratory melting pot

Held in late July on the verdant banks of the Salmo River, **Shambhala Music Festival** is a dazzling symphony of electronic music and transformative art. This four-day sonic adventure is a melting pot of cultures, where the beats of countless DJs resonate through the ancient forest. In early August, **Kaslo Jazz Fest** is orchestrated on an over-water floating stage against the breathtaking backdrop of Kootenay Lake and the Purcell mountains. In late September, **LUNA Fest** in Revelstoke is a nocturnal festival that transforms the city into a vast, open-air gallery of art, performances, sound and innovation. As the sun sets, the cityscape comes alive with a kaleidoscope of light installations, interactive art displays and immersive performances.

**Haida Gwaii**

 ## PLACES TO STAY IN THE KOOTENAYS

**Snow Valley Tiny Homes**
Meticulously designed homes in Fernie that are central and blend comfort, functionality and community. $$

**Boulder Mountain Resort**
This breathtaking Revelstoke portal to four-season outdoor adventure has fully equipped cabins, glamping and camping. $$

**Logden Lodge**
Chic lodge and cabins 20 minutes south of Nelson that are fully equipped but also offer catering. $$

# Haida Gwaii & the North

Vancouver

**ENGAGING INDIGENOUS HISTORY AND WILDERNESS**

Northern British Columbia is where the wild-hearted come to play in the most untamed, remote and sparsely populated part of this vast province. Here, the air hums with the vibrant cultures of Canada's Indigenous communities on the world-famous Haida Gwaii archipelago and in the many mainland Nations. Expect the thrill of mystery and the feeling of pathfinding and being very disconnected while navigating the remote trails, highways and gravel roads that traverse this wilderness with all of the nature and none of the people.

Whether you're on your way to Alaska or the Yukon or out for a truly remote expedition amid Canadian wilderness, revel in your own insignificance and find your place next to nature in British Columbia's north.

## Haida Gwaii

**Ethereal archipelago with Indigenous heritage**

Nicknamed 'Canada's Galapagos,' this 150-island archipelago is the ancestral territory of the Haida Nation. This vibrant culture has been traced back 13,000 years via carbon-dated artifacts from some of the first humans this part of the world ever saw. The storm-battered islands are rich in natural wonders, Pacific Ocean wildlife and 500 archeological sites most famously found at **Gwaii Haanas National Park Reserve, National Marine Conservation Reserve & Haida Cultural Site**. Getting here requires flying into Masset or Sandspit airports or taking BC Ferries from Prince Rupert. DIY trips are possible with careful planning and your own vehicle (there is no public transport here) unless you have a guided package trip. If you're self-driving, stop in at the **Daajing Giids Visitor Centre** for maps and expert advice on trail conditions, where to go and how to visit responsibly.

**Haida Style Expeditions** is a cultural adventure and fishing expedition company that offers authentic Indigenous experiences and respectful adventures. Explore the dagger-shaped island via human-powered adventures by kayak with **Green**

### ☑ TOP TIP

Distances are vast and roads long. Be prepared with food, water, maps, a portable battery and road-trip essentials. Mid-June to mid-September are the best times to travel. Many tourism businesses close outside these months.

# DRIVING THE ALASKA HIGHWAY

The world-famous Alaska Highway was built by US Army engineers in 1942 as an emergency war measure and winds almost 900km from Dawson Creek, BC, to the Yukon border. Starting at Mile 0 in **1 Dawson Creek**, where you can find local art and handicrafts at the Dawson Creek Art Gallery and self-guided tours that step back in time at the Walter Wright Pioneer Village. Train nerds will love the NAR Station Museum and the Pouce Couple Trestle Bridge just outside town. Head north from Dawson Creek to Fort St John, where you can learn about and purchase northern Indigenous art at the **2 Indigenous Artists' Market**. Much, much further north you can learn about the Alaska Highway construction at the **3 Fort Nelson Heritage Museum**. From Fort Nelson, head east to **4 Stone Mountain Provincial Park**, where you'll either see for the first time, or

once again, stunning Rocky Mountain scenery. Camp overnight at Summit Lake, fish, or stay for some epic hiking. Continue on to **5 Muncho Lake Provincial Park** to find jade-colored waters and the squished limestone of Folded Mountain, along with unbeatable paddling and wildlife-viewing opportunities. Join a flightseeing tour, a fly-in fishing trip, camp, or stay at Northern Rockies Lodge. If there were a hot springs competition in BC, **6 Liard River Hot Springs Provincial Park** would definitely be a finalist. This true wilderness hot springs swimming experience has lush boreal forests with a steamy ecosystem that allows 250 plant species to thrive, and after a long day in the car, you'll thrive too. Camp overnight or stay at the Liard River Hot Springs Lodge. From here, it's another 220km northwest to Watson Lake and the Yukon.

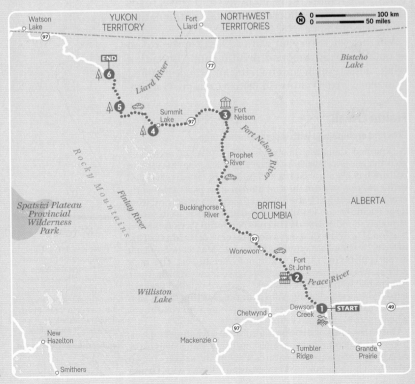

**Ninstints, Haida Gwaii**

**Coast Kayaking** or by paddleboard with **Ocean Edge Expeditions**. At the **Haida Heritage Centre** and the adjacent **Haida Gwaii Museum**, Haida wisdom, science, natural artifacts, oral history and exhibits boast an internationally recognized collection of Haida artifacts and contemporary art, and host events and programs that spotlight Haida art, culture, and current issues. And for the daring souls ready to plunge into the icy embrace of the sea, **North Beach Surf Shop** stands ready with surfboard and wetsuit rentals. Before arriving, plan ahead and take the **Haida Gwaii Pledge** at **gohaidagwaii.ca** and **haidatourism.ca**.

## GWAII HAANAS

The Unesco World Heritage Site of the Gwaii Haanas National Park Reserve, National Marine Conservation Reserve and Haida Cultural site is a collection of Moresby Island and 137 smaller islands, with over 500 ancient Haida sites including **SGang Gwaay** (Ninstints) on Anthony Island, where time-worn totem poles stand like silent guardians. Discover the antiquity of Skedans village on Louise Island, and the thermal wonder of Hotspring Island. The park in its entirety is safeguarded by the Haida Watchmen. Access is an adventure in itself, via boat or floatplane. However, due to visitor limits, pre-planning is essential. To simplify your journey, consider booking a tour with licenced Parks Canada operators via this QR code.

## PLACES TO STAY IN HAIDA GWAII

**Haida House**
Oceanside cabins with hot tubs and a lodge offer unique Haida cuisine and adventures. **$$$**

**Heillen Village Longhouses**
Authentic longhouses with kitchens that sleep small and large groups. Tent pads are also available. **$$**

**Haida Gwaii Glamping Co**
Chic glamping tents nestled in the forest and just steps away from the ocean. **$$**

Above: Three Sisters Mountains, Canmore; right: Peace Bridge over Bow River, Calgary

## THE MAIN AREAS

**CANMORE & KANANASKIS**
Front ranges of the
Canadian Rockies. **p152**

**WATERTON LAKES
NATIONAL PARK &
CROWSNEST PASS**
Crown of the Continent.
**p158**

# Alberta

## MOUNTAINS, FORESTS, PRAIRIES, LAKES AND BADLANDS

Explore vast and varied landscapes that include a mix of rugged mountains, dense forests, lakes, prairies, cosmopolitan cities and otherworldly badlands where dinosaurs once roamed.

Alberta does mountains like Rome does cathedrals and Florence does art. Banff National Park was established in 1885 as Canada's first national park and the world's third. Even today, it is the stunning landscapes of the Rocky Mountains that many visitors associate with Alberta, but there is beauty to be found both inside and outside the mountain parks. In 27,525 sq km of protected land, you'll find rugged mountains, dense forests, foothills, grasslands, rolling prairies, pristine lakes, boreal forest and desert badlands.

Small prairie communities and large metropolitan cities hold their own appealing adventures. Calgary is the largest city in Alberta and one of the most ethnically diverse cosmopolitan centers in Canada with people from 240 different ethnic origins calling it home. Edmonton, the province's vibrant capital city, was dubbed the 'festival city,' because it hosts more than 60 festivals each year. Both cities have impressive museums, art galleries, restaurants, craft breweries, activities, events and international airports.

The Canadian Badlands region is a landscape that transports you to another time when dinosaurs roamed. Home to the largest deposits of dinosaur bones in the world, this region stretches east of Drumheller to the Saskatchewan border and south to the United States. There is much to discover here including beautiful canyons, sacred Indigenous sites, abandoned coal mines, ghost towns, farms and ranches.

Most international visitors fly into Calgary or Edmonton. Calgary is the gateway to **Banff National Park** (p210) and the Canadian Badlands. Edmonton serves as the gateway to **Jasper National Park** (p224).

| **DRUMHELLER** | **CALGARY** | **EDMONTON** |
|---|---|---|
| Dinosaur fossils and otherworldly badlands scenery. **p164** | Alberta's largest city. **p170** | The capital city of Alberta. **p175** |

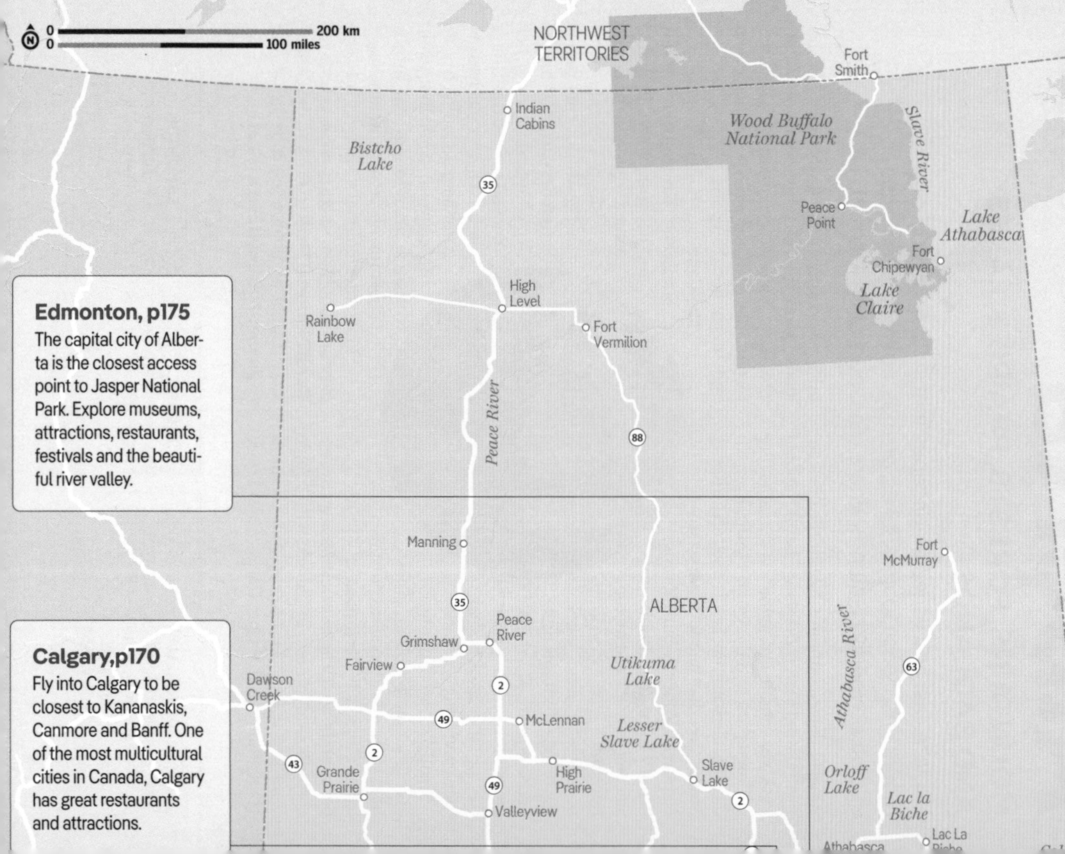

## CAR

Having your own vehicle is by far the best option for exploring Alberta. This allows you the freedom to stop at roadside pullouts, trailheads, attractions, parks, towns and cities.

## BUS

Most major cities have public bus services. Red Arrow connects Calgary and Edmonton with several other communities in Alberta and British Columbia. Banff Airporter and Brewster Inc offer bus services from Calgary Airport to the mountain parks and Sundog Tours connects Edmonton with Jasper and Banff.

## TRAIN

Via Rail has scheduled train services from Edmonton to Jasper twice per week. Rocky Mountaineer offers a luxury train service that connects Vancouver with Banff or Jasper and a motorcoach service to Calgary or Edmonton.

### Edmonton, p175

The capital city of Alberta is the closest access point to Jasper National Park. Explore museums, attractions, restaurants, festivals and the beautiful river valley.

### Calgary, p170

Fly into Calgary to be closest to Kananaskis, Canmore and Banff. One of the most multicultural cities in Canada, Calgary has great restaurants and attractions.

0 ──── 200 km
0 ──── 100 miles

NORTHWEST TERRITORIES

ALBERTA

Fort Smith

Slave River

Lake Athabasca

Fort Chipewyan

Lake Claire

Wood Buffalo National Park

Peace Point

Indian Cabins

Bistcho Lake

Rainbow Lake

Fort Vermilion

High Level

35

Peace River

Manning

Grimshaw

35

Peace River

2

Fairview

Dawson Creek

Grande Prairie

43

Valleyview

49

High Prairie

49

McLennan

2

Lesser Slave Lake

Utikuma Lake

88

Slave Lake

2

Fort McMurray

63

Athabasca River

Orloff Lake

Lac la Biche

Athabasca

Lac La Biche

## Drumheller, p164

The Canadian Badlands region in southeast Alberta features landscapes like nowhere else and the largest concentration of dinosaur fossils on the planet.

## Waterton Lakes National Park & Crowsnest Pass, p158

In the southwest corner of Alberta, the biologically diverse Crown of the Continent region is where prairies meet mountains.

## Canmore & Kananaskis, p152

Ski resorts, hiking and cycling trails and many beautiful vistas can be enjoyed in the parks of Kananaskis and the mountain town of Canmore.

# Find Your Way

With a total area of 661,858 sq km, Alberta is slightly bigger than France. The Rockies are on the southwestern part of the province along the British Columbia border. Prairies and badlands are in the southeast and boreal forest dominates the northern region.

SASKATCHEWAN

Rosetown

Bonnyville

St Paul

Lloydminster

Provost

Oyen

Medicine Hat

CANADA

USA

MONTANA

Lethbridge

Milk River

Cardston

Fort Macleod

Vulcan

Longview

Turner Valley

Calgary

Airdrie

Drumheller

*Royal Tyrrell Museum of Palaeontology*

Huxley

Red Deer

Bowden

Kananaskis

Banff

Lake Louise

Canmore

*Peter Lougheed Provincial Park*

*Banff National Park*

Saskatchewan River Crossing

Nordegg

*Yoho National Park*

*Kootenay National Park*

*Glacier National Park*

*Mt Revelstoke National Park*

*Rocky Mountains*

Kamloops

*Wells Gray Provincial Park*

*Bowron Lake Provincial Park*

BRITISH COLUMBIA

*Athabasca River*

Grande Cache

*Wilmore Wilderness Park*

Pocahontas

Jasper

*Jasper National Park*

*Mt Robson Provincial Park*

Hinton

Edson

Drayton Valley

Stony Plain

Leduc

Edmonton

Vegreville

Camrose

Wetaskiwin

Donalda

Castor

Waterton Lakes National Park

Bonnyville

Castor

149

# Plan Your Time

You can pack a lot into a few days or take your time and dig deeper into the culture, scenery, wildlife and interesting attractions in Alberta – outside Jasper and Banff.

Walterdale Bridge, Edmonton

## One Day to Explore

● If you're short on time, head straight to the Canadian Badlands. Explore the **Royal Tyrrell Museum** (p164) in Drumheller, which contains one of the world's largest displays of dinosaur fossils. Snap a picture of the World's Largest Dinosaur in downtown Drumheller.

● Then head to **Horseshoe Canyon** (p165) and enjoy otherworldly badlands scenery at the viewpoint or on a hike. If time permits, don a hard hat and take a tour of the historic **Atlas Coal Mine** (p166).

● Cap off the day with a cool drink at the **Last Chance Saloon** (p166) in the ghost town of Wayne.

### Seasonal Highlights

Alberta is an all-season destination, but July and August are busiest. Visit in late spring, summer and fall to hike mountain trails and view wildlife. Winter visitors experience some of the world's best skiing and snowboarding.

**JANUARY**

The High Performance Rodeo in Calgary is the largest festival of its kind in Western Canada, featuring theater, music, dance and art.

**FEBRUARY**

The third Monday in February is Family Day, a provincial holiday in Alberta. There are winter festivals and events throughout the province.

**JUNE**

The **Badlands Passion Play** (p165), depicting the life of Christ on Canada's largest outdoor stage, begins at the end of June.

ANTHONY MANCE/SHUTTERSTOCK ©

KARORI PRODUCTION/SHUTTERSTOCK ©, SAL AUGRUSO/SHUTTERSTOCK, ARTMEDIAWORX/SHUTTERSTOCK ©

## Three Days to Explore

● After a day in the Drumheller area, head to **Dinosaur Provincial Park** (p167) for more badlands dinosaur fossil fun. Participate in an interpretive program, enjoy the Scenic Loop Road and hike the 1.3km Badlands Interpretive Trail.

● On the third day, drive to **Head-Smashed-In Buffalo Jump Interpretive Centre** (p169) to see one of the largest and best-preserved buffalo jumps in North America and learn about Indigenous culture.

● From there, head to **Waterton Lakes National Park** (p160). Hike the short but steep Bear's Hump trail for one of the best views in the Canadian Rockies.

● Take a **scenic cruise** (p160) across Upper Waterton Lake into US waters and back.

## A Week or More

● It's worth lingering longer to explore Alberta beyond Banff and Jasper and there are plenty of places beyond what was included in the aforementioned itineraries to fill out a week or more. Several days could be spent enjoying hikes and activities in the Crown of the Continent region in Waterton Lakes National Park and Crowsnest Pass.

● There are many amazing museums, attractions, restaurants and festivals in **Calgary** (p170) and **Edmonton** (p175), Alberta's two largest cities. The scenery, hikes and attractions in the foothills and front ranges of the Canadian Rockies in **Canmore and Kananaskis** (p152) rivals the national parks and is a delight to explore.

**JULY**
July 1 is Canada Day and celebrations happen throughout the province. The 10-day **Calgary Stampede** (p170) begins the second week in July.

**AUGUST**
The 10-day **Edmonton International Fringe Festival** (p179), the largest fringe theater festival in North America, starts in mid-August.

**SEPTEMBER**
Larch trees turn golden in late September to early October in the Canadian Rockies and you can go **larch hiking** (p155).

**NOVEMBER**
Canadian Finals Rodeo takes place in early November in Red Deer.

# Canmore & Kananaskis

**FRONT RANGES OF THE CANADIAN ROCKIES**

Canmore and Kananaskis is an outdoor adventure paradise in the foothills and front ranges of the Canadian Rockies southeast of Banff. The 4200 sq km of Kananaskis Country encompasses nine provincial parks and more than 50 recreation, wilderness and natural areas. There are more than 175 established trails in Kananaskis – used for hiking, horseback riding, cross-country skiing, fat biking and mountain biking. There are cross-country and downhill ski facilities, golf courses, rivers and lakes, campgrounds and a variety of accommodations – from backcountry lodges to upscale resorts. Kananaskis is also home to the only Nordic spa in the Canadian Rockies. Some areas of Kananaskis allow for activities that are forbidden in the national parks such as dogsledding, snowmobiling, motorized boating and ATVing. Canmore is a laid-back gateway city to the mountain parks – just 20 minutes outside of Banff. It has recreational facilities, restaurants and accommodations.

## Hit the Trails in Kananaskis

### Hiking, mountain biking and cross-country skiing

There are trails suitable for everyone in Kananaksis Country, a place with some of the most beautiful trails in the Canadian Rockies. In the more than 175 established trails in Kananaskis Country, there are many that are unique. Experienced hikers enjoy the challenging 13.5km **Heart Mountain Horseshoe Trail**, because it allows you to summit three peaks in a single day. The **Heart Creek Bunker Trail** is a moderate 4km out-and-back trail that leads to an abandoned Cold War–era bunker, built on the side of a mountain. Bring flashlights and you can explore the network of caves that make up the bunker. The **Troll Falls Trail** is a quick and easy 3.4km jaunt for hikers of all ages and it leads to a beautiful waterfall. There are amazing winter cross-country

### ☑ TOP TIP

If you'd like to try glamping, otherwise known as comfort camping, Mount Engadine Lodge is the best bet. Each canvas tent has a king-size bed, a sofa bed, a fireplace, an ensuite bathroom and a private deck. The insulated tents are open year-round and all meals are included.

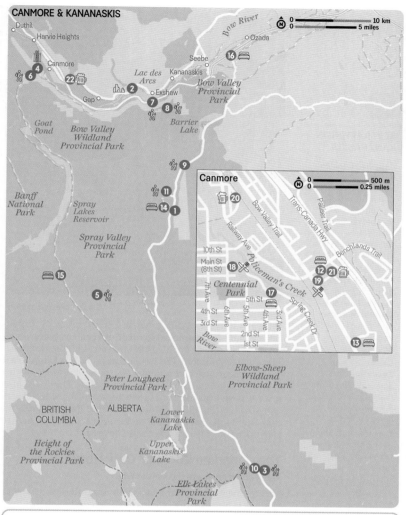

## CANMORE & KANANASKIS

### SIGHTS
1. Boundary Ranch
2. Grotto Canyon

### SIGHTS
3. Arethusa Cirque
4. Canmore Nordic Centre Provincial Park
5. Chester Lake
6. Grassi Lakes Loop Trail
7. Heart Creek Bunker Trail
8. Heart Mountain Horseshoe Trail
see 14. Kananaskis Nordic Spa
9. Mount Lorette Ponds Trail
10. Pocaterra Cirque
11. Troll Falls Trail

### SLEEPING
12. Canmore Downtown Hostel
13. Falcon Crest Lodge by Clique
14. Kananaskis Mountain Lodge, Autograph Collection
15. Mount Engadine Lodge
16. Stoney Nakoda Resort & Casino
17. The Malcolm

### EATING
see 14. Forte
18. Gaucho Brazilian BBQ
19. The Sensory

### DRINKING & NIGHTLIFE
20. Canmore Brewing Company
21. Grizzly Paw Taproom
22. Sheepdog Brewing

**BEST RAFTING IN KANANASKIS**

**Canadian Rockies Rafting**
Scenic floats on the Bow River, whitewater trips on the Bow and Kananaskis Rivers and surf rafting – where you paddle back into the flow to surf the current.

**Chinook Rafting**
Rafting trips on the Bow River, the Kananaskis River or the Kicking Horse River in British Columbia.

**Canmore River Adventures**
Specializes in scenic float trips on the Bow River. Also offers horseback riding.

**Canmore Raft Tours**
Scenic float trips or 3- to 4-day fully catered raft trips.

**White Wolf Rafting**
Whitewater rafting on the Kananaskis River that can be combined with dog carting adventures.

RICK SILVER/SHUTTERSTOCK ©

**Grassi Lakes, Canmore**

ski trails and fat biking trails in several areas of Kananaskis including **Canmore Nordic Centre Provincial Park** (p157), where there are also lessons and equipment rentals. Just outside Canmore, the 3.4km **Grassi Lakes Loop Trail** has an easy route and a moderate route that leads to two beautiful lakes surrounded by mountains. There are also several paved hiking trails that are good for wheelchairs and strollers including **Mount Lorette Ponds Trail**, an easy 1km loop trail that is a scenic spot for fishing, nature viewing and is also a popular picnic area.

## The Canadian Rockies' Only Nordic Spa
### Relax and rejuvenate the Nordic Way

Located next to the Kananaskis Mountain Lodge, the **Kananaskis Nordic Spa** is an oasis of relaxation and healing. A Nordic spa is a hydrotherapy experience that has hot pools, saunas, cold pools and warming spaces. The idea is to experience these facilities in a circuit of hot, cold, rest and repeat.

 **WHERE TO DINE IN CANMORE & KANANASKIS**

**Forte**
This restaurant at Kananaskis Mountain Lodge has a buffet breakfast and pizzas, pastas, salads and steaks. **$$**

**The Sensory**
For fine dining on a budget, try the chef's choice set menu at this Canmore restaurant. **$$$**

**Gaucho Brazilian BBQ**
Enjoy slow-roasted meats with delicious side dishes at this Brazilian barbecue restaurant in Canmore. **$$$**

BRADLEY L. GRANT/SHUTTERSTOCK ©

**Pocaterra Ridge, Kananaskis**

**Leigh McAdam,** bestselling author and owner of blog HikeBikeTravel. com shares her favorite larch hikes in Kananaskis.

What is larch hiking? Around the third or fourth week in September, larch trees begin to turn golden and for two or three weeks, it's one of the prettiest times to hike in Alberta.

**Pocaterra Cirque**
One of the most popular larch hikes in Kananaskis, this 7km hike leads to beautiful views of mountains and larches.

**Arethusa Cirque**
A lesser-known larch hike in the Highwood Pass area, this 4.5km loop trail has views of beautiful golden larches in a stunning mountain setting.

**Chester Lake**
This 9.8km, four-hour round-trip hike takes you through larch-filled meadows to a mountain lake ringed by larches and the cliffs of Mt Chester.

Nordic wellness rituals originated in Denmark, Finland, Iceland, Norway and Sweden and date back hundreds of years. Proponents of this type of therapy believe that exposing the body to extreme heat followed by extreme cold shocks the system, releases endorphins and improves immune response.

Nordic spa guests start by superheating their bodies in a hot pool, a dry sauna or a steam room. Then they cool their bodies in a cold plunge pool, an ice bath or by standing under an icy-cold waterfall. The rest phase brings the body back to its normal temperature and can be done by resting in a relaxation room, sitting around a bonfire or lying in a hammock.

If you want to completely bliss out, the circuit must be repeated several times over the course of a morning or an afternoon. For an extra charge, you can enjoy a healthy lunch or dinner at the on-site restaurant or a massage at the spa facilities.

 **WHERE TO STAY IN KANANASKIS**

**Kananaskis Mountain Lodge, Autograph Collection**
Full-service resort with five dining venues, a spa, a swimming pool and activities. $$$

**Mount Engadine Lodge**
Mountain lodge with lodge rooms, cabins, a yurt and glamping tents. All meals and afternoon tea are included. $$$

**Stoney Nakoda Resort & Casino**
Indigenous-owned hotel, with pool, waterslide, restaurants, casino and helicopter tours. $$

## EXPLORE BOUNDARY RANCH

If you want to experience the real west and the beauty of the foothills on horseback, **Boundary Ranch** in Kananaskis is the place to go. A dozen guided rides are on offer here – ranging from pony rides to multiday pack trips. All take you along trails with beautiful mountain views.

Rafting and dog carting can also be booked in summer. Sleigh rides and dogsled adventures are available in winter. There's a taxidermy museum, a cafe and a gift shop on-site.

LEVI LOOKE/SHUTTERSTOCK ©

**Dogsledding, Banaff National Park**

## Answer the Call of the Wild

### Enjoy a thrilling dogsled adventure

There's a special thrill that comes from riding in or driving a sled pulled by a team of excited dogs running along a snowy trail – especially when that trail comes with incredible mountain scenery. Dogsledding is a traditional mode of transportation in northern regions of Canada and one of the most popular recreational tours in Kananaskis. Most of the dogsled tour operators that sell tours in Banff actually operate the tours in Kananaskis.

A typical dogsled outing begins with the chance to meet the dogs – either at the kennels or near the sled before you hit the trail. You typically begin riding inside the sled under a warm blanket while an experienced musher drives the sled. Depending on the tour company and your own preferences, you may get the opportunity to drive the sled, shouting out 'Gee!' (turn right) or 'Haw!' (turn left) as the dogs skillfully traverse the trail.

 ## WHERE TO FIND A CRAFT BREWERY IN CANMORE

**Canmore Brewing Company**
Craft beers, seasonal brews and beer cocktails are served here. Bring your own snacks.

**Grizzly Paw Taproom**
Microbrewed craft beers and craft sodas are served with exceptional views and a full restaurant menu.

**Sheepdog Brewing**
Enjoy an ever-changing menu of craft beers and ciders alongside a basic menu of pretzels and other snacks.

Four companies operate dogsled tours in Kananaskis – Banff Adventures Unlimited, Howling Dog Tours Ltd, Snowy Owl Sled Dog Tours and Mad Dogs & Englishmen Dogsled Expeditions Inc.

Dogsledding is a winter activity, but some companies like Snowy Owl Sled Dog Tours also offer dryland dog carting during the summer months. With this type of activity, a sled dog team is used to pull a custom-designed cart on wheels through the forest along scenic trails.

## Learn to Cross-Country Ski

### Canmore Nordic Centre Provincial Park

Developed for the Nordic events of the 1988 Winter Olympics, **Canmore Nordic Centre Provincial Park** remains one of the top facilities of its kind in the world. It's the place where the Canadian national team trains for Nordic events and it has become an outstanding facility for those who enjoy cross-country skiing or for those who wish to learn how to ski.

There are more than 70km of groomed, machine-made and natural trails at the park, including 6.5km of trails that are illuminated for night skiing. Inside the Day Lodge, there are on-site equipment sales, repairs and rentals as well as an excellent cafe that serves everything from coffee and baked goods to soups, sandwiches, chili and butter chicken. You can arrange private or group lessons for skiers of all levels from beginner to advanced.

Winter is the most popular time to visit, but there are also summer activities at this provincial park. There's an 18-hole disc golf course and more than 100km of mountain bike and hiking trails to enjoy. There are also 6.5km of paved roller ski trails and a mountain bike skills park. Mountain bike rentals and lessons are available in the summer.

**BEST WINTER HIKES IN CANMORE & KANANASKIS**

Put on warm clothes and ice cleats to enjoy these amazing winter hikes.

**Grotto Canyon**
Follow a power line past an industrial plant before walking on the surface of a frozen creek through a narrow canyon to reach a frozen waterfall on this 4.2km round-trip hike. Look for ancient Indigenous pictographs on the canyon walls.

**Grassi Lakes**
A 3.4km loop trail leads to two glorious green lakes surrounded by mountains and towering cliffs that are popular with climbers.

**Troll Falls**
A beautiful frozen waterfall is the reward for a 1.7km one-way hike through foothills and aspen forest.

 **WHERE TO STAY IN CANMORE**

**The Malcolm**
Canmore's newest luxury hotel has comfortable modern rooms, restaurants, lounges and a pool. $$$

**Falcon Crest Lodge by Clique**
Spacious condos with full kitchens, a fitness room and two outdoor hot tubs. $$$

**Canmore Downtown Hostel**
Dorm beds or comfortable private rooms with a communal kitchen, lounge and laundry facilities. $

# Waterton Lakes National Park & Crowsnest Pass

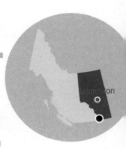

**CROWN OF THE CONTINENT**

Flat prairies collide dramatically with the rugged peaks of the Rockies in Waterton Lakes National Park. This 505-sq-km park is a meeting of two worlds with an unusual mix of plants, wildlife and incredible scenery that is found nowhere else. Waterton is part of a Unesco World Heritage site, a Unesco Biosphere Reserve and an International Peace Park. It is also part of the Crown of the Continent region that includes Glacier National Park in Montana, the Crowsnest Pass region of Alberta and some parts of British Columbia. The Crown of the Continent is known for remarkable biodiversity and incredible scenery. It's also far less traveled than other places in the Canadian Rockies. Crowsnest Pass has a fascinating history of coal mining and rum running. Together, Waterton Lakes National Park and Crowsnest Pass are a sublime pocket of tranquility in one of the prettiest places on the planet.

> ☑ **TOP TIP**
>
> There are two amazing viewpoints in Waterton Lakes National Park – one requires hiking and one does not. Stand on the bluff behind the Prince of Wales Hotel and take in the incredible view. Or if capable of tackling a short, steep hike, climb to the top of Bear's Hump for one of the best views in the Canadian Rockies.

## One of the World's Most Thrilling Trails

### Crypt Lake Trail's ledge walk

When it comes to the **Crypt Lake Trail**, both the journey and the destination are important. This adventurous 17.2km round-trip hike is widely considered to be one of the most thrilling hikes in the world.

The day begins with catching a boat taxi across Waterton Lake to the trailhead. From there the trail climbs 700m, passing four spectacular waterfalls along the way. To get to the final destination, you must climb a metal ladder, crawl through a 30m-long tunnel, and scramble across a ledge along a sheer rock face while holding onto a steel cable.

The mountain views are incredible all along the way and the reward at the end is a turquoise-blue lake and a 183m cascading waterfall.

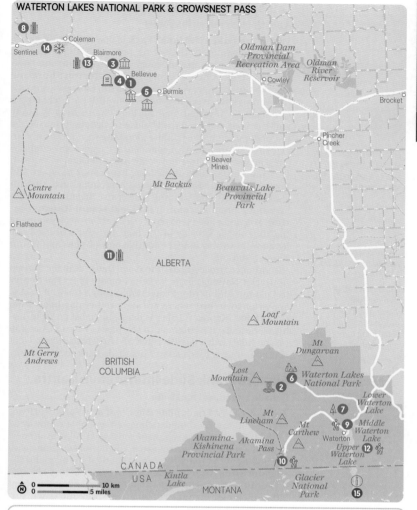

# WATERTON LAKES NATIONAL PARK & CROWSNEST PASS

## SIGHTS
1 Bellevue Underground Mine Tour
2 Blakiston Falls
3 Frank Slide Interpretive Centre
4 Hillcrest Mine Memorial & Cemetery
5 Leitch Collieries Provincial Historic Site
6 Red Rock Canyon
7 Waterton Lakes National Park

## ACTIVITIES
8 Allison Creek Nordic Ski Trails
9 Bear's Hump
10 Cameron Lake Trail
11 Castle Mountain Resort
12 Crypt Lake Trail
13 Pass Powderkeg Ski Area
14 Star Creek Falls Ice Walk

## INFORMATION
15 Goat Haunt Ranger Station

## TRANSPORT
see 9 Waterton Shoreline Cruise Co

# Cruise to the United States
### A boat journey across the border

**Waterton Lakes National Park** is one of the only places where you can cross the border between Canada and the United States without a passport. On a 75-minute non-landing Canada-USA Border Cruise with **Waterton Shoreline Cruise Co**, you'll travel across Waterton Lake past the cutline through the trees that marks the 49th parallel and the Canada/USA International Border. The scenery is lovely and the boat stays relatively close to the shoreline, so it's not uncommon to see wildlife along the way. The cruise includes lively interpretive commentary from local guides.

If you would like to enjoy some hikes in Glacier National Park on the USA side of the lake, bring your passport and take the 2¼-hour Interpretive Sightseeing Cruise that includes a Goat Haunt Landing. The cruise includes commentary and a 30-minute stop at the **Goat Haunt Ranger Station**. You don't need a passport to stretch your legs during the stop on the US side of the lake, but you will need one if you want to stay longer and hike beyond the Goat Haunt Ranger Station.

In order to proceed past the Goat Haunt Ranger Station in Glacier National Park, travelers must report their entry to Customs and Border Protection through the CPB ROAM app prior to arrival. There are several nice day-hikes from Goat Haunt. Kootenai Lakes is one of the most popular day-hikes, because it's common to see moose there. It's a 9km return hike, so it's best to catch an early boat ride to Goat Haunt and then catch a later boat ride back to Waterton.

# Explore Frank Slide Interpretive Centre
### Canada's deadliest rockslide

You won't miss Frank Slide when you drive past it. Heaps of rock and massive boulders line either side of Highway 22 in the Crowsnest Pass region of southwest Alberta. Underneath the rubble are buried homes and businesses along with the bodies of the 70 to 90 people that died in the rockslide.

**Frank Slide Interpretive Centre** tells the story of Canada's deadliest rockslide. At 4:10am on April 29, 1903, about 110 million metric tonnes of limestone rock slid down Turtle Mountain completely burying a large part of the mining town of Frank. In about 90 seconds, lives were lost and others were forever changed in the tight-knit mining community.

**BEST HIKES WITH A VIEW IN WATERTON LAKES NATIONAL PARK**

**Bear's Hump**
Views of the Waterton Lakes and surrounding mountains are the reward for this steep 2.8km hike.

**Blakiston Falls**
Two incredible viewing platforms overlooking Blakiston Falls are at the end of this 2.4km hike.

**Cameron Lake Trail**
This flat, paved trail follows the western shore of Cameron Lake for 1.6km with beautiful lake and mountain views.

 **WHERE TO EAT IN WATERTON**

**Wieners of Waterton**
Gourmet beef and veggie hotdogs served on homemade buns with interesting sauces and toppings. **$**

**Red Rock Trattoria**
Enjoy caprese salad, homemade pasta and tiramisu in this small restaurant with mountain views. **$$$**

**Lakeside Chophouse**
Enjoy a classic steakhouse menu – filet mignon with garlic butter, bison ribeye, teriyaki salmon and vegetarian options. **$$$**

**The Frank Slide**

The Interpretive Centre overlooks the wreckage of the rock-slide. There's an interpretive trail outside the center with lookouts over the site. Long before the tragedy occurred, the Blackfoot and Ktunaxa People called Turtle Mountain 'the mountain that moves.' Interpretive displays and a film inside the museum explain what scientists believe caused the rockslide and tell the stories of those that survived it.

## WHY I LOVE WATERTON LAKES NATIONAL PARK

**Debbie Olsen**, writer

Alberta is full of wonderful Rocky Mountain parks. But Waterton is the one that I grew up with and the one that always feels like home.

During summer visits with family, we always hike Bear's Hump, take a picture on the hill behind the Prince of Wales Hotel, get an ice cream cone at Big Scoop and visit Cameron Falls, Cameron Lake and Red Rock Canyon. Wildlife sightings are common – elk, deer, bighorn sheep, black bears and grizzlies.

Waterton is smaller and less visited than other Rocky Mountain parks, but that's what makes it special. Except for a couple of hotels and restaurants, the townsite shuts down in winter and it feels like this winter wonderland is all your own.

## WHERE TO STAY IN WATERTON

**Prince of Wales**
This iconic 1920s hotel overlooks one of the best views in the park and serves high tea every afternoon. **$$$**

**Kilmorey Lodge**
Completely rebuilt and opened in 2022, this lakefront hotel has spacious rooms and a great restaurant. **$$$**

**Northland Lodge**
Cozy rooms with coffee, tea, juice and hot homemade muffins for breakfast. **$$$**

## EXPLORE MINING HISTORY IN THE CROWSNEST PASS

**Leitch Collieries Provincial Historic Site**

Strikes, war and bad luck contributed to the failure of this sophisticated Canadian-owned coal-mining venture. A walking path with interpretive signs and listening posts is a window to the early 1900s. Open May 15 to Labour Day.

**Hillcrest Mine Memorial & Cemetery**

The worst coal-mining disaster in Canadian history happened on June 19, 1914 when an explosion killed 189 miners. Most victims were buried in a mass grave at Hillcrest Cemetery.

**Bellevue Underground Mine Tour**

Don a miner's helmet and lamp and go deep into the Bellevue Mine to see firsthand what it was like to be a coal miner. Book online in advance.

BGSMITH/SHUTTERSTOCK ©

Red Rock Canyon

## A Stunning Canyon & a Powerful Waterfall

### Red Rock Canyon and Blakiston Falls

Watch for bears and other wildlife as you drive up the Blakiston Valley to **Red Rock Canyon**. There you'll see a stunning red canyon that shelters a sparkling mountain stream. Stand on the bridge overlooking the canyon or take a walk on the trail that surrounds it. You can also enjoy a short 2.4km hike through the forest to reach two overlooks that provide fantastic views of stunning **Blakiston Falls**. The Blakiston Falls hike is not wheelchair friendly, but it is an easy hike that can be enjoyed by people of all ages and abilities.

 **WHERE TO STAY IN THE CROWSNEST PASS**

**Kanata Inns Blairmore**
This comfy hotel has a variety of rooms including some with kitchenettes and large family suites. **$$**

**York Creek B&B**
A hot tub, lounge and breakfast are included at this log cabin at the edge of Coleman. **$$**

**Country Encounters**
Nine rooms, a hot tub, patio, guest lounge and breakfast at this Coleman B&B. **$$**

# Ski Castle Mountain
## Alberta's second-largest ski area

It's a little surprising, but the second-largest ski resort in Alberta is also considered a hidden gem. **Castle Mountain Resort** was founded in 1966. It isn't operated by a massive corporation, but by skiers who are more driven by creating great terrain than by making a profit. The resort has more than 200 mostly local shareholders. Locals know and love this ski resort, but most visitors are completely unaware of its existence. That gives it a truly laid-back community vibe.

The resort is home to one of North America's only resort-based cat skiing operations, which was dubbed the Powder Stagecoach. Cat skiing takes skiers and boarders away from groomed slopes to backcountry areas with untouched powder using a snowcat machine. The powder skiing experience is comparable to heli-skiing at a fraction of the cost.

This remarkable resort is 50km west of Pincher. It boasts 3000 vertical feet spread over two mountains. Some 94 trails are accessed by seven lifts that are rarely crowded. The resort also has some of the longest, continuous fall line runs in North America.

Equipment rentals and lessons can be arranged at the day lodge, which also has a cafeteria. There's a hostel and a basic hotel on-site, and vacation homes and condo rentals are available through lodging partners affiliated with the resort.

In the summer, there's disc golf, hiking trails and road cycling to enjoy at the resort.

**Star Creek Falls**

ANTHONY HINGSBURGER/SHUTTERSTOCK ©

## WHAT TO DO IN WINTER IN THE CROWSNEST PASS

### Allison Creek Nordic Ski Trails
Explore the more than 30km of Nordic ski trails along the eastern Continental Divide that are maintained by local volunteers. It's also a great place to go fat biking.

### Star Creek Falls Ice Walk
A 2km loop trail takes you to Star Creek Falls. In winter you can walk on the frozen creek with ice cleats. Take a guided tour with Uplift Adventures and the gear is supplied.

### Pass Powderkeg Ski Area
This uncrowded family-friendly ski area has two t-bars and a day lodge that offers rentals and lessons. This ski area offers free bunny hill access and it's lit for night skiing.

 ## DINING IN THE CROWSNEST PASS

**Encounters Wine Bar & Small Plate Kitchen**
A great menu with everything from mussels to Moroccan lamb and chocolate fondue. $$

**The Pass Beer Co**
Enjoy small-batch craft beers and wood-fired pizzas on a great outdoor patio. $$

**Crowsnest Café and Fly Shop**
Free trade coffees and Rooibos teas are served alongside healthy organic bowls, wraps and sandwiches. $$

# Drumheller

**FOSSILS AND OTHERWORLDLY BADLANDS SCENERY**

As you approach Drumheller, the road dips down dramatically into the Red Deer Valley, looking like a big layered cake. This community was founded on coal but now thrives on another subterranean resource – dinosaur bones. A small town set amid Alberta's enigmatic badlands, it acts as the nexus of the so-called Dinosaur Trail.

Paleontology is a serious business here (the fantastic Royal Tyrrell Museum is as much research center as tourist site), and downtown the cartoon dino statues on most street corners add some color and character to an otherwise average town.

With broad desert-like expanses, it's hard to imagine this region as a subtropical paradise, but 75 million years ago that's exactly what it was. Dinosaurs roamed through a landscape of lush forests with towering redwoods, sycamore trees and giant ferns. The Canadian Badlands is home to the largest deposits of dinosaur bones in the world – including every known group of Cretaceous dinosaurs.

## The World's Largest Display of Dinosaurs
### Visit the Royal Tyrrell Museum of Palaeontology

This fantastic museum in Drumheller is one of the pre-eminent dinosaur museums on the planet. Even if you have no interest in dinos, you'll come out feeling like you missed your calling as a paleontologist. The exhibits are nothing short of mind-blowing. Unlike some other dinosaur exhibits, there's nothing dusty or musty about this super-modern place. Children and adults alike love the interactive displays.

The Royal Tyrrell (pronounced Teer-uhl) Museum's Dinosaur Hall houses one of the world's largest displays of dinosaur remains. As you explore, look for the skeleton of the 'Hellboy' dinosaur, a cousin of triceratops that was discovered in 2005. You should also look for the skeleton nicknamed 'Black Beauty,' a massive black T-rex rearing its head into the sky. You can learn how the dinosaur fossils are extracted from the ground

---

☑ **TOP TIP**

Dinosaur Trail Golf & Country Club lays the unsubstantiated claim of having the toughest back nine in North America. With greens and tee boxes interspersed through colorful badlands, it's challenging and unique.

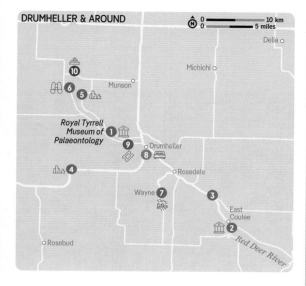

**DRUMHELLER & AROUND**

0 · 10 km
0 · 5 miles

Delia

Michichi

Munson

Royal Tyrrell Museum of Palaeontology

Drumheller

Rosedale

Wayne

East Coulee

Rosebud

Red Deer River

**HIGHLIGHTS**
1 Royal Tyrrell Museum of Palaeontology

**SIGHTS**
2 Atlas Coal Mine National Historic Site
3 Drumheller Hoodoos
4 Horseshoe Canyon
5 Horsethief Canyon
6 Orkney Viewpoint
7 Wayne

**ACTIVITIES**
see 1 Badlands Interpretive Trail

**SLEEPING**
see 8 Jura
see 8 Jurassic Inn by Canalta Hotels
8 Ramada by Wyndham Drumheller Hotel & Suites

**ENTERTAINMENT**
9 Badlands Amphitheatre

**TRANSPORT**
10 Bleriot Ferry

and even peer into the fossil lab to see researchers at work.

Interpretive programs geared to children and adults run throughout the year and include such activities as guided hikes, simulated dig experiences, fossil casting, assembling a dinosaur skeleton and summer science camps. Some interpretive programs are included and some cost an additional fee and require advance reservations.

The **Badlands Interpretive Trail** lies just outside the museum and it's free to explore. It's a 1.4km paved loop trail in Midland Provincial Park that is interspersed with interpretive signage. It will take you past stunning badlands scenery. Stay on the trail – especially if it rains. The hills in the badlands are filled with a clay mineral called bentonite, also known as 'dinosaur snot.' Bentonite is used as an industrial lubricant and it gets extremely slippery when wet.

## Hike Among Hoodoos in Horseshoe Canyon
### Stunning scenery and hidden fossils

This huge u-shaped canyon, 17km west of Drumheller, is one of the best lookouts and hikes in the badlands region. The powerful forces of natural erosion are on display in the striped canyon walls. Enjoy the view from the lookouts and then make

> **BADLANDS PASSION PLAY**
>
> For nearly three decades, a play based on the life of Christ has been performed on Canada's largest outdoor stage in the 2500-seat **Badlands Amphitheatre**. The three-hour performance is put on by a professional production crew and hundreds of volunteer actors. The costumes and music are exceptional. The dramatically beautiful natural amphitheater is used to host concerts and other events throughout the rest of the year.

 **GREAT VIEWPOINTS NEAR DRUMHELLER**

**Orkney Viewpoint**
Benches and views of badlands scenery in the Red Deer River Valley make this spot west of Drumheller special.

**Horsethief Canyon**
A hundred years ago, outlaws hid stolen livestock in this beautiful canyon. Today it's a pretty viewpoint and hike.

**Drumheller Hoodoos**
These dramatic hoodoos southeast of Drumheller stand 5m to 7m tall and took millions of years to form.

## STEP BACK IN TIME IN & AROUND DRUMHELLER

### Atlas Coal Mine National Historic Site
Take a train ride, explore Canada's last wooden tipple in the coal processing plant or put on a hard hat and headlamp to go inside this historic coal mine southeast of Drumheller.

### The Ghost Town of Wayne
Once a thriving coal mining town with a population of 3000, this ghost town is an interesting look at the rise and fall of coal in North America. Stop for a cold drink at the Last Chance Saloon and if you don't mind ghosts, stay overnight in the Rosedeer Hotel.

### Bleriot Ferry
Take a free ride on this 1913 ferry on your way to Orkney Viewpoint and Horsethief Canyon.

TODAMO/SHUTTERSTOCK ©

**Horseshoe Canyon, outside Drumheller**

your way inside the canyon for a one-of-a-kind hiking experience that can be enjoyed year-round.

It's a steep walk into and out of the canyon, but once you're in the canyon it's easy going. The official trail inside the canyon is 0.8km one way, but you could spend the better part of a day exploring the two arms of the canyon beyond the end of the trail. The trail surface is a mix of gravel and dirt. Be careful if you do this hike when the trail is wet as the formations get very slippery. It gets hot inside the canyon. Take plenty of water and go early in the day during the peak summer months.

It's entirely possible to find fossils inside the canyon. In 2020, a 12-year-old boy discovered several enormous hadrosaur fossils while hiking in the canyon with his father. If you find a fossil, leave it in place and take a picture, so you can report it to officials at Kneehill County. This region lies in the nomadic territory of the Niitsítapi, or Blackfoot People. They were the first to discover dinosaur fossils in the badlands. They believed the large bones belonged to giant ancestors of the bison. To them the badlands was a giant graveyard for ancient creatures.

 ## WHERE TO STAY IN DRUMHELLER

**Jurassic Inn by Canalta Hotels**
Comfy rooms with kitchenettes and a free hot breakfast are available at this hotel. $$

**Heartwood Inn**
This property has 12 rooms and two guest houses for families or groups. Breakfast is an extra charge. $$

**Ramada by Wyndham Drumheller Hotel & Suites**
This family-friendly hotel has a pool with a waterslide and an included hot breakfast. $$

# Beyond Drumheller

The Canadian Badlands region is vast and scenic. East and south of Drumheller are three Unesco World Heritage sites.

The Canadian Badlands region stretches east of Drumheller to the Saskatchewan border and south to the US. Interspersed between vast expanses of farmland and prairie are remarkable historic sites and breathtaking scenery that is unique in the world. There are three Unesco World Heritage sites in the Badlands region beyond Drumheller – Dinosaur Provincial Park, Head-Smashed-In-Buffalo Jump and Áísínai'pi/Writing-on-Stone Provincial Park. Exploring these sites requires some driving and the journey will take you by surprise. One minute you are driving past flat fields of grain and the next you are gazing at the otherworldly landscape that early explorers described as 'bad lands to cross.'

## Dinosaur Provincial Park

TIME FROM DRUMHELLER:
2HR SOUTHEAST 🚗

### Rub shoulders with paleontologists

This Unesco World Heritage Site contains the highest concentration of late Cretaceous Period fossils in the world in a starkly beautiful landscape of semi-arid steppes, gorges, buttes and hoodoos. When you're standing in the dry, lunar-like landscape of **Dinosaur Provincial Park**, it's hard to imagine it as a subtropical paradise, but millions of years ago palm trees, ferns and dinosaurs roamed at the edge of a great inland sea.

Today, this site is a tourist destination and a paleontology hot spot where scientists are still working and making discoveries. Every known group of Cretaceous dinosaurs is found here. Over 300 specimens have been extracted from the Oldman Formation in the park including more than 150 complete skeletons which now reside in museums around the world.

The on-site visitor center is open from April through mid-October with dinosaur displays and information. You can explore some areas of the park on a driving loop and on four short interpretive trails, but about 70% of the park has restricted access and can only be seen on guided hikes or bus tours that operate from May to October.

### TOP TIP

Stay in Brooks and explore nearby Dinosaur Provincial Park. Stay in Lethbridge and explore Head-Smashed-In-Buffalo Jump and Áísínai'pi/Writing-on-Stone Provincial Park.

## ROSEBUD THEATRE

Alberta's largest rural professional theater company is located 20 minutes southwest of Drumheller in a tiny hamlet with a population of about 100 people. Most of the actors in the performances are graduates or students at Rosebud School of the Arts.

About 35,000 theatergoers take in performances at the 232-seat opera house annually. A delicious lunch or dinner buffet is included with performances. See what's playing and purchase tickets in advance at rosebudtheatre.com.

Unearthed dinosaur bone, Dinosaur Provincial Park

To get the most out of a visit here, book a guided experience in advance. In the restricted area, you'll see unusual rock formations and fossils still waiting to be uncovered. There are more than 20 experiences ranging from guided hikes to bus tours and excavations. The tours range in price from about $25 to $200 per adult with lower prices for children, youths and seniors. A one- or two-day excavation is the ultimate experience if you want to know what it's like to be a paleontologist. You'll work alongside researchers collecting and uncovering 75-million-year-old dinosaur fossils.

## Áísínai'pi/Writing-on-Stone Provincial Park

TIME FROM DRUMHELLER: 3.5HR SOUTHEAST

### Rock art on the Great Plains

There's a mysterious energy in the landscape of this remote provincial park in the southeast corner of Alberta. The Niitsítapi, or Blackfoot People, have long believed that Spirit Beings dwell in the hoodoos and hills that make

### WHERE TO STAY WHEN YOU VISIT DINOSAUR PROVINCIAL PARK

**Comfort Camping**
Alberta Parks has seven wall tents with beds, mini-fridges, BBQs, a table and chairs, firepits and picnic tables. **$**

**Ramada by Wyndham in Brooks**
Rooms have kitchenettes and there's a pool and an included hot breakfast here. **$$**

**Days Inn and Suites in Brooks**
This property has comfy rooms, an included breakfast, a pool and a hot tub. **$$**

up **Writing-on-Stone Provincial Park**. Young warriors came here on vision quests seeking sacred knowledge and strength from the spirit world as they entered adulthood. Messages from the spirit world took the form of pictures carved into and painted on the sandstone. The Niitsíta-pi called this place Áísínai'pi, which means 'it is pictured or written.'

This Unesco World Heritage Site was actively used by the Niitsítapi from about 4000 BCE until the early 20th century, but you can still feel an undefinable power here. There's a special feeling that comes from standing in a place that has held meaning and purpose for thousands of years.

There is an excellent on-site interpretive center and a self-guided interpretive trail that takes you to some of the spectacular viewpoints and accessible pictographs and petroglyphs. The best art is preserved in a restricted area of the park to protect it from vandalism. Park rangers, many of whom are Indigenous, give informative guided tours into the restricted area of the park where you can see many pictographs and petroglyphs.

There's a riverside campground with 61 sites, running water, showers, flush toilets, a playground and a camp store. There are also three fully equipped cabins. There's a small sandy beach along the edge of the Milk River that is lovely on a hot summer day.

This park isn't on the way to anywhere, but those who are willing to head off the main thoroughfare are rewarded.

## HEAD-SMASHED-IN BUFFALO JUMP

One of the world's oldest and best-preserved buffalo jumps is contained in this unique Unesco World Heritage Site near Fort MacLeod. The buffalo jump was used by Indigenous people of the North American plains to hunt bison for nearly 6000 years.

An impressive on-site interpretive center tells the story of the buffalo jump and the Indigenous people who used it. There's drumming and dancing every Wednesday in July and August, and there's a cafe and a gift shop on-site. It's open from the May long weekend through Labour Day. This interesting site is a three-hour drive southwest of Drumheller.

 **WHERE TO STAY WHEN VISITING WRITING-ON-STONE PROVINCIAL PARK** —

**Comfort Camping**
Alberta Parks has three cabins with beds, mini-fridges, BBQs, a table and chairs, firepits and picnic tables. **$**

**Sandman Signature Lethbridge Lodge**
This hotel has 190 renovated rooms. There's a pool, hot tub and an included hot breakfast. **$$**

**Coast Lethbridge Hotel & Conference Centre**
This hotel has a game lounge, a pool, a hot tub and a fitness center. **$$**

# Calgary

**ALBERTA'S LARGEST CITY**

Calgary has long been associated with its ties to the Wild West and the annual Calgary Stampede, but it's so much more. Alberta's largest city will surprise you with its beautiful architecture, stunning green spaces, cool eateries, nightlife beyond honky-tonk, and long, worthwhile to-do list. Calgary is one of Canada's most culturally diverse metropolises – people from 240 ethnic origins call the city home. You'll find pretty much every kind of food in the city's award-winning restaurants, and an incredible array of cultural festivals and celebrations year-round.

Close proximity to the Canadian Rockies has attracted a young, active and adventurous populace. The city has the most extensive urban network of pathways and bikeways in North America – including long stretches of scenic riverside trails. For many travelers, Calgary serves as a gateway city to Kananaskis, Canmore and Banff, but this city's incredible urban adventures also warrant setting time aside for exploration.

## ☑️ TOP TIP

For a unique and fun way to explore Calgary, raft the Bow River through the heart of the city. It usually takes two to four hours depending on the current and the paddlers. Lazy Day Raft Rentals or the Paddle Station offer raft rentals and shuttle service.

## Attend the Calgary Stampede

### An unmatched celebration of western culture

For 10 days every July, Calgary celebrates its western roots with a rodeo, exhibition and festival that is so epic it attracts over one million visitors every year. The entire city transforms during Stampede as residents and visitors alike 'get their cowboy on' wearing cowboy hats, jeans and cowboy boots. The Greatest Outdoor Show on Earth kicks off with the Calgary Stampede Parade, which is led by a different parade marshal every year. The honorary role has been bestowed upon Indigenous chiefs, actors, Olympians, athletes, singers and politicians. Kevin Costner was parade marshal in 2023.

You can eat free pancakes every day if you want to during the Stampede. Businesses and organizations all around the city hold free pancake breakfasts to celebrate. Most pancake

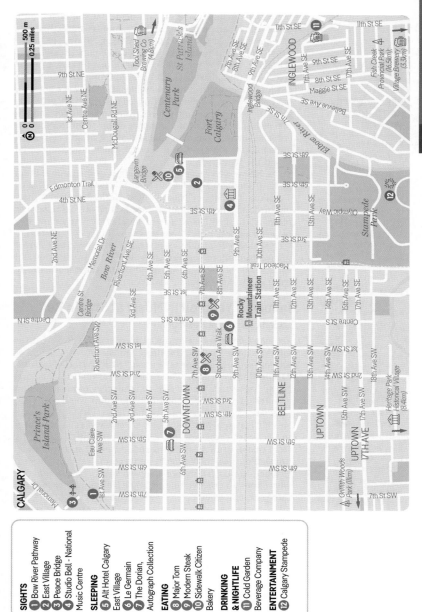

# CALGARY

## SIGHTS
1. Bow River Pathway
2. East Village
3. Peace Bridge
4. Studio Bell – National Music Centre

## SLEEPING
5. Alt Hotel Calgary
   East Village
6. Le Germain
7. The Dorian, Autograph Collection

## EATING
8. Major Tom
9. Modern Steak
10. Sidewalk Citizen Bakery

## DRINKING & NIGHTLIFE
11. Cold Garden Beverage Company

## ENTERTAINMENT
12. Calgary Stampede

breakfasts include live entertainment that can be anything from a clown and a petting zoo to a country music band.

The rodeo is at the heart of the Calgary Stampede, and it draws some of the world's best rodeo competitors in barrel racing, chuckwagon racing, bull riding, tie-down roping, steer wrestling, bareback and saddle bronc. It's the largest outdoor rodeo on the planet and like all rodeos, it's not without controversy. Animals are injured and die every year – despite the best prevention efforts. Humane societies and animal rights activists strongly oppose endangering animals for entertainment and money-making, and spotlight calf roping and chuckwagon races as two of the most dangerous activities at the Stampede.

The Elbow River Camp is a highlight of the annual Stampede. It's a chance to learn about Siksika, Piikani, Kainai, Tsuut'ina and Stoney Nakoda First Nations that have lived on this land since time immemorial. There are 26 tipis to explore, traditional foods, a traditional craft market and lively performances including a powwow dance competition.

The Stampede also has a midway with rides and interesting foods, outdoor concerts and live entertainment, agricultural displays and a nightly grandstand show featuring acrobatics, fireworks, music and dancing.

## Immerse Yourself in Music at Studio Bell

### Canada's National Music Centre

You don't need to be a music junkie to enjoy yourself at this fabulous museum. It's everything a music museum should be. Explore on your own or take a tour. **Studio Bell - National Music Centre** has five floors of musical instruments, artifacts, displays and more that tell the story of music in Canada. It's one of the most hand-on museums you'll ever visit.

Who doesn't like pretending they're a rock star? There are specific instruments that guests are allowed and encouraged to play with the assistance of video tutorials – everything from piano, drums, keyboard and guitars to a theremin, an unusual musical instrument that you don't actually physically touch to play. There are also two vocal recording booths where you can practice singing and have a computer program rate your skill level.

The collection of rare musical instruments is impressive – everything from Elton John's songwriting piano to an extremely rare Hammond Novachord. One of the museum's most prized items is TONTO (The Original New Timbral Orchestra), which was built in 1968 by the late Malcolm Cecil and is widely considered the 'holy grail' of synthesizers.

### HERITAGE PARK HISTORICAL VILLAGE

Step back in time and explore the history of Calgary at this 51-hectare park. Costumed interpreters and historic buildings tell the story of life during Calgary's early years. There's a steam train, a paddle wheel ship, a First Nations area and an area that explores the history of oil and gas discovery and development. The Gasoline Alley Museum contains one of the world's largest public collections of antique vehicles.

There's also an antique midway with fully operational heritage midway rides. There are a dozen dining venues including the Selkirk, a year-round fine dining restaurant located just outside the park gates. The park is open from the May long weekend to the first weekend in September.

## WHERE TO STAY IN CALGARY

**The Dorian, Autograph Collection**
This boutique-style downtown hotel is one of the newest and most luxurious in the city. **$$$**

**Le Germain**
Across from the Calgary Tower, this elegant hotel has luxurious in-room amenities and a great on-site restaurant. **$$$**

**Alt Hotel Calgary East Village**
Rooms have contemporary furnishings and large windows. There are three good on-site restaurants. **$$$**

**Peace Bridge over Bow River**

Studio Bell is also home to the Canadian Country Music Hall of Fame, where you can learn about the history of music and the lives of many musicians.

## Calgary's Extensive Urban Trail Network
### Walk, hike, cycle or Segway

Calgary is home to the most extensive urban pathway and bikeway network in North America. The city maintains about 1000km of regional pathways and 96km of trails. Whether it's walking, running, in-line skating, cycling or a guided Segway PT tour, there are plenty of great ways to explore Calgary actively.

For a pretty ride along the river, take a guided tour or rent an e-bike from Bow Cycle. Explore the **Bow River Pathway** to the **Peace Bridge**, one of the most eye-catching Instagrammable bridges in the city, designed by the renowned Spanish architect Santiago Calatrava.

If you'd like to do some bird-watching, **Griffith Woods Park** is a great place to go. There are paved and unpaved trails along the banks of the Elbow River and a series of wetlands inside the park.

**WHY YOU NEED TO DRINK A CAESAR COCKTAIL IN CALGARY**

The Caesar, or the Bloody Caesar as it is also known, is Canada's most popular cocktail and it was invented in Calgary. It has been estimated that Canadians drink 400 million Caesar cocktails annually and you'll find it on many menus.

The Caesar was created in 1969 by bartender Walter Chell for the grand opening of a new Italian restaurant in Calgary. The cocktail contains vodka, clam juice, tomato juice, hot sauce, Worcestershire sauce, a celery stalk and a lime wedge. There are many variations of this cocktail and some restaurants go over the top with so many garnishes it's a meal and a drink in one.

 **THREE GREAT MICROBREWERIES IN CALGARY**

**Village Brewery**
The new taproom at this longtime microbrewery offers 16 beers on tap and a full BBQ-inspired menu.

**Tool Shed Brewing Co**
This microbrewery has won a slew of awards for its beers and their BBQ. You'll find both on the menu.

**Cold Garden Beverage Company**
Twenty-five beers and craft bevies are on the menu here as well as a selection of snacks.

### EXPLORE CALGARY'S EAST VILLAGE

There was a time when nice people didn't venture into Calgary's East Village, but this revitalized area along the Bow River is now one of the hippest areas of the city. There are great hotels, restaurants and attractions.

Visit **Studio Bell - National Music Centre** (p172) to explore music in Canada. Check out the award-winning architecture of the Calgary Central Library. See public art and get in touch with nature on St Patrick's Island. Rent a bike at Bow Cycle E-Bikes and hit the trails. Enjoy great coffee at Phil and Sebastian or Sidewalk Citizen Bakery. Eat chocolate at Cochu Chocolatier and delicious Alberta beef at Charbar. There's a lot to see and do in the East Village.

MAGICVOVA/SHUTTERSTOCK ©

**Fish Creek Provincial Park**

**Fish Creek Provincial Park** is another great spot for hiking. One of the largest urban parks in Canada, the park has more than 100km of paved and unpaved trails that pass through a natural forested area. There's an artificial lake with a beach for swimming, a bike skills park, picnic shelters and a learning center.

There are many companies offering bike tours and rentals in Calgary. If you want to explore the amazing trail system in a unique way, consider booking a Segway PT tour with River Valley Adventure Co – Calgary in the East Village.

 **WHERE TO EAT IN CALGARY**

**Major Tom**
This stylish award-winning restaurant has sweeping city views, a global menu and great craft cocktails. Book well in advance. **$$$**

**Modern Steak**
This is one of its best steakhouses in a place that loves beef. Alberta beef, fish and one vegetarian option are on the menu. **$$$**

**Sidewalk Citizen Bakery**
Artisan sourdough bread, sandwiches, pastries and baked goods are served with great coffee here. **$**

# Edmonton

**THE CAPITAL CITY OF ALBERTA**

Alberta's vibrant capital city is incredibly green. Locals and visitors alike enjoy hiking, cycling and paddling through the beautiful River Valley, the longest stretch of connected urban parkland in Canada.

Edmonton is home to amazing attractions such as the Art Gallery of Alberta, the Royal Alberta Museum, Fort Edmonton Park and West Edmonton Mall, North America's largest shopping mall, spanning the equivalent of 48 city blocks and housing incredible entertainment, shopping and dining. Nearby attractions like the Ukrainian Cultural Heritage Village, Elk Island National Park and Métis Crossing are also worth exploring.

The city is a cultural hub, hosting more than 50 festivals year-round, including the oldest and largest fringe theater festival in North America. Sometimes considered a gateway city to Jasper National Park, which is a four-hour drive west of the city, Edmonton's many attractions, trendy shops and great culinary scene are worth stopping for.

☑ **TOP TIP**

The Old Strathcona and Whyte Avenue area of Edmonton is filled with historic buildings and a ton of unique boutiques, galleries, restaurants and shops. At first glance it may look old, but it's got a youthful bohemian spirit. There's no shortage of cool things to see and do in the historic district. It's a great place to shop and explore.

## North America's Largest Shopping & Entertainment Complex

### The massive West Edmonton Mall

North America's largest shopping mall spans the equivalent of 48 city blocks and is filled with world-class attractions, numerous entertainment venues, a hotel with unique theme rooms and more than 100 dining venues. Even if you don't like shopping, you could spend several days exploring West Edmonton Mall.

**Galaxyland Powered by Hasbro** is one of the key attractions here. North America's largest indoor theme park has more than 27 rides, play areas, concessions, games and fun for all ages.

The **World Waterpark** is another anchor attraction. At the center of the waterpark is the world's largest indoor

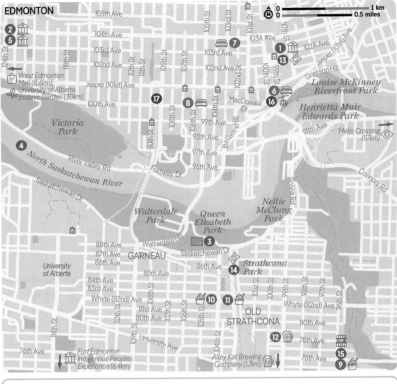

**SIGHTS**
1 Art Gallery of Alberta
2 Bearclaw Gallery
3 Indigenous Art Park
4 North Saskatchewan River
5 West End Gallery

**SLEEPING**
6 Fairmont Hotel Macdonald
7 JW Marriott Edmonton ICE District
8 Matrix Hotel

**EATING**
9 Kind

10 Made by Marcus
11 Yelo'd

**DRINKING & NIGHTLIFE**
12 Bent Stick Brewing
see 15 Blind Enthusiasm

**ENTERTAINMENT**
13 Francis Winspear

Centre for Music
14 Yardbird Suite

**SHOPPING**
15 Ritchie Market

**TRANSPORT**
16 100 Street Funicular
17 High Level Bridge Streetcar

wave pool. There's a concession, cabanas, a kiddie pool, kids play areas, a surfing area and many waterslides in three levels of difficulty.

The **Sea Life Caverns** are another major attraction featuring an underground aquarium with more than 100 species of fish, sharks, sea turtles, penguins, reptiles, amphibians and inverte-

## WHERE TO SCREAM FOR ICE CREAM IN EDMONTON

**Made by Marcus**
There are nine signature flavors, three seasonal ones and three vegan ice cream flavors at this popular shop. **$**

**Kind**
Elevates classic dairy and vegan ice cream by making it in small batches from the highest-quality ingredients. **$**

**Yelo'd**
You'll probably have to wait in line to try the Filipino- and Asian-inspired cold treats at this mom and pop shop. **$**

NICK FOX/SHUTTERSTOCK ©

**World Waterpark, West Edmonton Mall**

brates. There's a full-sized replica of Christopher Columbus' *Santa Maria* ship in the middle of a lake inside the mall.

Other mall attractions include paddle boats, race karts, bowling, mini-golf, a shooting range, movie theaters and an Ice Palace with an NHL-sized skating rink. You can purchase individual attraction passes or multi-attraction passes.

The **Fantasyland Hotel**, right inside the mall, has standard rooms and luxury theme rooms that let visitors live out the fantasy of sleeping inside an igloo, in a Victorian coach, in the back of a pickup truck or a variety of other themes.

## Explore the North Saskatchewan River Valley

### Long stretch of urban parkland

The **North Saskatchewan River** winds its way right through the city of Edmonton and the deep river valley provides the longest stretch of urban green space in North America. In 7400 hectares are 22 major parks and more than 150km of trails used for hiking and cycling in summer and cross-country skiing, fat biking and snowshoeing in winter.

There are many ways to access and explore the North Saskatchewan River Valley. From downtown Edmonton, you can take a free ride on the **100 Street Funicular** to

### UNIVERSITY OF ALBERTA BOTANIC GARDEN

Alberta's largest botanic garden is a 45-minute drive from downtown Edmonton.

It's a 97-hectare plant-lover's paradise. Alongside extensive natural areas, there's a Japanese garden, an Indigenous garden, an indoor tropical garden with colorful butterflies, and North America's largest Islamic garden.

The Aga Khan Islamic Garden was made possible through a $25 million donation from His Highness, the Aga Khan, the spiritual leader of the Shia Ismaili Muslims. Native plants were used in a contemporary interpretation of a traditional Islamic garden. It is meant to be an expression of culture and cooperation. It is the most northerly Islamic garden in the world.

 **WHERE TO STAY IN EDMONTON**

**Fairmont Hotel Macdonald**
Built in 1915, this grand dame luxury hotel has beautiful views of the river valley. $$$

**JW Marriott Edmonton ICE District**
One of the newest luxury hotels in downtown Edmonton is modern and high-tech. $$$

**Matrix Hotel**
This luxury hotel has lovely rooms and one of the best complimentary breakfasts you will ever have. $$$

## EXPLORE RITCHIE MARKET

This multiuse market space is filled with positive energy and some great local businesses.

### ACME Meats
This family-owned butcher shop has been in business since 1921. It's the place to go if you're planning to BBQ.

### Transcend Coffee and Roastery
The beloved specialty coffee roaster has been in business since 2006, sourcing and roasting sustainable, high-quality coffee.

### Blind Enthusiasm Brewery & Biera Restaurant
Neighborhood brewery and restaurant coexisting together. Chef Christine Sandford's focus is on pairing delicious European bistro fare with great beer.

### Little Duchess Bake Shop
Enjoy macarons, delicious cakes, cookies and pies at this French bakery, a second location for the beloved Duchess Bakery.

SAL AUGRUSO/SHUTTERSTOCK ©

**High Level Bridge Streetcar**

a promenade and lookout point. The **High Level Bridge Streetcar**, a restored trolley car that dates back to the early 1900s, is another great way to see the river valley. It's the highest streetcar river crossing in the world.

If you want to see more of the river valley, River Valley Adventure Co can help. This company offers guided Segway PT tours, bike rentals, running tours and walking tours. In winter, they also offer snowshoe rentals and tours and fat bike rentals and tours. You can also rent a wide variety of sports equipment including footballs, soccer balls, croquet and bocce sets.

Paddling a canoe is another fantastic way to see more of the beautiful river valley. Edmonton Canoe offers canoe and kayak rentals as well as shuttle service to drop you off or pick you up. Lifejackets are supplied and the river's current makes paddling easy. No previous paddling experience is necessary.

## THREE GREAT EDMONTON BREWERIES

**Alley Kat Brewing Company**
Founded in 1995, there are 14 house beers on tap at this brewery known for double IPAs and smooth brews.

**Blind Enthusiasm**
The tap room, the Monolith, runs one of largest barrel-fermented beer programs in Canada.

**Bent Stick Brewing**
This nanobrewery produces high quality unfiltered ales and serves them up with prepackaged snacks.

# Arts & Culture in Edmonton

### Festivals, art galleries and local theater

Canada's 'Festival City' has more than 50 annual festivals – most of which celebrate arts and culture. There are also a slew of art galleries and live performance venues where you can enjoy the arts and culture of Alberta's capital city.

There are many festivals celebrating arts and culture. Get your fringe on in August at the **Edmonton International Fringe Theatre Festival**, the oldest and largest fringe theater festival in North America. The three-day **Edmonton Heritage Festival**, also in August, is the world's largest outdoor celebration of multiculturalism. The **Edmonton International Jazz Festival** and the **Edmonton Folk Music Festival** are two top music festivals. Check to see what's happening when you plan to be in the city.

There are many art galleries in Edmonton. The **Art Gallery of Alberta**, an architectural marvel in the heart of downtown, is one of Canada's largest galleries. A wide range of art has been exhibited here, from classical art by renowned artists to abstract installations. The gallery also sells art from local up-and-coming artists. **West End Gallery** showcases the works of internationally recognized, contemporary Canadian artists. **Bearclaw Gallery** highlights the works of Canadian Indigenous artists including paintings, sculptures, carvings, clay, jewelry and crafts.

When it comes to live entertainment you have plenty of options – a concert at the **Francis Winspear Centre for Music**, a jazz performance at the legendary **Yardbird Suite**, contemporary ballet and dance or live theater from one of 25 local theater companies.

## DISCOVER THE INDIGENOUS SIDE OF EDMONTON

**Amiskwacîwâskahikan** is an Indigenous name for Edmonton, the city with the second-largest Indigenous population in Canada.

**Fort Edmonton Indigenous Peoples Experience**
Indigenous leaders informed the content of this new walkthrough experience at Fort Edmonton Park.

**Talking Rock Tours**
Let a Métis guide take you through the river valley to share Indigenous history and culture.

**Indigenous Art Park**
This unique outdoor park features six artworks by Canadian Indigenous artists.

**Métis Crossing**
About a 90-minute drive northeast of Edmonton, this site is a great place to explore Métis culture. There is a cultural gathering center, a guest lodge, a campground, a restaurant and a wildlife park where you can see traditional animals including white bison, an animal sacred to Indigenous Peoples. Activities include voyageur canoe excursions, traditional art workshops, snowshoeing and stargazing.

# Yukon Territory

## CARVED OUT OF GOLD

Hate traffic jams? Done with crowds? Craving clean air and a week without wi-fi? You've come to the right place.

Bigger than Sweden and slightly smaller than Spain, but with a population that would barely fill a medium-sized sports stadium, the Yukon doesn't lack breathing space. Popularly considered to be the most accessible and visit-worthy of Canada's three immense territories, its dramatic headline act is Dawson City, a once bawdy boomtown in the mid-north that garnered fame and notoriety during the 1897–99 Klondike gold rush, often billed as the 19th-century's last great adventure.

The Klondike story permeates many of the territory's other sights, from the vintage Yukon and White Pass railway to the Yukon River's antique paddle-steamers. There's even a road named after it. The Klondike Highway, a 708km-long ribbon of asphalt that intersects with the territory's two other great arteries: the Alaska and the Dempster. Gear up, you're in road-trip heaven.

Providing way more than just a support act are the Yukon's three vast national parks. Kluane, in the southwest, sits flush up against Wrangell-St Elias in Alaska (the world's second largest national park) and is home to the imposing hump of Mt Logan, Canada's highest mountain. The conjoined Arctic parks of Ivvavik and Vuntut contain the remote calving grounds of the porcupine caribou who migrate en masse to and from Alaska in herds 200,000 strong. It's an epic combination.

JESSE HASUP/SHUTTERSTOCK ©

## THE MAIN AREAS

**WHITEHORSE**
Vestibule to the
Wilderness. **p186**

**DAWSON CITY**
Terminus of countless
historic adventures. **p196**

Above: caribou; left: glacier, Kluane National Park     **181**

# Find Your Way

Remote Yukon has a pretty scant public transportation network. Cars and planes are the main means of getting around. Summer buses run between Dawson City and Whitehorse and a tourist train connects to Skagway in Alaska.

## AIRPLANE

Flying provides a quicker way of getting between Whitehorse and Dawson City and is the only way to reach Old Crow in the north. Air North (flyairnorth.com), the Yukon's main airline, is part Indigenous-owned and regularly touted as one of the best airlines in North America.

## CAR

Probably the easiest way to get around, especially if you bring your own vehicle. Rental cars are expensive and only available in Whitehorse and Dawson City. The Alaska Hwy and Klondike Hwy are paved and have services and EV chargers every 100km to 200km.

## BUS

Services are limited unless you're willing to fork out for an organized tour. In the summer, Husky bus (klondikeexperience.com) runs shuttles every other day between Whitehorse and Dawson City.

Beaufort Sea

Eskimo Lakes

Sitidgi Lake

Inuvik

Fort McPherson

Peel River

Mackenzie River

Richardson Mountains

NORTHWEST TERRITORIES

Eagle Plains

Ivvavik National Park

Vuntut National Park

Old Crow

Ogilvie M

ALASKA

## Dawson City, p196

Perched on the cusp of a brawny wilderness, Dawson is a town-sized historical site that stands as testament to the remarkable events of the Klondike gold rush.

100 miles
200 km

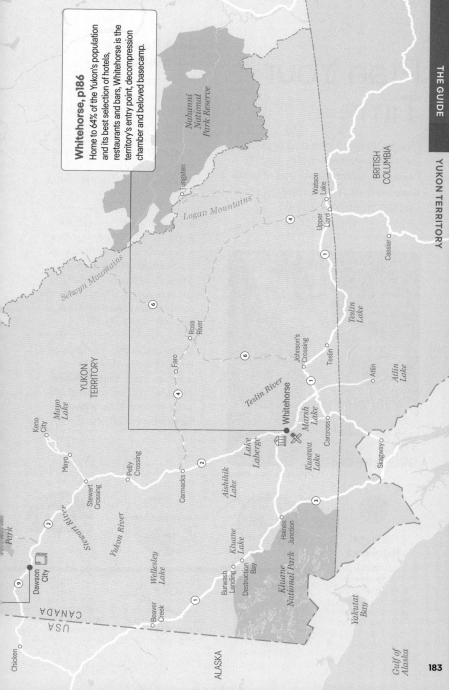

**Whitehorse, p186**
Home to 64% of the Yukon's population and its best selection of hotels, restaurants and bars, Whitehorse is the territory's entry point, decompression chamber and beloved basecamp.

BRITISH COLUMBIA

YUKON TERRITORY

ALASKA

CANADA

USA

Nahanni National Park Reserve

Logan Mountains

Selwyn Mountains

Tungsten

Watson Lake

Cassiar

Teslin Lake

Upper Liard

Atlin

Atlin Lake

Teslin

Johnson's Crossing

Ross River

Faro

Teslin River

Whitehorse

Marsh Lake

Carcross

Skagway

Kusawa Lake

Lake Laberge

Aishihik Lake

Carmacks

Pelly Crossing

Stewart Crossing

Mayo

Keno City

Mayo Lake

Yukon River

Stewart River

Kluane Lake

Haines Junction

Burwash Landing

Destruction Bay

Kluane National Park

Wellesley Lake

Beaver Creek

Dawson City

Chicken

Yakutat Bay

Gulf of Alaska

Park

# Plan Your Time

Due to its immense size and the long journey involved in getting here, the Yukon deserves at least a week. If you're heading off grid, you'll probably need two.

Miles Canyon, Yukon

## Just Passing Through

● Celebrate your arrival in Whitehorse with an orientation walk along the waterfront, investigating recent history in the **McBride Museum** (p186) and much deeper Indigenous roots in the **Kwanlin Dün Cultural Centre** (p186).

● On day two, grab breakfast at **Burnt Toast** (p187) before renting a bike and traveling further along the river to the **Miles Canyon Suspension Bridge** (p188). If you still have energy, attempt the tough ascent of **Grey Mountain** (p188) or stupendous city views.

● Devote day three to venturing outside town to admire the ungulates in the **Yukon Wildlife Preserve** (p191) before decamping to the exquisite **Eclipse Nordic Hot Springs** (p192) next door.

## Seasonal Highlights

Around 95% of visitors come in the summer. In the winter, the Yukon is cold, dark and (apart from the Yukon Quest or Eclipse Nordic's frozen hair competition) bereft of a lot to do.

**FEBRUARY**
This legendary Yukon Quest dogsled race travels 1600km from Whitehorse to Fairbanks, braving winter darkness and -50°C temperatures.

**APRIL**
Months of winter solitude end when the river ice breaks up and the days slowly lengthen.

**JUNE**
Yukon River Quest, the world's premier canoe and kayak race, covers the classic 742km run of the river from Whitehorse to Dawson City.

MARK-WU/SHUTTERSTOCK ©

SCALIA MEDIA/SHUTTERSTOCK ©, SCALIA MEDIA/SHUTTERSTOCK ©, A. MICHAEL BROWN/SHUTTERSTOCK ©

## Five-Day Bonanza

● Spend your first two days enjoying Whitehorse's salubrious riverside with a side-visit to the **SS _Klondike_** (p186), a national historical site.

● On day three, rent a car or take a bus along the North Klondike Highway to Dawson City, stopping off at **Braeburn Lodge** (p194) for cinnamon buns and **Five Finger Rapids** (p194) for river views.

● Spend your first day in Dawson hiking to the **Midnight Dome** (p198) and perusing the town's many historical heirlooms, including the fascinating **Jack London Museum** (p198).

● On your final day, find out where it all started at the **Bonanza Creek Discovery Claim** (p201) and seal the evening at **Diamond Tooth Gertie's Gambling Hall** (p199).

## Two-Week Tour

● After exploring Whitehorse, head out to **Kluane National Park** (p195) or a couple of days overnighting in Haines Junction.

● Reserve another day for the magnificent **train journey** to Skagway (p189), saving time for shopping and sightseeing in tiny **Carcross** (p189) fterwards.

● Decamp to **Dawson City** (p186) on day five and spend a couple of days digesting the gold rush paraphernalia.

● On day eight, load up your car with provisions and hit the **Dempster Highway** (p204). Stop in **Tombstone Territorial Park** (p202) or some leg-stretching hikes before pitching north via Eagle Plains to Inuvik. After a day admiring the chilly Arctic tundra, retrace your steps.

**JULY**

Days are warm with long hours of daylight. Hit the trails, rivers and lakes and make the most of it.

**AUGUST**

Dawson's Discovery Days celebrates the gold bonanza of 1896, with parades, picnics and art shows.

**SEPTEMBER**

You can feel the north winds coming in September when the trees erupt in color for a fleeting taste of autumn.

**DECEMBER**

For diehards only. Temperatures plummet, nights extend into daytime, rivers freeze over and many tourist businesses close.

# Whitehorse

**VESTIBULE TO THE WILDERNESS**

**GETTING AROUND**

Whitehorse's transit buses run through the center of the city. There are seven routes: route 3 serves the airport, route 5 passes the Robert Service Campground.

The downtown area is highly walkable, with various paths paralleling the riverbank.

☑ **TOP TIP**

Whitehorse is a good base for daytrips. You can get as far as Kluane National Park, Teslin, Carcross and Skagway and still be back in time for dinner. If you don't have access to a car, numerous agencies run excellent tours.

Long before it was a city, 'White Horse' was famed as the site of the most fearsome set of rapids on the Yukon River, a formidable obstacle that struck fear into the heart of many a tenderfoot gold rush stampeder. Today, the rapids have been drowned beneath a lake and Whitehorse has grown to become the Yukon's territorial capital.

The city rose to prominence during World War II and only became capital in 1953 when Dawson City's star seriously began to wane. In many ways, it was a natural choice: it's the crossroads of the territory's two great highways, the Alaska and the Klondike, and the one-time terminus of its only public railway, the White Pass and Yukon Route.

Whatever your daring wilderness ambitions – from a bus trip to Kluane National Park, to canoeing solo down the Yukon River – it can probably be organized here. Whitehorse is the lynchpin for most adventures in the territory.

## History & Heritage

### Museums and cultural centers

The Kwanlin Dün First Nations used the area around Miles Canyon and Whitehorse rapids (now Schwatka Lake) as a seasonal fishing camp and trading post long before the arrival of Europeans. Their **cultural center** on the north side of downtown explains the details of their story. Nearby, both Indigenous and 20th-century history is on show at the encyclopedic **McBride Museum**, which has a special section dedicated to the gold rush. The building has cleverly incorporated an old log telegraph office dating from 1900 into its modern exterior.

Whitehorse's historical pièce de résistance is the **SS *Klondike***, a paddle-steamer built in 1937 to carry freight along the Yukon River. Decommissioned in 1955 after the Klondike Highway was opened, the steamer has been rehabilitat-

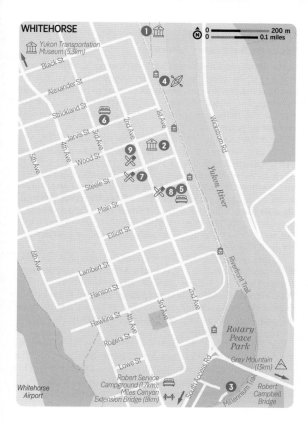

**WHITEHORSE**

Yukon Transportation Museum (5.3km)

Black St
Alexander St
Strickland St
Jarvis St
4th Ave
3rd Ave
Wood St
2nd Ave
1st Ave
Steele St
Main St
Elliott St
5th Ave
6th Ave
Lambert St
Hanson St
Hawkins St
4th Ave
Rogers St
3rd Ave
Lowe St
2nd Ave

Wickstrom Rd
Yukon River
Riverfront Trail

Rotary Peace Park

Whitehorse Airport

Robert Service Campground (1.7km);
Miles Canyon
Extension Bridge (8km)

South Access Rd

Grey Mountain (13km)

Robert Campbell Bridge

Millennium Trail

0    200 m
0    0.1 miles

**SIGHTS**
1 Kwanlin Dün Cultural Centre
2 MacBride Museum
3 SS Klondike

**ACTIVITIES**
4 Kanoe People

**SLEEPING**
5 Edgewater Hotel
6 Elite Hotel

**EATING**
7 Burnt Toast
9 Dirty Northern
9 Tony's

**BEST PLACES TO STAY**

**Robert Service Campground**
It's a pretty 15-minute walk from town on the Millennium Trail to the 70 sites at this tents-only campground on the river. Facilities include wi-fi, water, showers and a store. $

**Elite Hotel**
Elite Hotel probably doesn't fit in many people's 'elite' category, but it is a good, cheaper option with clean, spacious rooms in a convenient location. $$

**Edgewater Hotel**
Whitehorse's poshest option is slap-bang downtown and its bright modern rooms come with numerous bonuses, including bathrobes, Nespresso machines and a pleasant on-site restaurant. $$$

ed and made into a national historic site. The boat, with its giant stern wheel, has its own visitor center and offers daily guided tours. It sits handsomely in dry dock next to the Lewes Blvd Bridge.

Also on the waterfront is the wooden **White Pass and Yukon Railroad Depot**, the city's erstwhile train station built after an earlier model burnt down in 1905. No trains call here now, but it still functions as a ticket office and pick-up point for buses transferring to Carcross.

Much of the Yukon's recent history is related to transportation. Bush planes, the White Pass and Yukon Railroad, and the Yukon Quest dogsled race are three of the many themes explored at the **Yukon Transportation Museum** next to the airport. Outside stands a DC3 aircraft that doubles as one of the world's largest weather vanes.

## GREY MOUNTAIN BIKE & HIKE

Looking temptingly climbable from downtown Whitehorse, 1495m-tall Grey Mountain, with its humped profile and rounded rocky ridgeline, is best accessed via the 12km Grey Mountain Road, which quickly disintegrates from asphalt to gravel to bumpy stone-fest as you climb past the town cemetery. The last 5km are steep and exhausting (if you're cycling) or a jolting ride in a 4x4 (if you're driving) to a lofty trailhead beneath two communication towers only 2.5km short of the summit. From here, a well-trodden path undulates through open subalpine terrain with lake and river views falling away on either side. The summit ridge is punctuated with three smooth rocky peaks offering satellite-like views of Whitehorse.

# On the Waterfront

### Beside the fast-flowing Yukon River

In the days before a coherent settlement existed, 'White Horse' was the name given to a set of ferocious rapids on the Yukon River that gold rush prospectors had to portage around or attempt to 'shoot' in hastily built rafts. Dams pacified the river in the 1920s and the former portage site has been submerged by Schwatka Lake.

These days a sense of calm pervades over most of the riverside and you can stroll its wooded banks on the paved **Millennium Trail**, a short 5km loop that traces a rough circle between downtown's Lewes Blvd bridge and the Rotary Centennial bridge (just before the dam). For a longer 15km loop, carry on south to the **Miles Canyon Suspension Bridge**, where the Yukon River is pushed through a narrow gorge. The canyon hike involves some road walking on the river's west bank complemented by prettier forest trails on the east side.

Further north, the Yukon flows directly through downtown with most of the metro action centred on the west bank where a paved trail hugs the waterside. Here, you'll find many of Whitehorse's premier sights sandwiched between Rotary Peace Park at the southern end and Shipyards Park with its growing collection of historic structures in the north. Watch out for aggressive seagulls!

North of the dam, the Yukon is navigable as far as the Bering Sea, and Whitehorse is a popular embarkation point for canoers heading solo or en masse to Dawson City. For trip logistics, rentals and intriguing day paddles, head to the riverside office of **Kanoe People** (kanoepeople.com).

### PADDLE-STEAMER ON THE YUKON

For more on the fascinating history of Yukon River paddle-steamers that lasted from 1900 to around 1955, proceed to **Dawson City** (p196) where you can admire the SS *Keno* and even visit a 'paddlewheel graveyard.'

 **WHERE TO EAT IN WHITEHORSE**

**Burnt Toast**
Join the queue for brunch or come back for an early dinner in this casual sit-down cafe with an eclectic menu. $

**Dirty Northern**
Whitehorse's favorite pub-restaurant is feted for its draught beers, affordable pizzas and friendly 60° North ambience. $$

**Tony's**
The best of the city's Italian joints resides in the Sternwheeler hotel and leans heavily toward seafood. $$

# Beyond Whitehorse

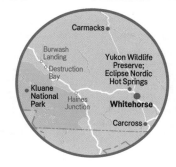

Less than 100km from the BC border, Whitehorse abuts the Yukon's Southern Lakes region, the traditional territory of the Tagish and Teslin Tlingit First Nations.

Beyond Whitehorse, civilization quickly fizzles out as the Yukon starts to reveal its true face: long, lonely highways; huge tracts of mostly uncultivated land; and not a lot of people (only around 36% of the territory's 44,000 population lives outside the capital). To the west, the Alaska Hwy cuts through low-rise taiga to Kluane, a world-class national park where sky-scraping mountains guard equally humongous glaciers. To the south lies the pretty southern lakes region anchored by the railway town of Carcross and the Indigenous community of Teslin. Head north and you'll hit the Klondike Hwy, the territory's metaphoric spinal cord, littered with the broken dreams of the gold rush.

## Carcross

TIME FROM WHITEHORSE 50 MINS

### Riding the Yukon & White Pass Railway

Dramatic landscapes conspire with gritty history to add luster to this vintage train ride between Carcross and Skagway in Alaska, with a brief international border crossing in British Columbia en route. Your host? A super well-maintained diesel locomotive coupled to a set of elegant parlor carriages, some dating from the 1880s.

Completed in 1900, just as the Klondike gold rush was losing its glitter, the **White Pass and Yukon Route** (wpyr.com) arrived too late for most stampeders, but just in time for a new breed of intrepid traveler keen to navigate the vast under-explored lands of the Yukon in more comfort.

Transporting the territory's earliest tourists between Skagway and Whitehorse, the train climbed through a spectacular steep-sided valley on a 4% grade to 873m White Pass. Heading in the other direction, freight in the form of copper and lead from rugged Yukon mines was exported to the sea.

The railroad closed for economic reasons in 1982 but was rehabilitated six years later when profit-eyeing authorities reopened it as a heritage railway aimed at Alaska's growing cohort of cruise passengers.

### Places

### GETTING AROUND

Carcross is at the junction of the Klondike Hwy and Hwy 8 (a shortcut to the Alaska Hwy) going east. The White Pass and Yukon Route train (wpyr.com) makes it up this far from Skagway, Alaska, in summer; it also operates buses that link to Whitehorse.

Husky Bus (klondikeexperience. com) serves the Klondike Hwy between Dawson City and Whitehorse in the summer only.

The Alaska Hwy and the Haines Hwy follow the edges of Kluane National Park and both are excellent roads. There is very little road access into the interior.

## ☑ TOP TIP

Load up on supplies, including food and drink. Beyond Whitehorse, roads are long and potential refueling stops few and far between.

## BEST STOPS ON THE ALASKA HIGHWAY

**Watson Lake**
The first town in the Yukon on the Alaska Hwy is a good rest stop, with a superb visitor center, which has a small museum about the highway.

**Teslin**
On the long, narrow lake 260km west of Watson Lake, Teslin is home to the Tlingits who maintain a superb heritage center with totems and a canoe exhibit.

**Burwash Landing**
Located 17km northwest of Destruction Bay in a spectacular setting next to Kluane National Park, this is an excellent place to stretch your legs and visit the local Kluane Museum.

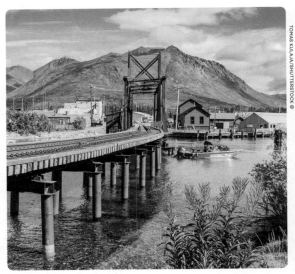

Carcross, Yukon

Today, the rail section operates between Carcross and Skagway, with buses connecting to Whitehorse.

Throughout the four-hour journey, you'll be treated to slightly anodyne commentaries about the ever-changing scenery, from subarctic alpine tundra to coastal forest. For a more visceral impression, stand on the carriage's outdoor viewing platform and try to picture thousands of erstwhile gold prospectors toiling through mud and rain to the summit.

Various packages can be organized as day excursions with a coach return. Train riders will need a valid passport to enter the US.

### Trains, bikes & Indigenous culture at Carcross

Known formerly as Caribou Crossing, Carcross is a railway hub turned touristic village that sits at the north end of Bennett Lake, a few kilometers from the BC border. It's anchored by the **Carcross Commons**, an artistic celebration of Indigenous culture replete with totem poles, a wood-carving house and the historic **Caribou Hotel**, once home to a notorious opera-singing parrot with a penchant for whiskey.

 ## WHERE TO CAMP BY A LAKE BEYOND WHITEHORSE

**Lake Laberge**
Located 50km north of Whitehorse, with outhouses and a boat launch. A great spot to view the northern lights. **$**

**Kathleen Lake**
Attractive and accessible campground in Kluane, with trailheads, outhouses and firepits abutting the water. **$**

**Conrad Campground**
On Tagish Lake, 16km south of Carcross, this 35-site campground has a playground and its own hiking loop. **$**

TOMAS KULAJA/SHUTTERSTOCK ©

The local Carcross-Tagish First Nation played a key role in developing a nearby bike trail network on **Montana Mountain**. The peak has long had a special spiritual significance for the Tagish, but was surveyed and exploited for silver mining by an American financier from Montana named John Conrad in the early 1900s. In 2006, when the Tagish took back the mountain in a land claims settlement, young members of the Nation reactivated many of the abandoned mining paths as biking trails. There are now over 40km worth of trails, from short steep connectors to the exhilarating 24km-long 'Mountain Hero.' Rentals are available at **Icycle Sports** (icyclesports.com/service/icycle-sports-carcross) and you can fuel up on java afterwards at Caribou Crossing Coffee.

Carcross has strong gold rush connections. Skookum Jim, aka Keish, was born nearby and lived for a time in the village. You can see his carefully crafted post-gold rush house, a replica of an 1899 original, in the Carcross Commons complex, richly decorated with motifs of the wolf clan. Skookum used some of his Klondike fortune to build another house for his sister Kate in Carcross after she was deserted by her husband, George Carmack. Fellow Tagish prospector Dawson Charlie once owned the Caribou Hotel.

Train passengers utilizing the White Pass and Yukon Railway usually stop off in Carcross with time to peruse a few of the shops, along with the modern **Visitor Information Centre**.

With its exceptionally low rainfall, the village is known for harboring the world's smallest **desert**, a curious collection of sand dunes that look more like scattered golf bunkers.

# Yukon
# Wildlife Preserve     TIME FROM WHITEHORSE 30 MINS 🚗

### Uncovering the Yukon's Ungulates

If you've struggled to spot fauna while in the Yukon, or didn't have the time or equipment to abscond to the wilds, help is at hand. The **Yukon Wildlife Preserve** (yukonwildlife.ca), 29km northwest of Whitehorse, is a large, sprawling wildlife park spread over 140 hectares that's replete with a wide selection of the territory's largest non-predatory fauna (spoiler: you won't find any bears or cougars).

Ungulates (hooved animals) is the buzzword here and among the native species on show are wood bison, moose, mountain goats, thinhorn sheep, musk oxen and elk. Several non-hooved animals also feature, including arctic foxes and the highly elusive lynx.

**TAGISH FIRST NATION**

The Tagish are a self-governing First Nation based mainly around Carcross in the Southern Lakes region of the Yukon. They maintain a learning center in the Carcross Commons where you can admire a selection of their totem poles representing the Nation's six clans, along with other art pieces emblazoned on the local buildings. With deep ancestral roots in the region, the Tagish are central to the Yukon story on many levels. Three of the four prospectors responsible for the original gold discovery at Bonanza Creek in the Klondike in 1896 were Tagish: Keish (usually known as Skookum Jim), his nephew Káa Goox (Dawson Charlie), and his oft-forgotten sister, Shaaw Tláa (Kate Carmack).

 **WHERE TO EAT BEYOND WHITEHORSE**

**Caribou Crossing Coffee**
Urban-quality coffee backed up by Parisian-standard pastries and Indigenous aesthetics in tiny Carcross. $

**Village Bakery & Deli**
This log cabin–style cafe in Haines Junction offers glazed scones and enough 'joe' to fuel you through a Kluane hike. $

**Coal Mine Campground**
A walk-up window beside the Klondike Hwy in Carmacks that dispenses no-nonsense nosh: burgers, pizza and hot dogs. $

With hectares of space to call upon, this is no zoo. The enclosures are huge and closely mimic the animals' natural surroundings (swamps for the moose, cliffs for the goats, woodland for the caribou). It takes a couple of hours to walk around the two interconnecting loops on 5km of dirt roads. Alternatively, you can drive. Each enclosure has a viewing platform with reams of info about the majestic critters within.

**EPIC HUMAN-POWERED JOURNEYS**

**Chilkoot Trail Hike**
Popular 53km trail between Dyea, Alaska and Lake Bennett, BC, that crests Chilkoot Pass and follows in the footsteps of the 1897–98 stampeders. Usually done over three to four days with camping.

**Yukon River Canoe**
Shadows the 742km route of the Klondike stampeders between Whitehorse and Dawson City along the Yukon River. Can be done solo or as part of an organized trip.

**Canol Heritage Trail Hike or Bike**
Remote 350km jaunt across the Northwest Territories and eastern Yukon following the route of an old oil pipeline. Requires advance planning and food drops.

## Eclipse Nordic Hot Springs

TIME FROM WHITEHORSE 30 MINS 🚗

### The Deluxe Hot Springs Treatment

Formerly known as Takini Hot Springs, this plush spa complex, 30km northwest of Whitehorse, underwent a radical overhaul in the early 2020s when it was rebuilt and rebranded as **Eclipse Nordic Hot Springs** (eclipsenordichotsprings. ca). Numerous outdoor pools are now supplemented by a raft of indoor facilities, including steam rooms, saunas, meditation rooms and a cafe.

Gushing from the earth at a temperature of 46.5ºC before being cooled to around 40ºC in the complex's sumptuous pools, the spring site has been utilized for centuries. Prior to its commercialization in the early 1900s, it was called Jim Boss's bathtub after a local First Nations chief. In the 1940s it provided solace for construction workers building the Alaska Highway.

In the winter, the springs stage an eccentric hair-freezing competition.

## Carmacks

TIME FROM WHITEHORSE 2HR 🚗

### Road-trip staging post

With a population of 580-ish, **Carmacks** is the biggest settlement on the North Klondike Hwy between Whitehorse and Dawson. This is where the road crosses the Yukon River on a three-span truss bridge and intersects with the Robert Campbell Highway, a partly paved thoroughfare that branches east to **Faro**, a former lead- and zinc-mining town named after a gamblers' card game. Faro's population plummeted in the mid-1990s when the mines closed. Today it tries to pull in crowd-averse tourists with an esoteric sheep- and crane-viewing festival and an off-the-beaten-track nine-hole golf course.

Some people use Carmacks as the finish point for a multi-day paddle down the Yukon from Whitehorse. Others carry

 **WHERE TO SNAP A PHOTO ON THE WHITE PASS & YUKON RAILWAY**

**White Pass**
Pulling out of Fraser station, look for the border flagpoles as you rattle across the rocky wilderness of this alpine pass.

**Bennett station**
Cute station-turned-museum next to an abandoned gold rush town, where boats set off to sail down the Yukon.

**Denver Caboose**
An old railway caboose 8km northeast of Skagway marks the the trailhead to the Denver glacier.

JEF WOONIACK/SHUTTERSTOCK ©

**Klondike Highway, Yukon**

## POET'S LAKE

Lake Laberge, a half-hour drive north of Whitehorse on the Klondike Highway, is the name given to a 50km-long widening in the Yukon River. Slender and relatively deep, the rippling lake is notorious for its cold water and inclement weather, both of which provide a formidable barrier for canoers heading downstream as they struggle with the strong winds and almost complete lack of current. Many row, sporadically, for the shoreline to rest, recuperate and camp overnight (the stargazing is trippy). The lake has entered Yukon folklore thanks to the British-Canadian poet, Robert Service, who referenced it in his famous 1907 poem, 'The Cremation of Sam McGee.' To fit in with his intricate rhyming scheme, Service altered the lake's spelling from Laberge to Lebarge.

on to Dawson City. Disembarking in Carmacks means you avoid the choppy waters of Five Finger Rapids. A locally produced walking tour directs visitors around a small ensemble of historic buildings, most of them log cabins, some related to mining. There's also a local grocery store, campground and walk-up restaurant.

## Klondike Highway Road-Trip

STARTS FROM WHITEHORSE 🚗

**Hit the north**

The Yukon's most quintessential road is a 708km driving extravaganza split into two distinct sections, both haunted by the ghosts of the 1898 Klondike gold rush.

The 176km South Klondike runs between Skagway and Whitehorse and is speckled with the road's most spectacular scenery as it crests the Boundary Range roughly paralleling the course of the White Pass and Yukon Railroad.

North of Whitehorse, the road follows the route of an old wagon trail to Dawson City, first laid down in 1902 with a

## WHERE TO STAY BEYOND WHITEHORSE

**Air Force Lodge**
This welcome apparition in Watson Lake has spotless rooms with shared bathrooms in an historic 1942 barracks. **$$**

**Parkside Inn**
Five self-catering units in the middle of Haines Junction, with kitchens and mountain views. Open year-round. **$$**

**Yukon Motel**
The lakeside Yukon Motel in Teslin offers simple motel rooms, an RV park with 70 sites and a licensed restaurant. **$**

## THE ALASKA HIGHWAY

War has long acted as a catalyst, speeding up technology and making seemingly impossible tasks appear possible. In 1942, during World War II, 27,000 soldiers and civilians, stoked by fears of a Japanese invasion, managed to build the 1600km Alaska highway in a miraculous eight months.

Running between Dawson Creek in BC and Delta Junction in Alaska, the Yukon segment of the road bisects the southern lakes region and Whitehorse before tracing the eastern boundary of Klaune National Park. Initially 'the Alaska' served as a military road designed to supply US bases in the territory vulnerable to Japanese attack. It was opened to the public in 1948 and remains the main route for people driving from the contiguous US or Canada up to Alaska.

Kluane National Park, Whitehorse, Yukon

roadhouse built every 20 miles. Paved these days but still dotted with occasional potholes, it's embellished by majestic river bridges, slender montane forest and ribbons of pink flowers that line the verges in summer.

Fancy services aren't abundant. The best places to quench your thirst with sugar-laced energy drinks and gas station coffee are the blink-and-you'll-miss-them communities of Carmacks, Pelly Crossing and Stewart Crossing that guard the Yukon, Pelly and Stewart rivers, respectively.

For an even bigger sugar spike, pull over at the **Braeburn Lodge**, 103km north of Whitehorse, where an old wooden roadhouse, long feted for its quirky backcountry ambience, serves soccer-ball-sized cinnamon buns that can sustain a small family for a week. The adjacent airport is facetiously called Cinnamon Bun Airstrip.

Another essential stop is **Five Finger Rapids**, 200km north of Whitehorse, where four river islands generate the roughest aquatic obstacle between Whitehorse and Dawson. A stairway leads off the road to a viewpoint.

For a detour, pitch northeast at Stewart Crossing to remote Keno City along the Silver Trail where a local **mining museum** illustrates what life was like during Klondike's less glittery sequel.

## WHERE TO SEE INDIGENOUS CULTURE BEYOND WHITEHORSE

**Da Ku Cultural Centre**
This Haines Junction facility has a variety of exhibits showcasing the culture of the Champagne and Aishihik people.

**Tagé Cho Hudän Interpretive Centre**
A center in Carmacks with volunteers who explain their Indigenous life past and present.

**George Johnston Museum**
This engrossing museum in Teslin details the life and culture of a 20th-century Tlingit leader.

# Kluane
# National Park

A giant among national parks

Vast, wild and mostly roadless, Kluane makes all other Canadian national parks look positively tame. Herein lie 17 of Canada's 20 highest mountains (including Logan, the highest), over 2000 glaciers and endless tracts of unadulterated backcountry. Seasoned mountaineers have been known to describe it as 'more Himalayan than the Himalayas' and they have a point: Kluane, along with its conjoined national park neighbors, Wrangell-St Elias and Glacier Bay (both in Alaska), comprise the largest protected area on Earth.

So, where do you start? Haines Junction is the best option, a typically diminutive Yukon outpost at the intersection of the Haines and Alaska Highways, unremarkable except for its super modern **Visitor Information Center** that's also home to a Parks Canada desk, an Indigenous cultural center and a fabulous mini-museum about the park.

While no main roads penetrate Kluane, the Haines and Alaska Highways track its eastern boundary for 150km and are dotted with various spots to pull over and enjoy some relative domesticity (campgrounds, fire pits and picnic areas).

The most popular stopping-off point is **Kathleen Lake**, 24km south of Haines Junction, dominated by the steep slopes of **King's Throne**, a rugged baptism-of-fire hike that climbs over loose rock to an ultra-windy cirque (bring poles and layers). This is also the trailhead for the **Cottonwood hike**, 85km of creek crossings, alpine passes and animal sightings that will still only offer you a small glimpse of Kluane's boundless wilderness.

If you're desperate to see more of Logan and Kluane's ice-encrusted interior, sign up for a flightseeing trip. **Alpine Aviation** (alpineaviationyukon.com) runs half-day tours out of Whitehorse.

### ANOTHER MOUNTAIN DRIVE

For another elemental drive through endless mountains speckled with lakes, glaciers and a selection of short touch-the-wilderness hikes, fuel up for a journey along the **Icefields Parkway** (p220) in Banff and Jasper.

## MT LOGAN

The highest peak in Canada and the second highest in North America, 5959m Mt Logan is an intimidating, high-altitude monster that sits atop the largest mountain massif in the world. Mt Blanc, Kilimanjaro and the Eiger could all squeeze inside its expansive girth. Hidden deep within the St Elias range in Kluane National Park, the remote peak is invisible from any road. To see it, you'll need to either charter a plane or be in possession of enough time and tenacity to climb it. Don't expect an easy 'hike.' Logan creates its own weather system and, in 1991, it registered the coldest ever temperature on Earth outside of Antarctica, a deathly -77.5°C. Among experienced mountaineers, higher Denali is generally considered a much easier climb.

---

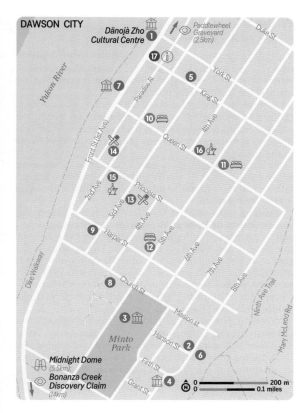

**HIGHLIGHTS**
1 Dänojà Zho Cultural Centre

**SIGHTS**
2 Berton House
3 Dawson City Museum
4 Jack London Museum
5 Palace Grand Theatre
6 Robert Service Cabin
7 SS Keno
8 St Andrew's Church
9 Strait's Auction House

**SLEEPING**
10 Downtown Hotel
11 Triple J Hotel
12 Westmark Inn

**EATING**
see 12 Belinda's Dining Room
13 Bonton & Co
14 Red Mammoth Bistro

**DRINKING & NIGHTLIFE**
15 Bombay Peggy's
16 Diamond Tooth Gertie's Gambling Hall

**INFORMATION**
17 Dawson City Visitor Information Centre

Some, such as the **Palace Grand Theatre** are faithful replicas of the originals. Helping you piece together the story, the whole town is chock-a-block with pictorial signboards documenting the historical significance of the various tenements and the charismatic characters who once frequented them.

Historically speaking, the 'rug' that ties the room together is the town **museum** housed in the landmark 1901 Old Territorial Administration building. Inside, fascinating gold rush paraphernalia (including old gold pans) is complemented by numerous Indigenous artifacts.

Part of the beauty of Dawson is its gritty realism. Not everything has been ruthlessly restored. Check out the gloriously ruined **Strait's Auction House**, the hopelessly lopsided **St Andrew's church** (1901) and the spectacularly wrecked **Paddlewheel Graveyard** on the west bank of the Yukon River (take the free ferry and walk 10 minutes north).

# Writer's Row

### London, Service and Berton

Much of the enduring legacy of the Klondike gold rush is rooted in the work of three seminal writers who used their evocative prose to record, document and romanticize the remarkable spectacle for posterity.

The most famous, by far, was Jack London, who is memorialized in a small but poignant **museum** on Ninth Ave, which contains a reconstructed portion of his original cabin found at Henderson Creek by literary sleuth Dick North in the 1960s.

The museum offers superb daily interpretive talks narrated by passionate staff who'll enlighten you about the details of London's Klondike adventures and the subsequent search for his cabin.

Less than 100m away in the same street lies the equally modest **cabin of Robert W Service**, a British-born poet and writer whose rhythmic verse earned him the sobriquet, the 'Bard of the Yukon.' A decade too late to witness the gold rush first-hand, Service lived in Dawson from 1909 to 1912 using the town's seedy atmosphere to evoke expressive narrative poems such as 'The Shooting of Dan McGrew.'

Every day in summer, the cabin hosts dramatic readings, guided walks and tours.

Directly opposite Service's cabin is the childhood home of Pierre Berton, author of the seminal non-fiction tome, *Klondike: The Last Great Gold Rush*. Born in Whitehorse in 1920, Berton moved to Dawson as a young child. His time living in the town put him in touch with many of the eccentric gold rush characters and veterans that would later inspire his work.

The house is now a **writer's retreat** run by the Writer's Trust of Canada.

# Hiking Midnight Dome

### Dawson's sentinel lookout

The famous slide-scarred hill that overlooks Dawson and appears in numerous old gold rush photos is known as the **Midnight Dome**, an 880m-high viewpoint with both a road and trail to the summit. The main path starts at the top of King Street winding up past the town cemetery. Get a map from the info office first. For drivers, New Dome Rd

 **WHERE TO EAT IN DAWSON CITY**

**Belinda's**
The town's most reliable restaurant serves plentiful Canadian staples in the Westmark Hotel. **$$**

**Red Mammoth Bistro**
The best place in town for breakfast, lunch and coffee. Don't miss the exceptional stuffed pretzel buns. **$**

**Bonton & Co**
Proving the words 'arctic' and 'gourmet' aren't an oxymoron, Bonton molds local ingredients into spectacular dishes. **$$$**

Dawson City, Yukon

branches off the Klondike Hwy about 1km south of town, climbing in broad curves for about 7km.

Summer solstice has been celebrated at the top of the Dome by townspeople since 1899. The views of Dawson and the Yukon River are stupendous.

## Biking the Ridge Road

### Cycling bonanza

You can explore much of the Dawson area by bike, including the 33km **Ridge Road Heritage Trail**, which winds through the gold fields south of town along an old wagon trail built in 1899 to supply the mines. The lower trailhead is close to the junction of Bonanza Creek Rd and the Klondike Hwy, 3km southeast of town. There are two campgrounds en route and an old boxcar nestled amid the spruce, birch and alder trees. On completion, cyclists can return to the main trailhead via the Bonanza Creek Rd (total distance 63km).

### WHY I LOVE DAWSON CITY

**Brendan Sainsbury,** writer

It was a longstanding fixation with Jack London and the Klondike gold rush that first led me to Dawson City. I arrived on a long-light evening in June after a jolting bus ride along the Top of the World Hwy from Alaska. It was a golden intro.

Sallying forth from my comfortable room in the Triple J Hotel, Dawson seemed diminutive and handsome but, at the same time, hardnosed and authentic. It was easy to imagine London and his stampeding sidekicks boisterously roaming the streets.

Years later, I would follow the Klondike story to Skagway, Whitehorse and up the Chilkoot trail to Lake Bennett, but it was in Dawson that I first felt its magic.

 **WHERE TO GO FOR A NIGHT OUT IN DAWSON CITY**

**Bombay Peggy's**
Former brothel reincarnated as a super-friendly pub and inn with local beers, whiskeys and a large martini selection.

**Downtown Hotel**
Where tourists line up to drink a shot of booze that has a pickled human toe floating in it.

**Diamond Tooth Gertie's Gambling Hall**
This re-creation of an 1898 saloon has gambling, honky-tonk piano and the can-can.

## DREDGES

The Klondike's initial prospectors came armed with only the most rudimentary of tools (a gold pan and shovel were standard), but as big business and smarter technology took over in the early 1900s, dredges became the primary modus operandi.

Beginning in the 1910s, dredges lasted 50 years and introduced the concept of gold mining on an industrial scale to Dawson. Huge machines were fitted with revolving buckets and mechanical arms in order to shift up to 14,000m³ of material a day and leave the endless piles of gravel tailings still visible today. The era's legacy can be investigated at Dredge No 4, a floating sluice plant turned historical site near Bonanza Creek, 14km south of Dawson. Guided tours are available.

PECOLD/SHUTTERSTOCK ©

**Gold panning, Bonanza Creek, Yukon**

## Dänojà Zho Cultural Centre

### Pre-gold rush history

The area of Dawson City is the traditional territory of the Tr'ondek people. Inside this impressive riverfront wood building there are displays and interpretative talks by the Tr'ondëk Hwëch'in (River People) First Nations. The collection includes traditional artifacts such as canoes and fish-drying racks, as well as photos and historical information about the village of Moosehide where the displaced Indigenous people migrated after the gold rush began.

 **WHERE TO STAY IN DAWSON CITY**

**Westmark Inn**
Dawson's poshest hotel, ever-popular with cruise tourists, offers modern rooms with period touches, plus pub. **$$$**

**Triple J Hotel**
Authentic frontier-style hotel with a selection of hotel rooms, annexes and separate cabins, some with kitchenettes. **$$**

**Downtown Hotel**
Wild West frontage and modern bedrooms make an excellent combo at the birthplace of Dawson's 'sourtoe'. **$$$**

# Bonanza Creek Discovery Claim

### Klondike's ground zero

This is where it all started on August 16, 1896, the strike that was heard around the world, when Skookum Jim, George Carmack and Dawson Charlie found placer gold in Rabbit Creek (quickly renamed Bonanza Creek), a languid tributary of the Klondike. Now a national historic site, an interpretive trail with info boards leads you around the eerily quiet creek surrounded by brush and trees (and mosquitoes!).

The **Discovery Claim** is 14km from Dawson City and can be reached by heading south on Bonanza Creek Road. It's possible to visit the area as part of a guided tour with Klondike Experience (klondikeexperience.com).

There is some dispute about who was the first to spot the placer gold gleaming in the river. At the time, credit was given to Carmack, an American miner married to an Indigenous woman who registered the first claim in his name. Skookum Jim and Dawson Charlie were both members of the Tagish First Nation (Indeed, Jim, whose real name was Keish, was Carmack's wife's brother) and, in the discriminatory atmosphere of the 19th-century, a claim registered by an Indigenous person was often not recognized.

These days, a growing number of historians cite Skookum Jim as the true 'discoverer' of the gold, with some proposing his sister (Carmack's wife, Kate) as another potential candidate. First or not, Jim and his nephew, Dawson Charlie, quickly filed claims alongside Carmack and, by the end of August 1896, the whole creek had been staked by excited prospectors, as word quickly spread far beyond Dawson City. The rest, as they say, is history.

You can still pan for gold for free at nearby Free Claim #6.

### EARLIER RUSHES

Klondike wasn't Canada's only gold rush. In the 1850s and '60s, discoveries were made in the Cariboo region of BC igniting a frenzy and leading to the emergence of whole new towns such as **Barkerville** (p128), now preserved as a heritage site.

### RAGS OR RICHES?

When the ship *Portland* sailed into Seattle harbor in July 1897 with the equivalent of over $1 billion-worth of gold on board, the local newspaper proclaimed 'Gold! Gold! Gold!' Rallied by the call, it is estimated that 100,000 people set out for Klondike over the following year, with around 35,000 ultimately reaching Dawson City where less than 15,000 became bona fide prospectors. The rest merely walked the muddy, pot-holed streets shell-shocked and disconsolate, or set up small business to serve others, from plying whisky to digging graves. Only around 4000 of the wannabe prospectors successfully mined gold and a paltry couple of hundred became rich as a result. For most aspiring miners, Klondike was less a bold spin of the fortune-wheel and more an exhausting but life-changing adventure.

# Beyond Dawson City

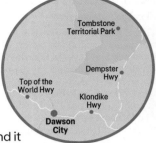

Tombstone
Territorial Park

Dempster
Hwy

Top of the
World Hwy

Klondike
Hwy

**Dawson
City**

If Dawson is the frontier, the territory beyond it is the frontier on the frontier, a land of unpaved roads and zero-bar phone reception.

### GETTING AROUND

There is no regular public transport on the Dempster or the Top of the World highways.

For car-hire, commercial transport and other logistics, call into the Northwest Territories Information Centre in Dawson City.

### ☑ TOP TIP

The Top of the World Highway is only open seasonally between June and September. The Klondike and Dempster highways are operational year-round.

Dawson is small. Venture beyond its false-fronted houses and warped wooden sidewalks and it doesn't take long for the wilderness to close in. If you're after shopping malls and skinny decaf lattes, you could be in for a long wait. The town's nearest neighbor, tiny Mayo (population: 188) is 233km away (and has neither).

Emanating from Dawson's tight downtown grid, roads head out in three directions. To the west, across the Yukon River, lies the Top of the World Hwy, a bumpy backroad to Alaska. To the south, the Klondike Hwy offers paved but sporadically rutted passage down to Whitehorse. To the north, the Dempster Hwy carves its gravelly path through a mixture of taiga and tundra to the Arctic Ocean. Take your pick.

## Tombstone Territorial Park

TIME FROM DAWSON CITY 1½HR 🚗

**Enjoy the silence**

Not everyone has the time or the driving chops to tackle the Dempster Highway in all its glory. But to get a taste of this famously feral road, you can drive along a portion of it on a day trip from Dawson and explore **Tombstone Territorial Park**.

Named for a local mountain rather than a cemetery, Tombstone stretches between the 50km and 120km markers of the Dempster, guarding the road's most majestic mountains and accessible trails. Driving through, you'll pass a well-curated **interpretive center** and a front-country campground. Soon after, the road crests the Continental Divide between the Pacific and Arctic watersheds as the green and charcoal landscape transitions from boreal forest to tundra. Purple wildflowers burst forth in July as clouds sweep across the tundra, bringing squalls punctuated by brilliant sun.

Several trailheads offer short leg-stretching hikes. The 3.4km **North Klondike River Trail** leads through trees and then low brush from the Tombstone campground. Placards explaining the flora and fauna dot the first segment. Beware: moose are common in the area.

**Tombstone Territorial Park**

## TOP OF THE WORLD HIGHWAY

Apart from the Klondike, the only other road leading out of Dawson City is the Top of the World Hwy, which runs for 127km to an intersection with the Taylor Hwy just across the border in Alaska. The road starts on the west bank of the Yukon River, directly opposite Dawson where, in true Yukon fashion, there's no road-bridge, just a free 24-hour ferry service that swings back and forth like a pendulum in summer.

The unpaved road that winds through bleak, undulating tundra has no services or turn-offs until it reaches Alaska at North America's most isolated and laid-back border post. From there, it's 64km to the eccentric outpost of Chicken (population 12), so named because the original inhabitants couldn't spell the word 'ptarmigan.'

The **Goldensides Trail**, a little further up the road, is 4km out-and-back across open mountainside dotted with small shrubs and big views, including the raised rocky obelisk of Tombstone Mountain (2192m) in the Ogilvie Range. Bring some sandwiches from Red Mammoth Bistro in Dawson and enjoy a picnic outside the interpretive center. Inside, you can warm up with a cup of mountain wild tea.

The **Grizzly Lake Trail** is a gutsier 22km round-trip backpacking adventure, much of it along a stony but spectacular ridgetop. There's a campground at the lake and inspiring views of Mt Monolith.

 **WHERE TO CAMP ON THE DEMPSTER**

**Tombstone Mountain**
Handy location next to the interpretive center and various trailheads with outhouses, picnic tables and cooking shelters. **$**

**Engineer Creek**
A small eight-site campground at the foot of a limestone ridge, with outhouses, picnic tables and good river fishing. **$**

**Rock River**
At the Dempster's 447km mark, this 20-site campground is sheltered by a steep gorge in the Richardson Mountains. **$**

## DEMPSTER DRIVING TIPS

It takes around 10 to 12 hours to drive to Inuvik without stopping for a break. However, it's much nicer to split the journey over two days, followed by a night in Inuvik and two extra days on the way back.

Graveled almost its entire length, the highway has a well-deserved reputation for being rough on vehicles. Travel with extra gas and tires, and expect to use them.

Bring plenty of food and water; the only source on the Dempster in the Yukon is at Eagle Plains.

The Yukon government maintains three roadside campgrounds and there are another three across the border in the Northwest Territories. Before setting out, call into the Northwest Territories Information Centre in Dawson City for trip advice and road conditions information.

# The Dempster Highway

TIME FROM DAWSON CITY 1½HR

### To the shores of the Arctic

The only road in North America to reach the Arctic Ocean, the daunting Dempster Hwy stretches for 740km from just east of Dawson City to Inuvik. En route, it goes through more scenery changes than an episode of *Game of Thrones,* encompassing boreal forest, tussocky tundra, two mountain ranges, migrating caribou, continental divides, the lake-dotted MacKenzie River Delta and the barren arctic.

No other drive on the continent can compare with it: the eerie silence, the unnerving solitude and the roaming bears – black, grizzly and polar!

Conceived in the late 1950s to link new oil and gas discoveries with the rest of Canada, the Dempster was beset by high costs and fickle weather during its early development and didn't finally open until 1978. In 2017, a new 150km section was added between Inuvik and Tuktoyaktuk on the Arctic Ocean, an Inuvialuit hamlet famed for its distinctive pingos (conical ice-cored hills).

Built on a thick base of gravel to insulate the permafrost underneath (which would otherwise melt and cause the road to disintegrate), the highway includes two ferry crossings over the Peel and MacKenzie rivers. In winter, the rivers freeze to form ice bridges and, for a few weeks during the spring thaw and winter freeze-up, the road is closed.

The most beguiling and user-friendly section of the highway is through Tombstone Territorial Park. Further north, the **Eagle Plains Hotel**, at the 370km mark, only 35km from the Arctic Circle, is open year-round and offers 32 rooms in a low-rise building in a stark setting. The next service station is 180km further north at Fort McPherson in the Northwest Territories.

TOMAS PAVELKA/SHUTTERSTOCK ©

**Above: Icefield Parkway, Banff; right: Moraine Lake**

# Banff & Jasper National Parks

## THE CANADIAN ROCKIES' GREATEST HITS

The two pioneering parks that helped lay the foundations of Canada's modern national-park movement.

Standing as gateways to an alluring mix of front-country activities and backcountry adventure, the two conjoined national parks of Banff and Jasper sit flush up against the Continental Divide in Alberta where they form part of a much larger web of contiguous parks protected as a Unesco World Heritage Site.

Glaciers, mountains, canyons and waterfalls are all part of the landscape here and are complemented by copious species of wildlife and a rich Indigenous and post-European contact history.

As Canadian as maple syrup and lumberjack shirts, Banff is the crucible of the national-park movement and a central pillar of Canada's tourist industry. Compared with other national parks, it has a well-oiled infrastructure with hot springs, three ski resorts, numerous hotels and a huge network of trails.

Jasper is the cooler, less commercial, more challenging alternative to Banff. It's particularly noted for its mountain biking, wildlife-spotting, glacier-viewing and opportunities to get off the beaten track. A compact townsite keeps one foot planted in the natural world, and minimal light pollution creates ideal conditions for stargazing. Old-school and friendly, the well-organized townsite feels wholesome and blue-collar, a little less staged than Banff's.

Amid the plethora of activities on offer, cycling, backcountry hiking and whitewater rafting stand out.

The two parks are linked by the 233km Icefields Parkway, popularly considered to be Canada's most spectacular road trip.

ATTILIO PREGNOLATO/SHUTTERSTOCK ©

## THE MAIN AREAS

### BANFF & AROUND
Accessible wilderness with 21st-century conveniences. **p210**

### ICEFIELDS PARKWAY
Made-in-heaven road trip with copious pull-overs. **p220**

### JASPER & AROUND
Biking, rafting, stargazing and glacier-walking. **p224**

# Find Your Way

Major highways cut through Banff, and in recent years, authorities have increased the provision of public transport. Jasper is less well served, and a car will offer you more flexibility, particularly outside of the high summer season.

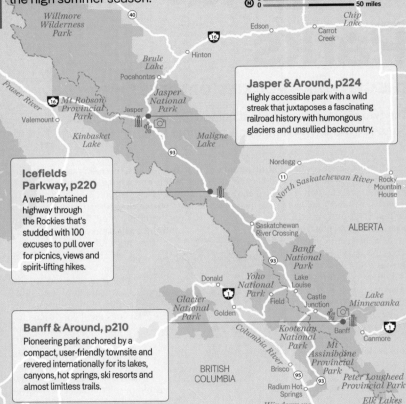

### Jasper & Around, p224

Highly accessible park with a wild streak that juxtaposes a fascinating railroad history with humongous glaciers and unsullied backcountry.

### Icefields Parkway, p220

A well-maintained highway through the Rockies that's studded with 100 excuses to pull over for picnics, views and spirit-lifting hikes.

### Banff & Around, p210

Pioneering park anchored by a compact, user-friendly townsite and revered internationally for its lakes, canyons, hot springs, ski resorts and almost limitless trails.

## CAR

Most visitors arrive by car. The Trans-Canada Hwy cuts through Banff before veering west via Yoho to Vancouver. The Icefields Pkwy heads north from Lake Louise to Jasper where it intersects with the Yellowhead Hwy (Hwy 16).

## BUS

The Roam Transit (roamtransit. com) bus network covers Banff Town, Canmore and Lake Louise, with reduced provision in the winter. Sundog Tours (sundogtours.com) plies the Icefields Pkwy as far as Jasper. Both parks run summer shuttles to tourist sites.

STEPA87/SHUTTERSTOCK ©

**Chipmunk, Peyto Lake, Banff**

# Plan Your Time

These two conjoined parks are well organized and blessed with easy access and good infrastructures. You can see a great deal in a week and really get under the skin of them in two.

## Whistle-Stop

Get oriented in Banff Town on **'the Ave'** (p210). Then hike to the top of **Sulphur Mountain** (p212), have lunch at the summit and descend on the gondola for a soak in the **Upper Hot Springs** (p213). Drive Icefields Pkwy, stopping at **Peyto Lake** (p221) and **Columbia Icefield** (p223) en route. In Jasper's survey the townsite on the circuitous **Discovery Trail** (p224) and explore **Pyramid Bench** (p226).

## Take It Easy

With more time in Banff, hit the **Fairmont Banff Springs Hotel** (p213) for afternoon tea and the **Cave and Basin** (p214) for park history. Spend two days in Lake Louise hiking the **Larch Valley** (p219) and the **Teahouse Trail** (p218) and another day in **Sunshine Meadows** (p217) enjoying the wildflowers. In Jasper, explore the **Maligne Canyon** (p229) and **Jasper Park Lodge** (p229) with its **planetarium** (p227).

### Seasonal Highlights

| SPRING | SUMMER | AUTUMN | WINTER |
|---|---|---|---|
| Skiing is possible until early May. Late May means open valley trails, double-figure temps and fully operational parks. | Alpine areas are mostly snow-free from early July. Most trails are open for hiking, cycling and outdoor activity. | Early fall brings a blaze of color, making for spectacular hiking, especially around Lake Louise's Larch Valley. | The ski season gets underway, with snow descending on Banff's Big Three resorts and Jasper's Marmot Basin. |

# Banff & Around

**WILDERNESS WITH 21ST-CENTURY CONVENIENCES**

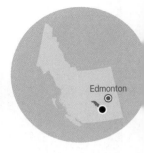

Edmonton

### GETTING AROUND

Banff has an excellent bus service for a national park with regular scheduled services running between Banff Town and Canmore, and Lake Louise. There's also a summer service to Lake Minnewanka. Check the Roam Transit website (roamtransit.com) for timetables.

Banff Town and its immediate surroundings are easily walkable and Canmore and Lake Minnewanka are both popular bike rides in the summer. Bike rental is readily available.

### ☑ TOP TIP

Most of Banff's hotels and inns line the north side of Banff Ave. They offer good facilities but are pricy and hard to procure in summer. Book well ahead. For old-school luxury, head south of the river to the **Fairmont Banff Springs** (p213).

Banff is a Canadian icon. Created as the world's third national park in 1885, this finely sculpted corner of the Rocky Mountains helped shape Canadian history and pave the way for the growth of modern tourism in North America in the late 19th century. As an early exponent of environmental protection, Banff was a blueprint for national parks that came later and, in more recent times, has emerged as a litmus test for how they should act today, balancing ecological integrity with all-round visitor experience.

Geographically, the park is split into two opposing parts. There's the cozy comfort of Banff Town anchored by its busy main avenue versus the raw energy of the expansive wilderness that lies beyond. It's the juxtaposition of these two very different worlds that make Banff so intriguing. One minute you're sinking a beer on crowded Banff Ave, the next you're scrambling up a scree slope with only mountain goats for company.

## Essential Business in Banff Avenue

### Banff's main drag

The street that 99% of national-park tourists visit, and many never really leave, **Banff Avenue** is the town's commercial artery, a 5km-long conglomeration of shops, restaurants, pubs and lodges. On a busy day in summer, up to 30,000 people descend here to stroll, shop, eat or relax after an energetic day in the mountains. To ease the congestion, in 2023 the town elected to close several blocks of the street to car traffic.

It wasn't always so busy. A little over a century ago, Banff Ave was Banff, home to a handful of hotels, homesteads and trail outfitters vying to accommodate the park's tiny trickle of tentative tourists. Development of the town took off following the arrival of the Canadian Pacific Railway in 1885 and the opening of the Banff Springs Hotel three years later.

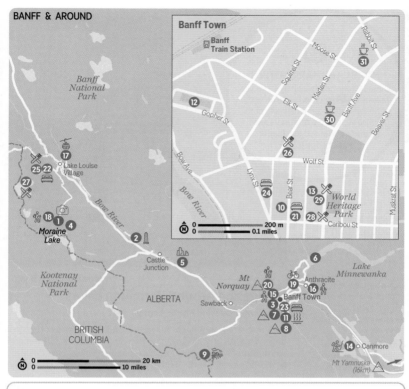

BANFF & AROUND

Banff Town

Banff Train Station

**HIGHLIGHTS**
1 Moraine Lake

**SIGHTS**
2 Castle Mountain Memorial
3 Cave & Basin National Historic Site
4 Consolation Lakes
5 Johnston Canyon
6 Lake Minnewanka
see 5 Lower Falls
7 Sanson Peak
8 Sulphur Mountain
9 Sunshine Village

see 5 Upper Falls
see 15 Vermilion Lakes

**ACTIVITIES, COURSES & TOURS**
10 Banff Adventures
11 Banff Upper Hot Springs
12 Brewster
13 Discover Banff
14 Elevation Place
15 Fenland Loop
16 Johnson Lake
17 Lake Louise Summer Gondola

see 6 Lake Minnewanka Cruise
18 Larch Valley
19 Legacy Trail
see 2 Marsh Loop
20 Mt Norquay Via Ferrata

**SLEEPING**
21 Brewster's Mountain Lodge
22 Chateau Lake Louise
23 Fairmont Banff Springs
24 Peaks Hotel & Suites

**EATING**
25 Lake Agnes Teahouse
26 Lupo Ristorante
27 Plain of Six Glaciers Teahouse
28 Tooloulou's
29 Zyka Elevated Indian Restaurant

**DRINKING & NIGHTLIFE**
see 13 Evelyn's Coffee World
30 Good Earth Coffeehouse
31 Whitebark Cafe

 **WHERE TO GO FOR COFFEE & CAKE IN BANFF TOWN**

**Good Earth Coffeehouse**
Where hot, smooth, earthy coffee pairs beautifully with unique coconut and beetroot muffins. $

**Whitebark Cafe**
Trendy and popular cafe in the Aspen Lodge with a modish interior and an abundance of non-stodgy snacks. $

**Evelyn's Coffee World**
Old Banff stalwart that sells assorted coffee paraphernalia and giant cookies shaped like scones. $

## MORE LANDMARK HOTELS

Other historic hotels built by Canadian railway companies and more recently acquired by the Fairmont luxury hotel chain include the **Chateau Lake Louise** (p218) and the **Jasper Park Lodge** (p229).

**Vermilion Lakes, Banff**

## SHORT HIKES AROUND BANFF TOWN

### Johnson Lake
A lovely pond-sized lake ringed by fir forest and encircled by an easy 3km trail with views of Cascade Mountain.

### Marsh Loop
Easy, sometimes muddy 3.4km loop alongside the Bow River that combines well with a visit to the Cave & Basin Springs. Waterfowl and beavers abound.

### Fenland Loop
Popular with Banff dog-walkers and joggers, this 2.1km circular trail travels through a variety of natural habitats – woodland, marsh, fen, riverbed and wetland – around placid Forty Mile Creek.

# Navigating Around Vermilion Lakes

### Water, wildfowl and photography

As the nearest navigable lakes to Banff Town, these tranquil havens are an attractive nexus for water activities, hiking and communing with nature. You can spot a diverse stash of wildlife here: elk, beavers, owls, bald eagles and ospreys are all common around the lakeshore, especially at dawn and dusk. A paved path – part of the Legacy bike trail – parallels the lakes' northern edge for nearly 6km, but the proximity of the Trans-Canada Hwy means an almost constant buzz of traffic noise.

Noise or not, the calm, glassy water is an excellent spot for painters and photographers with the surrounding mountains clearly mirrored on the surface.

The best way to reach the lakes on foot from Banff is via the 2.1km **Fenland Trail**, which starts at the Forty Mile Creek picnic area, just north of the 'Welcome to Banff' sign.

# Two Ways up Sulphur Mountain

### Hiking trail and gondola

For drone-like views of Banff Town and the Bow Valley, it's necessary to ascend Sulphur Mountain (2451m), Banff's sentinel peak named for the famous hot springs that bubble beneath

## WHERE TO STAY IN BANFF TOWN

**Fairmont Banff Springs**
Royalty, Hollywood stars and Banff pioneers have all stayed at these iconic accommodations. **$$$**

**Peaks Hotel & Suites**
Handsome Scandi-inspired design with log-shaped desks. wall-sized photos and fancy coffee machines. **$$**

**Brewster's Mountain Lodge**
Comfy wood-embellished lodge owned by the sixth generation of Banff's original outfitters and travel operators. **$$**

its wooded slopes. There are two ways up: a physically taxing hike that zigzags skyward for 5.6km incorporating a series of increasingly steep switchbacks, or a seductive gondola ride.

If you don't hike up, you can make use of your stored energy on a short summit walk via boardwalks and stairways to adjacent **Sanson Peak**, the site of the old weather station and an erstwhile Cosmic Ray research facility. The former – a small stone structure – is still intact; the latter was dismantled in 1981.

## A Landmark Hotel

### Symbol of Banff

Looking like a cross between Harry Potter's Hogwarts and a Loire Valley castle, the **Fairmont Banff Springs Hotel** (fairmont.com/banff-springs) competes with the surrounding Rocky Mountains for size and grandeur. Constructed as one of the nation's 'grand railway hotels' in 1928, it replaced an earlier wooden structure that was built to serve the park's first tourists in the 1880s but was destroyed by a fire in 1926. The remodel was designed in the prevailing Canadian Châteauesque style that sought to imitate the Renaissance castles of the Loire in France. It quickly became a leading contender for Canada's most iconic building.

Sleepy? Bed down in one of the 757 rooms. Hungry? Choose from one of a dozen restaurants. Afternoon tea is the hotel's quintessential if expensive Banff indulgence. There's a golf course, of course, and a terrace hosting opulent weddings. One of the real joys, however, is just wandering around the halls trying to work out who's staying over and who ain't.

## Soaking in Banff Upper Hot Springs

### Public spring-water pool

Banff's raison d'être is hot water. Not any old hot water but the soothing spring water that gushes out of the depths of Sulphur Mountain at temperatures that oscillate between 32°C and 46°C. This geothermal gift of nature contains numerous revitalizing minerals including sulphate, calcium, sodium and magnesium and is kept at temperatures of between 37°C and 40°C in the public pools (hotsprings.ca/banff)

The pools get busy in season, so aim for an early or late dip if you prefer smaller crowds. Towels and swimsuits – including 1930s retro garments – are available for hire, and there's a rudimentary cafe selling coffee and sandwiches on the 2nd floor of the bathhouse.

**CANOEING IN BANFF**

Canoes and kayaks have a long history in the Rockies, particularly among Indigenous people. With numerous rivers and lakes scattered around the park, oar-power remains popular with modern tourists. You can hire canoes from boathouses at Lake Louise, Moraine Lake and Lake Minnewanka, although they're rather expensive and only available when the water fully defrosts between May and October.

For a cheaper deal, head to Banff Canoe Club (banffcanoeclub. com) in town, ideal for paddles on the Bow River or Vermilion Lakes.

Alternatively, you can bring your own canoe, kayak or SUP and paddle on any number of lakes. Be sure to download a self-certification permit from the park website first. Lake Minnewanka is the only lake that permits motorboats.

 **WHERE TO GO FOR DINNER IN BANFF TOWN**

**Zyka Elevated Indian Restaurant**
An ambitious venture offering high-class Indian food and congenial service. **$$**

**Tooloulou's**
Cajun food with an Acadian twist. Bank on catfish, po'boys and jambalaya prepared with Canadian panache. **$$$**

**Lupo Ristorante**
Enjoy superbly authentic Italian food and a casual ambience in a large, attractive but informal dining room. **$$$**

## CLIMBING IN CANMORE

Canmore, 25km south of Banff Town, is the Rockies' rock-climbing hub and the spiritual home of the sport in Canada. It's no coincidence that the Alpine Club of Canada has its national HQ here. Numerous crags, all within a short distance of each other, surround the town, including Cougar Creek, Grassi Lakes and Grotto Canyon. The holy grail for multipitch routes is **Mt Yamnuska** (aka Mt John Laurie) with over 100 routes of all grades. In the colder months, Canmore shifts its focus to frozen waterfall climbing.

The one-stop shop for climbing courses, guided tours and gear is Yamnuska Mountain Adventures (yamnuska.com) in Canmore, with nearly 50 years of experience. For one of Canada's best indoor climbing walls, head to **Elevation Place**, Canmore's hi-tech sports center.

# Cave & Basin National Historic Site

### The site that launched the park

When three Canadian Pacific Railway employees stumbled upon these hot springs half-hidden in a cave on one of their days off in 1883, they probably didn't realize the deluge their discovery would unleash. Not only did they come up with an epiphanic business idea, but they inadvertently helped ignite a national-park movement and make Banff into the international phenomenon it is today.

The Cave and Basin National Historic Site, 1.6km west of the town center, is where it all started. While you can't bathe here anymore, the place has been preserved as a museum and National Historic Site allowing access to the shadowy cave, the original outdoor bathing pool and a terrace that covers the once popular lower mineral springs pool that welcomed spa-seeking visitors for 78 years. An adjacent boardwalk with interpretive signage leads uphill to additional springs and the cave's upper vent.

# Cycling the Legacy Trail

### Paved inter-town bikepath

Of all the initiatives introduced to Banff in the last 15 years, this hugely popular multi-purpose trail that parallels the Trans-Canada Hwy for 26.8km is arguably the most memorable – and sustainable.

Opened to celebrate the national park's 125th anniversary in 2010, the Legacy Trail between Banff Town and Canmore has logged well over one million users since its inception, sometimes amassing over 3000 cyclists in a single summer day.

The trail is mostly flat, wholly paved and armed with a number of user-friendly contraptions, including solar-paneled electrified rubber mats designed as invisible 'gates' to protect wildlife.

For most of the journey, the path cuts through low foliage and scattered trees sandwiched between the Trans-Canada and the railway line. There's one major stop-off point 8km northwest of Canmore called the Valleyview picnic area, where you can slump down in a red Adirondack chair and contemplate the giant buttresses of Mt Rundle opposite.

# Head for Heights on the Via Ferrata

### Fixed-protection climbing routes

Via Ferratas (iron ways) were popularized in the mountains of northern Italy during WWI when they were used for military purposes. Their rock-spanning ladders, metal bridges and fixed-line cables helped move armies across rugged Al-

 **WHERE TO ORGANIZE TRIPS AND ACTIVITIES IN BANFF TOWN**

**Brewster**
Now operating under the name 'Pursuit,' this company has been leading the way for tourists in Banff since 1892.

**Discover Banff**
Organizes rafting trips, wildlife tours, Columbia Icefield day trips and even a 10-hour grizzly-bear tour in BC.

**Banff Adventures**
Banff's main activity-booking company can organize a huge range of activities and combo packages.

**Cycling the Banff Legacy Trail, Banff**

pine terrain during the high-altitude war being played out on the Italian Front.

The idea migrated to Canada in the early 2000s and Mt Norquay's via ferrata (banffnorquay.com/summer/via-ferrata), which opened in 2014, is the only one in the national park, with five different route choices: the Explorer (2½ hours), the Ridgewalker (four hours), the Alpinist (4½ hours), the Skyline (five hours) and the Summiteer (six hours). The latter includes a three-wire suspension bridge to the top of Mt Norquay. Prices include full safety kit, accompanying guide and passage up the Norquay chairlift to the start point.

## Venturing Out at Lake Minnewanka

### The Rockies' largest lake

Minnewanka is a popular recreational lake, 28km long, that develops more of a wilderness feel the further you penetrate east. The western shore, only 10km from Banff Town, is a busy hub with a boat dock, picnic area, various trailheads and a seasonal cafe (the Black & Anchor). The narrated one-hour **boat cruises** bookable through Pursuit (banffjaspercollection.com) are worth it for their succinct history and jovial commentaries, but for a longer, quieter contemplation of what Indigenous people called the 'lake of spirits,' you'll need to hike its northern shoreline. The

### THE TOWN BENEATH THE LAKE

One of Alberta's more interesting diving sites, **Minnewanka Landing** is a former resort town that got submerged beneath the lake. The first log hotel was built in 1886 and the area quickly became a popular summer resort village for recreation-seeking Calgary-ites. Within a couple of decades, there were several hotels, a handful of restaurants and numerous cottages spread along four parallel avenues. However, the businesses were ultimately forced to yield to the growing hydroelectric demands of Calgary as the lake was dammed three times, in 1895, 1912 and 1941, causing it to rise by 30m (98ft). Thanks to Minnewanka's cold, clear glacial water, many of the town's submerged ruins have been well preserved. Divers today can view ghostly foundations, sidewalks, pilings of erstwhile wharves and even an old bridge.

 **WHERE TO EAT IN SUNSHINE VILLAGE**

| **Mad Trapper's Saloon** | **Creekside Bar & Grill** | **Eagle's Nest** |
|---|---|---|
| Pub grub in an ever-popular 1920s-era log cabin perched at 2159m. Open year-round. **$$** | Winter-only hub for breakfast waffles and lunch-time poutine located in the gondola base station. **$$** | The mountain's only fine-dining restaurant offers ski-in coq au vin and rack of lamb. **$$$** |

## INTERNMENT CAMPS

Part of a regrettable chapter in Banff's history, the **Castle Mountain Internment Camp** was established in WWI when the Canadian government, invoking the 1914 War Measures Act, rounded up over 8000 so-called 'enemy aliens' and sent them to internment camps where they were forced to work in slave-labor conditions on national-park building projects. The prisoners were civilians whose only 'crime' was their ethnic background – in this case mostly Austro-Hungarians and Ukrainians allied with the Axis powers in WWI. Ironically, many of them had been enticed to emigrate to Canada only years before by a freedom-extolling government desperate for hard-working settlers. A memorial entitled 'Why?' was installed next to the Bow Valley Pkwy at the site of the original camp in 1995.

**Upper Johnston Waterfalls, Banff**

lakeside path extends from **Stewart Canyon** (easy stroll) to the **Aylmer Pass** junction (day-hike) and, ultimately, **Ghost Lakes** (two days out-and-back). Kayaks and canoes are another transport option and are rentable from the boat dock.

## The Catwalks of Johnston Canyon
### Narrow gorge and thunderous waterfalls

This deep and narrow gorge is characterized by its dramatic limestone cliffs and two crashing cascades. To help negotiate it, a sturdy catwalk has been attached to the canyon wall offering a unique vertiginous perspective. Shrouded in foliage, the lofty cliffs are covered with mosses, lichen and ferns, and from late June to September, black swifts swoop to and from their moss-lined nests in the steep walls searching for flying insects.

There are three hiking options of varying lengths here. The path to the **lower falls** (1.2km) is mostly asphalt and partly accessible to wheelchairs/strollers. The **upper falls trail** (2.5km from the start) heads further upstream to a taller cascade that's particularly beguiling in spring when it cuts shapely holes in the ice. It's also worth pressing a further 3.2km beyond the upper falls through coniferous forest to the **inkpots**, a collection of half-a-dozen ultra-clear mineral pools.

 **WHERE TO EAT IN LAKE LOUISE**

**Bill Peyto's Cafe**
Local youth hostel that's best in the village for big breakfasts and economic burger and pasta dinners. **$**

**Station Restaurant**
Maple-glazed salmon and slow-braised bison ribs in Lake Louise's 1910-vintage railway station. **$$$**

**Fairview Dining Room**
Expensive afternoon tea in the Chateau Lake Louise with Devonshire-style cream and priceless views. **$$$**

# Bow Valley Parkway
### Traffic-calmed backroad

While most Banff visitors rush along the Trans-Canada Hwy in the slipstream of the car in front, savvier souls divert serendipitously onto quieter Hwy 1A, also known as the Bow Valley Parkway, which parallels Hwy 1 for 51km between Banff Town and Lake Louise.

Constructed in the days before SUVs and high-velocity cars, the road was designed for slow meandering rather than speed. Despite the ubiquitous trees, there are regular viewpoints where drivers and cyclists can hit the brakes and gaze out across the Bow Valley and its forest-meets-mountain landscapes. This is a prime place to spot wildlife, especially elk, bighorn sheep and even the occasional moose. The obligatory stop is Johnston Canyon and its thunderous cascades, but there are plenty of other meadows, monuments and pull-overs to ponder.

# Sunshine Meadows
### Summer wildflower extravaganza

Don't expect thatched cottages and a steepled church. **Sunshine Village** isn't a village in the traditional sense. Rather it's home to one of the national park's three main ski areas nestled amid a high-alpine nirvana of meadows, ridges and lakes that straddles the Continental Divide between Alberta and British Columbia. In winter, skiers congregate in the small purpose-built village to experience some of the best snow in the Rockies. In the spring thaw, the snow melts to reveal the majestic beauty of Sunshine Meadows, a sweeping expanse of ponds and flower meadows backed by crenelated peaks that stretches for 15km between Citadel Pass and Healy Pass. The presence of a gondola and seasonal bus service make this one of the easiest places in the Rockies for hikers to get above the treeline without chartering a private helicopter or expending copious gallons of sweat.

# Ski Sunshine
### One of Canada's snowiest resorts

People have skied at Sunshine since the 1930s and there has been the semblance of a resort here since the '40s. The pioneers knew good terrain when they saw it. In a comparative study of Rocky Mountain ski resorts, **Banff Sunshine** (skibanff.com) comes out top for quantity of snow: it receives double Lake Louise's snow-dump and three times that of Norquay. The reason? Altitude. Sunshine's base village is perched at a height of 2159m at the top of a gondola ride and abutting a huge

## SUNSHINE VILLAGE

Clustered around the top station of the Sunshine gondola at an altitude of 2159m, Sunshine Village consists of a handsome glass-and-wood hotel, the **Sunshine Mountain Lodge**, along with half-a-dozen cafes and restaurants, from the pub-like **Mad Trappers Saloon** housed in a 1928-vintage hunting cabin (that predates the ski resort) to the upscale **Eagle's Nest**. In the summer, the village provides a gateway to a circuit of short alpine trails, accessed via the Standish chairlift, and a couple of longer hikes, most notably the backcountry excursions to Egypt Lake and Mt Assiniboine Provincial Park.

The **Creekside Lodge** at the gondola base station sports a coffee shop and grill restaurant, and handles hotel check-in and ski rentals. It's also the summer trailhead for Healy Pass.

## WHERE TO FIND THE BEST LAKE LOUISE VIEWPOINTS

**Big Beehive**
Follow the grueling switchbacks above Lake Agnes to a historic CPR shelter for Lake Louise panoramas.

**Fairview**
Short uphill grind through forest from the lakeshore to a tree-framed vista of Lake Louise and the Chateau.

**Whitehorn Mountain**
Take the summer gondola above a protected wildlife corridor to Whitehorn Bistro and Michelin-star views.

GUNTER NUYTS/SHUTTERSTOCK ©

**Lake Agnes, Banff**

## LAKE LOUISE SUMMER GONDOLA

Whitehorn Mountain does a *volte-face* in the spring, switching from ski resort to summer activity center with a big focus on wildlife. The gondola still runs with its cabins grafted onto the Glacier Express chairlift where they alternate with alfresco quad-chairs. Lower Whitehorn, where skiers zigzag dexterously in winter, becomes a wildlife corridor that's closed to visitors. Aspiring hikers must ascend the mountain on the gondola/chairlift to a viewpoint halfway up where there's a restaurant, wildlife interpretive center and small trail network.

alpine bowl. There are very few trees in this neck of the woods and the views over toward the Continental Divide and BC will have you skidding to regular stops in admiration.

## Chateau Lake Louise

### Room with a view

This opulent Fairmont hotel (fairmont.com/lake-louise) dominates the eastern shore of Lake Louise in the same way that the glistening Victoria glacier dominates the west. Originally constructed in the 1890s but altered radically in 1924 after a serious fire, the Chateau Lake Louise is a railway-era twin of the Banff Springs, whose Renaissance Revival style it closely mimics. A newer wing was added in 2004.

While the imposing multi-story facade might not blend harmoniously with its natural surroundings, the soaring turrets and manicured gardens certainly add a dash of architectural panache to the Rocky Mountain landscape.

## Teahouse Hikes

### Tea and scones at 2100m

Once you've digested the beauty of Lake Louise's chateau and the luminosity of the water, there are a couple of other surpris-

 **WHERE TO CYCLE IN LAKE LOUISE**

**Bow River Loop**
Fine family-friendly trail that loops around both sides of Banff's river, starting at Lake Louise train station.

**Great Divide**
Relatively easy run on a rough paved road (Hwy 1A) between Lake Louise and Yoho National Park.

**Moraine Lake Road**
Paved but unrelenting uphill grind between Louise and Moraine lakes with only buses for company.

es waiting. Hidden away in the amphitheater of mountains that surround Lake Louise are two backcountry tea houses, inaccessible by road, which serve up the kind of light, flaky scones normally confined to dainty tea rooms in England.

Hikers have been calling in at the **Lake Agnes Teahouse** since 1901. The soup, sandwiches on homemade bread and apple crumble are as spectacular as the scenery.

The **Plain of Six Glaciers Teahouse** is of newer vintage and involves a slightly longer hike (5.5km). Constructed in 1927 as a way station for Swiss mountaineering guides on Mt Victoria, the twin-level stone chalet sits nestled in a quiet glade at 2100m and provides almost the same dishes as Lake Agnes Teahouse to a steady stream of sugar-depleted hikers.

## A Day at Moraine Lake

Canada's most famous view

Emblazoned on calendars, dish towels, coffee-table books and $20 bills, Moraine Lake is an eerily familiar sight even to first-time visitors. To say that the view from its rocky northern shore is cinematic would be an understatement: the water a deep teal, the surrounding forest a dark bottle-green, a rampart of 10 dagger-like peaks – the Wenkchemna Range – stacked up behind like a giant medieval fortress.

This is superb hiking terrain. There are four main trails emanating from the lakeshore, plus a short punt to the top of the 'Rockpile' (400m) on Moraine's north shore for a view that every single person who comes here wants (and has) to see. Two of the hikes are graded 'easy': a weaving path that tracks the lakeshore for 1.6km, and a slightly more adventurous trail to **Consolation Lakes**.

## Fall Hiking in Larch Valley

Banff's best autumnal hike

Banff has many memorable hikes, but there's only one contender for top spot in the fall. The wondrous Larch Valley comes into its own when the scent of autumn is in the air and its namesake trees blaze golden yellow.

The broad, well-signposted path into the valley branches off the Moraine Lake trail and travels up a set of switchbacks that gain over 350m in 2.5km before leveling out into alpine meadows interspersed with larch forest.

Larch Valley reaches its golden apex in the second half of September with the colors usually fading by the second week of October.

**ASK AN EXPERT**

**Victoria Hawley**, Promotions Lead, Banff National Park

**Favorite day-hike in Banff?**
One of my favorites with my young family is Boom Lake. This gradual ascent and packed trail is good for little feet or less-experienced hikers.

**See any wildlife?**
Yes! The last time a pika greeted us with its call and then we watched it meander up the slope.

**Tips for first timers?**
I make sure to make noise and carry bear spray.

**Where to eat afterwards?**
Every hike with my kiddos ends with ice cream! In Banff we like Cows and Beaver Tails.

# Icefields Parkway

**MADE-IN-HEAVEN ROAD-TRIP**

Edmonton

## GETTING AROUND

Sundog Tours (sundogtours.com) runs year-round buses along the parkway between Banff, Lake Louise and Jasper. In summer, you can do it as part of a guided tour with stops at Bow Lake, the Weeping Wall, the Columbia Icefield and Athabasca Falls.

If you're driving, start out with a full tank of gas. It's fairly pricey to fill up at Saskatchewan River Crossing, the only gas station in the 233km-long stretch between Lake Louise and Jasper.

### ☑ TOP TIP

With no commercial trucks, a generous shoulder and plenty of accommodation along the route, the parkway is a spectacular bike adventure. It's considered slightly easier to cycle from north to south, starting in Jasper and finishing in Lake Louise

The Icefields Parkway, or the Promenade des Glaciers as it's more romantically known in French, is one of the most spectacular slices of asphalt in North America, maybe the world. Running just east of the Continental Divide, which it parallels for 230km (144.7 miles), between Lake Louise and Jasper Town, the highway is shared between Banff and Jasper national parks and studded with a sensory overload of scenery. Landscape-shaping glaciers, foraging wildlife and gothic mountains will be your constant companions. When we say don't miss it, we mean *don't miss it!*

The Banff section of the parkway, rather like its Jasper counterpart, is punctuated with copious excuses to pull over and contemplate your speck-like importance in the vast natural universe of the Rocky Mountains. Some of the stops have accommodation (in campgrounds or rustic hotels and hostels) and simple eating joints. Others are the starting points for magnificent short trails.

## Reflections in Bow Lake

### Lake, lodge and waterfall

Bow Lake, 33km north of Lake Louise, has multiple reasons to apply a little pressure to the brakes. Firstly, there's the distracting view of **Crowfoot Mountain** from a roadside pullover with its craggy cliffs and scree-laden skirts perfectly reflected in the water. Then there's the **Crowfoot Glacier** spread across the mountain's upper flanks. Decades of glacial retreat mean its name is no longer 100% accurate: the lowest toe has melted making it look more like an ostrich's foot.

The four-story wooden structure on the lake's north shore was the erstwhile business and residence of one of Banff's most endearing legends, Jimmy Simpson. Reborn as the **Lodge at Bow Lake** (lodgeatbowlake.com) in 2023, it's the start of a 7.2km trail to the 100m-tall **Bow Glacier Falls**, a slender cascade that emanates from a small lake sitting above tall cliffs.

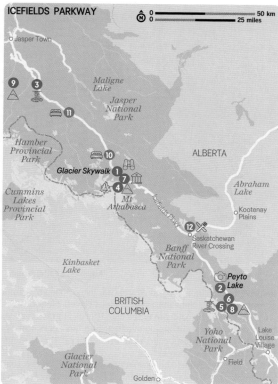

**ICEFIELDS PARKWAY**

0 — 50 km
0 — 25 miles

Jasper Town

Maligne Lake

Jasper National Park

Hamber Provincial Park

ALBERTA

Glacier Skywalk ①

Cummins Lakes Provincial Park

Abraham Lake

Mt Athabasca

Kootenay Plains

Kinbasket Lake

Banff National Park

Saskatchewan River Crossing

BRITISH COLUMBIA

Peyto Lake

Yoho National Park

Lake Louise Village

Field

Glacier National Park

Golden

**HIGHLIGHTS**
- ① Glacier Skywalk
- ② Peyto Lake

**SIGHTS**
- ③ Athabasca Falls
- ④ Athabasca Glacier
- ⑤ Bow Glacier Falls
- ⑥ Bow Lake
- ⑦ Columbia Icefield Discovery Centre
- **see** ⑧ Crowfoot Glacier
- ⑧ Crowfoot Mountain
- ⑨ Mt Edith Cavell

**SLEEPING**
- **see** ⑦ Glacier View Lodge
- ⑩ HI Beauty Creek Wilderness Hostel
- **see** ⑥ Lodge at Bow Lake
- ⑪ Sunwapta Falls Rocky Mountain Lodge

**EATING**
- **see** ⑥ Hanging Glacier Cafe
- ⑫ Mt Wilson Restaurant

# Magical Colors of Peyto Lake

## Summertime blues

Peyto Lake is 40km north of Lake Louise and one of the most popular stops on the Icefields Parkway. Only Moraine Lake makes it onto more magazine covers. Unlike other sights on the parkway, minimal hiking is required to see it. The viewing platform is a mere 15 minutes' walk from the Bow Summit parking lot, which recently reopened after significant infrastructure upgrades.

It's a lofty vantage point perched several hundred feet above the water and best visited in early morning, between the time the sun first illuminates the water and the first tour bus arrives.

# Mt Edith Cavell

## Jasper's most monumental mountain

Easily visible in the mid-distance from Jasper Town, **Mt Edith Cavell** (3363m) is one of the park's most distinctive and oft-visited peaks. The tallest mountain that's entirely in Alberta, it is known for its intimidating quartzite north face softened by

## WILD BILL PEYTO

You can't help logging Bill Peyto's face when you arrive in Banff. He's the rugged, steely-eyed gentleman who stares out from the 'Welcome to Banff' sign greeting visitors as they enter town. Born in England in 1869, Peyto came to Canada as a teenager and found work as a railway laborer for the CPR. But it was the Rocky Mountains that gave him his vocation. Peyto built a log cabin by the Bow River and set about reinventing himself as an outfitter and mountain guide for the park's early visitors. Cultivating a mystique as a man who loved solitude and simple backcountry living, he became a park warden, a position he held for nearly 30 years. His no-nonsense pioneering spirit has since become part of Banff folklore.

LARISSA DENNING/SHUTTERSTOCK ©

**Athabasca Falls, Jasper**

the presence of the so-called Angel Glacier, whose icy 'wings' fan out above the floral extravaganza of Cavell Meadows.

It's the meadows and the cracking (literally) glacier views that are the mountain's biggest attraction, all accessible via a winding, precipitous road that branches off the Icefields Pkwy 7km south of Jasper.

There are two hikes that depart from the end of the road both starting at the same trailhead. The **Path of the Glacier Loop** (1.6km) takes you through stunted trees on a well-built path to a viewpoint over small milky-blue Cavell Pond. The **Cavell Meadows trail** (8km) is longer and tougher, leading to two more dizzying viewpoints.

## Athabasca Falls

### Jasper's finest waterfall

Icefields aren't the only behemoths on the parkway. There's a duo of ferocious waterfalls too. The most dramatic is Athabasca Falls located on the namesake river, 30km south of Jasper

## WHERE TO STAY ON THE ICEFIELDS PKWY

**Sunwapta Falls Rocky Mountain Lodge**
Suites and lodge rooms with fireplaces or wood-burning stoves. South of Jasper. **$$$**

**HI Beauty Creek Wilderness Hostel**
Two small bunkrooms, propane-powered communal kitchen, tiny common room. **$**

**Glacier View Lodge**
Revamped hotel on the top floor of the Icefield Centre with panoramic glacier views. **$$$**

Town, a thunderous maelstrom of angry water that cuts deeply into the surrounding limestone rock, carving out an ever-changing patchwork of potholes, canyons and channels.

Winding pathways direct you toward multiple lookout points with views of the water in graphic close-up.

## Columbia Icefield

### The largest Rocky Mountains icefield

The Columbia is the largest icefield in the Rockies, feeding five major river systems and six glaciers, the most famous and accessible of which is **Athabasca Glacier**, which slides stealthily off the slopes of Mt Andromeda and Snowdome to within walking distance of the Icefields Pkwy.

Situated next to the parkway, close to the 'toe' of the Athabasca Glacier, the green-roofed **Columbia Icefield Discovery Centre** is the hub for all activities and a mini-museum to the Icefield's scientific significance. Decamp here to purchase tickets and board buses for the 'snocoaches' and Glacier Skywalk. You'll also find a hotel, cafeteria, restaurant, gift shop and Parks Canada information desk.

The most popular way to get on the glacier is via the **Columbia Icefield Adventure Tour**, which uses 56-seater 'snocoaches' to access the ice. The large hybrid bus-trucks grind a track onto the ice, where they stop to allow passengers to study the surface and take a billion selfies for around 20 minutes. Entertaining drivers offer jocular narrations. Tickets can be bought at the Discovery Centre or online; tours depart every 15 to 30 minutes.

## Glacier Skywalk

### Walking in the air

Opened in 2014 to ripples of architectural acclaim, this glass-floored, glass-sided, open-air lookout and walkway is suspended high above the Sunwapta River opposite Mt Kitchener, giving you the feeling of floating in midair over the valley. Numerous outdoor panels divulge the details of the surrounding geology, wildlife and architecture. The Skywalk must be visited via tour bus from the Columbia Icefield Discovery Centre, 6km to the south. Most people buy a combined Columbia Icefield Adventure-Glacier Skywalk ticket and are bused straight over to the Skywalk after getting off the Snocoaches.

### WONDER TRAIL

By 1911, Banff and Jasper were both busy national-park hubs equipped with railway stations. But to travel between the two towns still entailed a grueling three-week journey on horseback along the so-called 'Wonder Trail,' a rugged route first mapped out by surveyors marking the BC–Alberta border in the 1880s.

A long-dreamt-about road link through the mountains started to take shape in 1931 when Depression-era work gangs fashioned a 233km (146-mile) single-lane dirt road in a project that took nine years to complete. Opened in 1941, the pioneering 'parkway' served its purpose for 20 years before an increase in car traffic necessitated the building of a two-lane asphalt replacement along the same route. The modern Icefields Pkwy cut travel time down to 2½ hours.

### WHERE TO EAT ON THE ICEFIELDS PKWY

**Hanging Glacier Cafe**
New in 2023 on the shores of Bow Lake, this log cafe serves coffee, hot chocolate, sandwiches and beer. $

**Mt Wilson Restaurant**
The best eating option at the Crossing Resort does decent breakfasts and lunch, and buffets at dinnertime. $$

**Laggan's Mountain Bakery & Deli**
Grab fresh quiches and sausage rolls from this Lake Louise deli. $

# Jasper & Around

**BIKING, RAFTING, STARGAZING AND GLACIER-WALKING**

Edmonton

## GETTING AROUND

Jasper isn't as well serviced by public transport as Banff. Sundog Tours (sundogtours.com) run daily buses along Icefields Pkwy year-round and summer shuttles to and from the SkyTram. Maligne Adventures (maligneadventures. com) runs a summer hikers' shuttle to/from Maligne Lake.

## ☑ TOP TIP

Jasper Town is significantly smaller than Banff with no capacity to expand. As a result, its limited hotel and hostel rooms fill up quickly in summer, as do the cabins, bungalows and campgrounds in the surrounding countryside. Book well in advance between May and September.

Take Banff, stretch its borders, remove over half its tourists, sprinkle it with a bit more wildlife and endow it with a coarser, slightly more rugged edge and you've got Jasper. The less famous of the two main Rocky Mountain parks is sometimes (wrongly) regarded as a latecomer to the ball – it was designated 22 years after Banff but was still Canada's sixth national park when it was founded in 1907.

In some ways the park seems like a northern extension of Banff. The two conjoined areas have several commonalities: sizeable townsites, alpine ski resorts, hot springs and a rambunctious history connected to the trans-continental railroad. They also share the Columbia Icefield and the Icefields Pkwy, the spectacular road that cuts through northern Banff and southern Jasper like a Rocky Mountains rollercoaster. But overall, Jasper is a larger and wilder beast, with expansive tracts of gritty backcountry demanding detailed exploration.

## Following the Discovery Trail

### Jasper's quintessential orientation hike

Jasper's definitive 'urban' walking trail completely circumnavigates the town on a part paved, part rustic path that's split into three sections focusing on the town's natural, historical and railroad legacies. A wealth of fact-packed interpretive boards dotted along the route provide an educational introduction to both the town and national park.

You can jump on the 8km loop at any point along its course, although the best place to start is the **Discovery Trail info kiosk** at the foot of Pyramid Lake Rd, north of the train station.

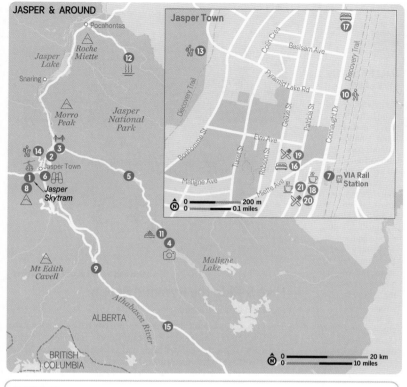

**HIGHLIGHTS**
1 Jasper Skytram

**SIGHTS**
2 Annette Lake
3 Fifth Bridge
see 6 Jasper Planetarium
see 3 Maligne Canyon
4 Maligne Lake
5 Medicine Lake
6 Old Fort Point
7 Rocky Mountaineer

8 Whistlers

**ACTIVITIES, COURSES & TOURS**
9 Athabasca River
10 Discovery Trail info kiosk
11 Maligne Lake Cruise
see 11 Mary Schäffer Loop
12 Miette Hot Springs
13 Mina & Riley Lakes Loop Trailhead

see 11 Moose Lake Loop
14 Pyramid Bench
15 Sunwapta River
see 6 Valley of the Five Lakes Trail

**SLEEPING**
16 Athabasca Hotel
17 Crimson
see 6 Jasper Park Lodge
see 6 Mt Robson Inn

**EATING**
see 3 Maligne Canyon Wilderness Kitchen
18 Other Paw
19 Bistro
20 Spice Joint Lounge
see 17 Terra
see 6 Wicked Cup

**DRINKING & NIGHTLIFE**
21 SnowDome Coffee Bar

 **WHERE TO MOUNTAIN BIKE AROUND JASPER**

**Overland Trail**
This flat historic trail parallels Hwy 16, passing an early-20th-century homestead en route.

**Pyramid Trail**
A speedy downhill jaunt from Pyramid Lake to Jasper Town on bumpy forest paths.

**Saturday Night Loop**
A technical 27km ride through a root-ridden and sometimes swampy forest, with plenty of nature-watching opportunities.

## VALLEY OF THE FIVE LAKES

If Jasper does one thing better than Banff – and every other Canadian national park – it's off-road mountain biking. The park's intricate network of trails fanning out from the central hub of Jasper Town is extensive, well maintained and incredibly varied. Its crowning glory? A scenic two-wheeled odyssey known as the Valley of the Five Lakes.

This technically challenging 27km loop is not for beginners. Get ready to be taken on a hair-raising journey over sinuous singletrack, bone-rattling rocks, sudden drops, abrupt inclines and twisted roots.

Like most of Jasper's best bike trails, the **Five Lakes** loop is easily accessible from the townsite via trail number 1, which cuts around the back of the mega-popular **Old Fort Point**.

SANDYS/SHUTTERSTOCK ©

**Mina and Riley Lakes Loop, Jasper**

## Hike & Ride the Pyramid Bench

### Plateau lakes and trails

The elevated plateau immediately northwest of Jasper Town is often referred to as the Pyramid Bench, a lattice of forested trails, diminutive lakes and reedy sloughs (swampy areas) that's refreshingly accessible from the townsite without a car – just choose your preferred trailhead and keep walking.

This is Jasper's all-season playground, the cherished domain of mountain bikers, hikers, snowshoers and horse-riders all sharing the same mouth-watering landscapes.

The Bench's two major lakes are accessed via the winding 6km-long Pyramid Lake Rd, the area's only paved thoroughfare that dead-ends just beyond the deluxe Pyramid Lake Resort.

The network of trails is well mapped with copious clearly numbered paths. A good first-day orientation hike is the 9km **Mina and Riley Lakes Loop** (trail number 8) that leaves from the northwest corner of the Jasper-Yellowhead Museum parking lot and climbs into a lake-speckled mini-wilderness where you'll spot ptarmigan, Barrow's goldeneye ducks and loons gliding across the green surface of the water.

## WHERE TO GO FOR COFFEE AND CAKE IN JASPER TOWN

**Other Paw**
Go on a long enough hike and you can easily justify the epic cakes at this well-loved cafe opposite the train tracks. $

**Wicked Cup**
Coffee, cake and more substantial snacks can be savored on a pretty patio at the quiet end of Connaught Ave. $$

**SnowDome Coffee Bar**
The best coffee in Jasper is served in the unlikely confines of the local launderette. $

# Stargazing in a Dark Sky Preserve
### Studying the Rocky Mountains' skies

Stargazing in Jasper has a long history dating back to ancient traditions practiced by Indigenous people. David Thompson, one of the area's earliest European explorers, was an expert surveyor and astronomer nicknamed Koo-Koo-Sint, or 'stargazer' by the First Nations.

Interest in outer space was ignited in 2011 when the park was named a 'Dark Sky Preserve' by the Royal Astronomical Society of Canada. In the years since, Jasper has held a Dark Sky Festival every October, hosting a diverse schedule of events, including visits from well-known astronomers and starlit musical concerts.

The **Jasper Planetarium** (jasperplanetarium.com) is bivouacked in an unusual inflatable structure at the Jasper Park Lodge. The 40-capacity auditorium runs regularly scheduled audiovisual shows about Jasper's night sky and offers the opportunity to steal a glance through the largest telescope in the Rockies.

# Ascending the Whistlers
### Instant alpine access

While Banff has three different gondola options, Jasper offers just one, an aerial tramway that utilizes a slightly different technology to its southern cousins, shunting two large passenger cabins up and down a moving cable to which they are fixed. The **Jasper Skytram** (jasperskytram.com) is the largest and highest of its type in Canada and whips visitors up the steep slopes of the Whistlers, a 2470m mountain 7km southwest of Jasper townsite, in a brisk seven minutes.

The Skytram doesn't actually call at the summit. For that you'll have to hike 1.3km further up the rocky ridge where 75km views justify the energy expenditure.

# Getting in Hot Water
### Keeping warm in the wilderness

The hottest springs (hotsprings.ca/miette) in the Canadian Rockies are ejected from deep beneath the Sulphur Skyline at a scalding 54°C (129°F) before being cooled to a more bearable 40°C in the pools of **Miette Hot Springs'** modern aquacourt. There is a warm pool, a hot pool and a couple of icy ones to get the heart racing – so it's a good idea to test

## LAKE ANNETTE

One in a necklace of diminutive lakes that graces the Athabasca River Valley east of Jasper Town, Lake Annette is hailed for its beach – a godsend in landlocked Alberta – and numerous picnic spots that entertain the crowds in summer. Short and narrow and backed by a large grassy area, the thin sweep of yellowish sand is popular on hot days when footsore hikers drop by to cool off.

As this is Jasper, you might want to pack some bear spray alongside your blow-up raft: grizzlies are sometimes spotted in the area, while elk and mule deer provide more innocuous company.

## WHERE TO STAY IN JASPER TOWN

**Athabasca Hotel**
No-frills centrally located hotel with shared bathrooms, decent prices and on-site bar and restaurant. **$$**

**Crimson**
Jasper's snazziest option is modern with an indoor pool and gym and one of Jasper's best restaurants. **$$$**

**Mt Robson Inn**
Jasper motel on the western edge of town with plush Jacuzzi suites and substantial breakfasts. **$$$**

## ASK AN EXPERT

**Kim Weir**, Product Development Officer, Jasper National Park

**Favourite day-hike in Jasper?**
Wilcox Pass. Since you begin at such a high elevation, you get far-reaching views almost right away. The viewpoint over the Athabasca Glacier is only a few kilometers up. After that, you're hiking to the pass through alpine meadows. The flowers can be unreal.

**See any wildlife?**
We almost always see bighorn sheep on this hike. We've also seen mountain goats a few times.

**Tips for first timers?**
If you're not used to hiking or being at this elevation (above 2000m), pace yourself, especially at the start.

**Where to eat afterwards?**
A picnic at Mt Christie on the way back to town! Great peak views and the river is right below. Nice place to chill.

**Rocky Mountaineer train, Jasper**

the water first before attempting a belly flop. Swimsuits and towels can be rented at the complex.

The modern facilities have a laidback natural ambience and are generally less crowded than Banff. On balmy summer days, the craggy mountains opposite look resplendent and close enough to touch, In fall, the pools are equally pretty when snow drifts in and steam envelops the assembled bathers.

It has an on-site gift shop and a cafe with a blackboard menu of wraps and paninis.

## Jasper by Train

### A spectacular arrival

Despite the late arrival of the railway in the northern Rockies, Jasper has always been more of a train town than Banff. The line runs directly through the town center where kilometer-long freight trains regularly hold up traffic and a cross-continental passenger service operated by VIA-Rail (viarail.ca/en) still stops at the historic station twice a week. Jasper is also the terminus for a separate thrice-weekly service to Prince Rupert on the BC coast.

For a more substantial fee, it's possible to ride with the private **Rocky Mountaineer** (rockymountaineer.com) along the same route but in a ritzier train that stops overnight in Kamloops to maximize mountain-viewing time. The Vancouver–Jasper route, called 'Journey Through the Clouds,' offers a specially curated package with professional guides and fine dining.

# Legendary Jasper Park Lodge

### Smart hotel beside attractive lake

Within golf-putting distance of Lac Beauvert and surrounded by manicured grounds and rugged mountain peaks, this classic national park lodge (fairmont.com/jasper), owned by the Fairmont group, is less showy than its Banff and Lake Louise counterparts. Eschewing the Renaissance Revival architecture of other grand railway hotels, its 1920s builders designed it as a diffused resort made up of individual log cabins surrounding a larger central lodge.

The aptly named Lac Beauvert (literally 'beautiful green' in French) is an all-season recreation lake popular for boating in the summer and ice-skating in winter when it's smoothed over by a Zamboni. There's a boathouse beside the lake along with a challenging Stanley Thompson–designed golf course attached to the Jasper Park Lodge. Shoes and clubs can be rented at the hotel.

# Climb Old Fort Point

### Short walk up a steep hill

You won't find any old forts atop this roche moutonnée – a bedrock knob shaped by glaciers – just south of Jasper Town. Rather, the name refers to the likely site of an erstwhile fur-trading post known as Henry House thought to have been built here in 1811 by William Henry, a colleague of Canadian-British explorer David Thompson. It was abandoned soon after and nothing visible remains today.

Instead, the hill has become one of Jasper Town's favorite local hikes, easily reachable on foot from the townsite and instantly rewarding with its broad mountain-studded vista across the Athabasca River Valley. The 4km loop starts in a parking lot beside a truss bridge that spans a majestic bend in the braided Athabasca River. Take the wooden stairway that ascends a tall crag overlooking the river.

# Delve into Maligne Canyon

### Steep cliffs, gushing water

One of Jasper's signature sights, **Maligne Canyon**, 8km northeast of Jasper Town, is a year-round attraction with two very different faces. From May to December, it's an attractive riverside hike that threads over half-a-dozen bridges with sheer drops into the abyss below. From December to May, it's an eerie stroll through a gorge full of ice sculptures and frozen waterfalls that are beloved by ice-climbers.

## MEDICINE LAKE

A geological rarity, Medicine Lake, 20km south of Jasper on the Maligne Lake Rd, is not technically a lake at all, but the point where the Maligne River disappears underground for several kilometers as a 'losing stream' before converging with the Athabasca River.

The water is absorbed into the ground through a series of small holes. When glacial meltwater is high in the summer, the holes aren't large enough to absorb all the water and the broad river valley clogs up like a slow-draining sink in need of some bleach. The back-up of water results in the formation of Medicine Lake, a shallow body of water that can measure up to 7km in length when it appears in late spring.

## WHERE TO EAT IN JASPER TOWN

**Terra**
Exceptional farm-to-table food in the Crimson Hotel offering gourmet salt-of-the-earth dishes in a casual setting. $$

**Spice Joint Lounge**
Jamaican-influenced food including jerk chicken wraps, Red Stripe beer and Blue Mountain coffee. $

**Raven Bistro**
Affordable fine dining in small European-style bistro. Vegetable-forward dishes with a Mediterranean bias. $$$

## RAFTING IN JASPER

Whitewater rafting is a Jasper specialty. There are two main rivers inside the park boundaries deemed rough enough for adrenalin-charged boat trips, both abutting Icefields Pkwy.

The **Athabasca River** is usually tackled downstream of Athabasca Falls where the mildly choppy water is graded as class II and deemed safe for beginners and families with kids.

The **Sunwapta River**, a tributary of the Athabasca, is an altogether wilder beast. Between its headwaters on the Athabasca Glacier and turbulent Sunwapta Falls, the river throws up class III rapids at its roughest point. Previous experience and an adventurous spirit are recommended in this neck of the woods. Rafting trips can be organized in Jasper Town with several agencies who charge generic prices. The season runs May to September.

The canyon is crossed by six bridges. The first was built in 1914. The newest, **Fifth Bridge**, opened in 2015 replacing an older model damaged in a flood.

The area is most easily accessed from the parking area on Maligne Lake Rd, near First Bridge, where you'll find the **Maligne Canyon Wilderness Kitchen**, a well-appointed eating joint on the site of a former teahouse.

# A Watery Wilderness

### Cruising or kayaking on Maligne Lake

**Maligne Lake** is the largest natural lake in the Rocky Mountains parks and only slightly smaller than artificially enhanced Lake Minnewanka in Banff.

Its appeal is legendary. The classic photo of Spirit Island situated two-thirds of the way along the lake's course is world famous. The sapphire hue of the water and the craning circle of glaciated mountains in the background only adds to the romance.

The easiest way to see the lake is on expensive summer **boat cruises** run by Pursuit (banffjaspercollection.com), who also manage Banff's Lake Minnewanka cruises. There are a couple of tour options ranging from 1½ to two hours. Neither are cheap.

Abutting the lake's north shore are two hiking trails, the short **Mary Schäffer** and **Moose Lake** loops, both within 15 minutes of the day-lodge car park.

**Spirit Island, Maligne Lake, Jasper**

# TOOLKIT

The chapters in this section cover the most important topics you'll need to know about in British Columbia & the Canadian Rockies. They're full of nuts-and-bolts information and valuable insights to help you understand and navigate British Columbia & the Canadian Rockies and get the most out of your trip.

**Arriving**
**p234**

**Getting Around**
**p235**

**Money**
**p236**

**Accommodations**
**p237**

**Family Travel**
**p238**

**Health & Safe Travel**
**p239**

**Food, Drink & Nightlife**
**p240**

**Responsible Travel**
**p242**

**LGBTiQ+ Travelers p244**

**Accessible Travel**
**p245**

**How to See the Northern Lights**
**p246**

**Nuts & Bolts**
**p247**

# Arriving

Vancouver International Airport (YVR) is the main entry point for visitors to British Columbia. Most visitors access the Canadian Rockies via Calgary International Airport (YYC) or Edmonton International Airport (YEG). Erik Nielsen Whitehorse International Airport (YXY) is the main entry point for visitors to the Yukon.

### Visas

Most travelers need a visa or an Electronic Travel Authorization (eTA) to enter Canada. American and Canadian citizens only need a valid passport.

### Border Crossing

Airport arrival kiosks and eGates are located at most major airports in Canada. If you arrive at an airport without this service, you must fill out a declaration card and present it to a border services officer.

### Wi-fi

Free wi-fi is available at all international airports in Canada. Most hotels, restaurants, shopping malls and coffee shops also offer free wi-fi.

### SIM Cards

A prepaid SIM card can be purchased at some international airports, in convenience stores and mobile provider stores. If your mobile phone supports eSIM cards, that can be less costly than a traditional SIM card.

## Public Transport from Airport to City Center

| | Vancouver | Calgary | Edmonton | Whitehorse |
|---|---|---|---|---|
| **TRAIN** | 26min $9.25 | N/A | N/A | N/A |
| **BUS** | N/A | 40min $11 | 60min $10 | 10 min $3 |
| **TAXI** | 30min $30 | 25min $45 | 35min $60 | 10min $25 |

## ELECTRONIC TRAVEL AUTHORIZATION (ETA)

Visa-exempt foreign nationals can apply for an eTA to visit Canada. It's a simple online application that costs $7. Most applicants get their approval within minutes, but it can take several days. The eTA is linked to a particular passport and is valid for up to five years. If you get a new passport number or enter the passport number incorrectly, you will need a new eTA. Citizens from select visa-required countries may also be eligible to apply for an eTA instead of a visa if arriving by air. Top Tip: Confirm the passport number on your eTA matches your passport number when you receive it by email.

# Getting Around

Major cities have good public transportation networks, but having a vehicle gives you more freedom to explore the Canadian Rockies and other places outside cities.

## TRAVEL COSTS

Car rental
**$40 per day**

Gasoline
**$1.93 per litre**

EV charging
**$4 per 100km**

All-day Vancouver transit pass
**$11.25**

## Urban Public Transportation

Major Canadian cities have extensive public transit systems that are relatively easy to navigate. Many also have bike and e-scooter sharing programs and extensive rail systems. Parking in large urban centers can be expensive and challenging. It's often easier to get around on public transit.

## Taxis

Traditional taxi companies and Uber are both available in Canada's major cities. Taxi rates are regulated by city bylaws and they vary slightly from city to city. Applicable rates are listed on a company's website.

**TIP**

Cell phones must be used hands free in Canada. A distracted driving ticket for texting and driving will cost $300 or more.

## RIGHT LANE CONSIDERATIONS

On multilane highways, the right lane is used for slower-moving traffic and the left lane is used for passing and for faster-moving traffic. Keep an eye on traffic behind you if you are in the left lane and move to the right lane to allow faster-moving vehicles to pass. In urban centers, you can turn right on a red light if you are in the right-hand lane – unless there is a sign indicating otherwise.

## DRIVING ESSENTIALS

Drive on the right and pass on the left

**50**

Speed limit is typically 50 km/h in urban areas and 90–100 km/h on highways

**.08**

Blood alcohol limit is 0.08%

### Renting a Car

For the best rate, book well in advance and then recheck the price a couple of months before to see if the rate has gone down. In general, renters must be over 21 years of age and have a credit card. Most rentals have an automatic transmission.

### Road Conditions

Road construction is common during the warmer weather months. Watch for reduced speed signs in construction areas. For snowy and icy driving conditions in winter, drive slowly and leave plenty of distance between vehicles. Keep your windows clear of ice and your gas tank at least half full in winter.

### Buses

There are buses that can take you from Calgary International Airport to Banff ($79 one way), Edmonton International Airport to Jasper ($99 one way) and Vancouver International Airport to Whistler ($110 one way) as well as other destinations. It's best to book in advance.

# Money

## CURRENCY: CANADIAN DOLLAR ($)

### Credit Cards

Credit cards are widely accepted in Canada and most merchants can accept digital tap payments from mobile phones and smart watches. If given the option to pay in the local currency or your home currency, always pay in local currency. Most credit cards charge additional fees for paying in your home currency.

### ATMs

ATMs are widely available in Canada. You'll find them in banks, shopping centers, hotels and other locations. Stay alert and aware of your surroundings when using an ATM late at night. Private ATMs not affiliated with a bank may charge higher user fees.

### Currency Exchange

Currency exchange counters are located at international airports and can be found in major cities and tourist destinations. Most larger banks can exchange currency, and rates are usually better. US dollars are often accepted in tourist towns such as Victoria, Whistler and Banff, but rates are typically not very favorable.

### HOW MUCH FOR A...

national park admission
**$10.50**

fast food hamburger
**$6**

museum entrance
**$20**

large pizza
**$30**

### HOW TO... SAVE Some Dollars

Low Season: travel in late spring or fall to save money on accommodations.
Get Out of Town: accommodations on the edge of town or in a neighboring community usually cost less.
Free Stuff: there are many amazing hikes and attractions that are completely free.
Pack a Picnic: a picnic is romantic, fun and usually less costly than a restaurant meal.

### LOCAL TIP

Canadian one dollar coins are locally called Loonies and two dollar coins are called Toonies. A picture of a water bird called a loon on the one dollar coin led to the nicknames.

### PAYING THE BILL

It's a good idea to ask a restaurant to give you a physical bill. Most restaurants do not automatically add a gratuity, but a few do – especially for larger groups. Tipping is generally expected when dining in a restaurant. It is customary to tip 15% to 20% of the bill before tax, but some establishments have a default setting that suggests a higher tip. Don't be afraid to click the button to pay a custom amount. You may choose to tip less if the service was poor or more if exceptional.

# Accommodations

## Hostels

There are hostels in major cities as well as in towns in the Canadian Rockies. You can get a dorm room or a room with a private en suite and the amenities of a hotel room at a much lower rate.

## Backcountry Lodges

Well off the beaten path, backcountry lodges offer a touch of luxury in high alpine areas that are only accessed by hiking, horseback riding, skiing or helicopter. Lodge accommodations typically include comfy beds, hot meals, flush toilets and hot showers. Some travelers use backcountry lodges as a base to hike further into backcountry areas that are normally only accessible to backpackers.

## B&Bs

Staying in a cozy bed and breakfast has its perks including a hot breakfast, a comfortable bed and a property with distinct character. These properties are operated by friendly locals who are happy to share tips about area attractions and restaurants. Some B&Bs have rooms with shared bathrooms, while others have private en suites.

## Airbnb

You'll find Airbnb accommodations throughout Canada and the options are vast. You can rent a fully equipped yurt, a cabin in the mountains, an apartment in the city or a house by a lake. Ensure a good stay by booking properties with good reviews and a superhost symbol. Always check the cancellation policy.

### HOW MUCH FOR A NIGHT IN...

a hostel dorm
$50

comfort camping
$140

a grand railway hotel
$450–800

## Camping

There is a wide range of camping options that range from modest facilities for tents with pit toilets to large complexes with flush toilets, electricity, wi-fi, showers, playgrounds, camp stores and comfort camping facilities. There are facilities operated by national parks, provincial parks and private companies. Camping equipment can be rented if you don't have it. You can also book a comfort camping facility like a tent or cabin with beds, tables, electricity and barbecues.

## GRAND RAILWAY HOTELS

Canada's grand railway hotels are bucket list historic properties built by the railways from the late 1800s to the 1950s to attract visitors to Canada. These historic properties have been compared to French châteaus and Scottish castles. The Fairmont Banff Springs, for example, is known as 'the Castle in the Rockies.' These historic properties are located in very desirable locations and tend to offer high-end amenities like luxury spas, fine dining, golf, mountain shuttles, concierge service and other features.

# Family Travel

British Columbia, Alberta, Yukon and the Canadian Rockies are filled with national and provincial parks, which are ideal family travel destinations. In these parks, there is amazing scenery, wildlife, family-friendly hikes and programs specifically designed for kids. In cities and towns in this region, you'll find wonderful attractions and hands-on museums that capture the imagination.

## Parks Canada Xplorers

Keep kids busy and happy by having them become Xplorers. Make the visitor center your first stop in national parks. Children will receive an Xplorers booklet filled with fun kid-friendly activities and information. The guide is unique to each national park. At the end of the visit, kids receive an official collectable souvenir that recognizes them as Xplorers. They can collect one for each national park they visit.

## Discounts

Admission to all national parks, national historic sites and national marine conservation areas operated by Parks Canada is provided free of charge to youths and children under the age of 17. Discounted admission for children and youths under the age of 18 is also available at most attractions. Many attractions have family rates that can also be a savings.

### Facilities to Reserve

Most hotels have cribs and cots. Car seats are compulsory for children under age six or until they weigh more than 18kg. In British Columbia, booster seats are compulsory for children under the age of nine or under 145cm tall.

### Sightseeing

The journey is part of the adventure. Stop at scenic lakes to let kids learn to skip rocks and dip their toes. Watch for wildlife while you're driving. Stop at waterfalls and take short hikes. Have a picnic at a scenic spot.

### KID-FRIENDLY PICKS

**Royal Tyrrell Museum (p164)**
Brings the prehistoric past to life with hands-on activities, educational programs and an extensive display of dinosaur fossils.

**Fort Edmonton Park (p179)**
The largest living history museum in Canada has costumed interpreters and fun activities for kids.

**Stanley Park (p62)**
Vancouver's largest urban park has four playgrounds, a miniature train, a waterpark, a swimming pool, beaches, a bike path and more.

**Sleigh ride**
Hear sleigh bells ring during the winter in Whistler, Banff, Lake Louise or Jasper.

## HIKING WITH KIDS

Whether you're pushing a stroller, hiking with a little one who tires out quickly or you're looking for a hike that will challenge and excite a teenager, you'll find trails to suit in national and provincial parks. Make the visitor center your first stop in any park for great advice on family-friendly trails. Bring along plenty of water, snacks and extra layers of clothing in case the weather changes. Keep your distance from wildlife and always carry bear spray. A small set of binoculars can let you see birds and other wildlife from a distance and kids love using them.

# Health & Safe Travel

## Wildlife Viewing

Observing wildlife is fascinating. If you see wildlife by the road, slow down. Pull over if there's enough room on the shoulder. Turn on hazard lights and stay in the vehicle. Watch for a few moments, take a photo and move on. If a wildlife jam develops, it's best to move on. Never feed or entice wildlife to come closer. It's unsafe and can lead to a $25,000 fine.

## Healthcare Facilities

Canada has an excellent healthcare system. Pharmacists can advise on medical matters and may even be able to prescribe medications for minor illnesses. There are also walk-in clinics for more serious issues and hospitals for emergency care. Make sure you have adequate medical insurance that is valid in Canada before you leave home.

### TAP WATER

Tap water is safe to drink in Canada, unless otherwise indicated. Using a refillable water bottle is a safe, environmentally responsible choice.

## WILDFIRES

Check provincial and national park websites for wildfire updates and follow the guidance from local authorities – including fire bans and restrictions. Provincial and territorial governments have a tiered fire ban system that helps to reduce the number of human-caused wildfires when the risk is high. Sometimes roads are closed and air quality advisories are issued when smoke from wildfires causes harmful air pollution.

## FIRE RISK

| Low | Moderate | High | Extreme |
|---|---|---|---|
| controlled campfires and other activities allowed | campfires allowed; take precautions | campfires are typically allowed with precautions | open campfires are prohibited |

## Hiking Safely

In mountainous regions and at higher elevations, weather can change quickly. Always dress in layers and carry extra clothes in a backpack. Carry water, snacks and bear spray when you're out on trails. Make plenty of noise and be aware of your surroundings. It's always safer to hike in a group than by yourself. Hike after breakfast and before dinner.

### CANNABIS

Travelers in BC, Alberta and Yukon who are 18 or older are legally allowed to purchase and consume cannabis in accordance with federal and provincial laws. But it is illegal to bring cannabis with you when you enter or leave Canada. Like alcohol, cannabis should be used responsibly. It is illegal to drive a motorized vehicle while under the influence of cannabis.

# Food, Drink & Nightlife

## When to Eat

**Breakfast** (7am to 10am) Coffee, juice, fruit, cereal, toast, bagels, yogurt, eggs, bacon, sausages, hash browns and pancakes are typical breakfast foods.

**Lunch** (Noon to 2pm) Lunch is usually simple and light – soup, sandwiches, salad and similar items.

**Dinner** (5pm to 8pm) Dinner tends to be more hearty featuring a meat main, vegetables, salad and a starch such as rice, pasta or potatoes.

## Rocky Mountain Cuisine

Rocky Mountain cuisine can be experienced in the Canadian Rockies regions in Alberta and British Columbia as well as in Montana, Idaho, Colorado, Utah and Wyoming. It features game meats like bison, elk, venison, moose, wild boar and pheasant as well as fresh fish like trout or Arctic char served alongside locally sourced vegetables and berries. Alberta is well known for high-quality beef and that has found its way onto menus in restaurants in the Alberta Rockies.

### HOW TO ORDER A COFFEE IN CANADA

Canadians love coffee and Tim Hortons is by far the most popular chain of coffee shops. Tim Hortons was founded in Hamilton, Ontario in 1964 by Tim Horton, a National Hockey League legend, and today there are nearly 4000 restaurants across the country. The Tim Hortons chain is so influential it has influenced Canadian coffee lingo. If you ask for a double double at a Tim Hortons restaurant (or any other coffee shop in Canada), they will know you're asking for a large coffee with two creams and two sugars. It's become part of the Canadian vernacular. If you want to sound like a local, call the restaurant Timmies instead of saying Tim Hortons. It's not the only place to get coffee in Canada; you'll also find Starbucks and many great independent coffee shops.

**HOW TO...**

### Enjoy British Columbia Wine

British Columbia is one of Canada's top wine-producing regions. The province is home to more than 325 licensed grape wineries, many of which have won prestigious international awards. Canada's cold winters and short growing seasons allow for the production of exceptional sparkling wines and icewines.

When you're traveling through BC, stop and explore some of the wineries. Most have tasting rooms and some also have on-site restaurants.

The Thompson Okanagan region has more than 120 vineyards and is considered the northernmost wine region in the world. The cool climate is ideal for producing pinot gris, riesling, pinot noir and other varieties.

There are wonderful wine festivals in British Columbia as well as several wine tours. There are also apple orchards nearby and a bustling cider industry. Look for BC wines on menus right across Canada – even the most passionate wine lover will find a vintage to love.

## HOW MUCH FOR A...

coffee
$3

beer
$5

small ice cream cone
$3

muffin or croissant
$2

large pizza
$25

lunch at a fast food restaurant
$12

dinner main at a fancy restaurant
$50

---

 **HOW TO...**

### Find a Great Microbrewery

Canada's brewery scene is booming. Microbreweries are found right across the country in big cities as well as sleepy little towns. There are curated craft beer itineraries, also known as ale trails, that will take you to award-winning breweries in different regions. Whether you want to walk from brewery to brewery in a city or enjoy a tour and tasting at an off-the-beaten path country brewery, there are plenty of options. If you're traveling with someone who is under the legal drinking age or someone who simply doesn't like beer, choose a brewery that also produces great craft sodas and has an on-site restaurant.

For many years, the craft brewing industry was suppressed in Canada by antiquated regulations tied to prohibition. Simplified regulations, improved brewing technology and consumer demand led to the microbrewery scene Canada is enjoying today.

In British Columbia, there are ale trails in Vancouver, Vancouver Island, Kootenay Rockies, Thompson Okanagan and Northern BC. You'll find many microbreweries in Calgary and Edmonton, Alberta's two largest cities. There are also ale trails in the Alberta Rockies, Crowsnest Pass, the Central Prairies and Red Deer County.

Whatever your preference you'll find a microbrewery that makes a drink you'll enjoy.

Fast Fact: in BC and the Yukon, the legal drinking age is 19. In Alberta, the legal drinking age is 18. It is illegal to drive in Canada with a blood alcohol concentration (BAC) of 0.08% or more.

---

### INDIGENOUS CUISINE

Indigenous cuisine is rich in tradition and history and it's experiencing a resurgence in Canada's culinary scene. First Nations, Inuit and Métis Peoples in Canada have long used seasonal local ingredients from the land and the water. Indigenous people lived in balance with nature, respected all forms of life and used every part of an animal by practicing no waste, nose-to-tail cooking.

Historically, recipes and cooking techniques were passed down from generation to generation, but there was a disruption for the Indigenous Peoples of Canada. Between the 1870s and the 1990s, Indigenous children aged four to 16 were taken from their homes and forced to attend Indian Residential Schools. Generations of Indigenous people grew up eating institutional food most of the year rather than enjoying traditional foods and learning how to prepare them. Residential schools had a devastating effect. Indigenous people lost their language and their connection to family, culture and traditions – including culinary traditions.

The resurgence of Indigenous cuisine in Canada's culinary scene is long overdue. It is a manifestation of the reconciliation process – the work the people of Canada are doing to renew the relationship with Indigenous Peoples.

Indigenous restaurants and food trucks are popping up right across Canada making delicious and interesting food. In many cases, chefs put a modern twist on traditional foods like bison, elk, salmon, berries, vegetables and herbs. Bannock, a type of fried bread, is also a common food in Indigenous cuisine. When Indigenous people were moved to reservations, they were given flour rations and they used the flour to make this simple food that was cooked on an open fire.

# Responsible Travel

### Climate Change & Travel

It's impossible to ignore the impact we have when traveling, and the importance of making changes where we can. Lonely Planet urges all travelers to engage with their travel carbon footprint. There are many carbon calculators online that allow travelers to estimate the carbon emissions generated by their journey; try resurgence.org/resources/carbon-calculator. html. Many airlines and booking sites offer travelers the option of offsetting the impact of greenhouse gas emissions by contributing to climate-friendly initiatives around the world. We continue to off set the carbon footprint of all Lonely Planet staff travel, while recognizing this is a mitigation more than a solution.

### Sustainable Transportation

Reduce the number of cars on the road by taking public transportation. You'll find excellent public transportation in major cities and in Whistler and Banff.

### Ethical Wildlife Viewing

Respect wildlife and stay a safe distance away to protect both yourself and the animal. If you see wildlife near a road, stay in your vehicle. Never feed, entice or disturb a wild animal.

Farmers markets are found right across Canada. They offer fresh, seasonal, locally grown food directly from the people who produce it. You'll also find crafts and art by local artisans.

Look for Indigenous art and crafts at gift shops at Indigenous attractions and at shops in cities and towns. You'll find unique souvenirs and purchasing them helps to support the artisans who create them.

### SHOP LOCAL

Tourism dollars really make a difference in small communities. Purchasing souvenirs and other items from small local shops selling items made by local artisans may also give you a more authentic and unique shopping experience.

## REDUCE WASTE

You'll find compost and recycle bins in many communities. These initiatives help reduce the amount of waste in landfill sites.

### Leave No Trace

When you spend time in nature, follow 'leave no trace' principles. Pack out everything that you take into a place. Keep your campsite clean to prevent attracting wildlife. Make memories and take pictures.

### Sustainable Accommodations

The Green Key Program (greenkeyglobal.com) is a voluntary program promoted by the Hotel Association of Canada (hotelassociation.ca) that recognizes hotels and other lodgings that are taking steps to reduce environmental impacts.

### Walking & Cycling

Walking and cycling is a great way to get to know a destination. Many cities and towns have excellent trails and bicycle or scooter rental programs to facilitate green transportation choices.

### Reuse

Many hotels and lodges have programs in place that allow guests to reuse towels and bedding. If you leave a towel on the floor, you want it changed. If you hang it up, you are willing to use it again.

### Eat Local

Small independent restaurants often offer a more authentic local dining experience than larger chain restaurants.

Get a fascinating tour and an Indigenous cultural experience by taking an Indigenous ecotour.

This fully automated rapid transit system is fast and convenient and offers travel along three lines.

# 20th

Canada ranked 20th globally out of 162 countries on sustainable development by the Sustainable Development Solutions Network (sdgindex.org). The index and ranking is based on the United Nations' 17 Sustainable Development Goals.

## RESOURCES

**natureconservancy.ca**
Canada's leading national land conservation organization.

**cwf-fcf.org**
The Canadian Wildlife Federation works to conserve Canada's wildlife.

**ducks.ca**
Ducks Unlimited Canada promotes waterfowl habitat conservation in Canada.

# ⭐ LGBTIQ+ Travelers

Canada is diverse and safe for LGBTIQ+ visitors. In 2005, Canada became the fourth country in the world to legalize same-sex marriage nationwide. It's also a nation that is proud and supportive of its LGBTIQ+ residents and communities holding some of the largest pride festivals and events in the world. Vancouver's annual pride parade is the largest in Western Canada, attended by more than 650,000 people.

## Vancouver's Davie Village

Located in the West End area of Vancouver, Davie Village is a vibrant gay district with buzzing bars and clubs, quirky fashion boutiques and LGBTIQ+ bookstores. It's known internationally for its thriving community located on Davie St between Burrard St and Jervis St and encompasses the side streets of the area as well. Grab a coffee and take a stroll on the Rainbow Crosswalk. Join a bingo game hosted by a drag queen. Visit a dance club, a sports bar or a multicultural restaurant.

### CELEBRATE PRIDE

Pride festivals happen across Canada. There's typically a pride parade as well as a festival that includes a diverse collection of vendors, entertainment, family activities and beer gardens. Pride festivals are typically very inclusive. Even if you don't consider yourself to be anywhere on the LGBTIQ+ spectrum, you're welcome to attend most events and show your support.

### Clubbing

Vancouver has a lively clubbing scene in Davie Village and even though Kelowna, Calgary and Edmonton do not have gay villages, you'll still find LGBTIQ+-friendly spots for a night out. This includes Friends of Dorothy Lounge in Kelowna, Infinity Ultra Lounge in Calgary and Evolution Wonderlounge in Edmonton.

### QUEER WALKING TOURS

Forbidden Vancouver (forbiddenvancouver.ca) offers a variety of unusual and fascinating walking tours including one called the Really Gay History Tour, which celebrates unsung heroes who changed Vancouver and Canada. It includes stories about drag queens, two spirit warriors, queer church ministers, transgender crime fighters and more.

### PRIDE EVENT DATES

Some visitors plan their trip around pride events. Here are the dates for some of the key ones in British Columbia, Alberta and the Yukon.
**Vancouver Pride Festival** first weekend in August
**Whistler Pride and Ski Festival** late January
**Banff Pride** Early to mid-October
**Jasper Pride and Ski Festival** early to mid-April
**Calgary Pride** Late August to early September
**Edmonton Pridefest** late August

### Resources

Egale is a national lesbian, gay, bisexual and trans (LGBT) human rights organization.

It Gets Better Canada: this site has a fantastic list of resources to help LGBTIQ+ people in crisis.

# Accessible Travel

Traveling with a physical disability can be challenging, but Canada is becoming more accessible every year. While some trails and places in the Canadian Rockies are almost impossible to access in a wheelchair, provincial and federal parks have worked to make most of the key viewpoints and sites accessible.

**Public Transit**
Public transit is fully accessible in Vancouver, Calgary, Edmonton and Banff and mostly accessible in other smaller centers.

**Handy Bus**
Many communities in Alberta, BC and the Yukon offer Handy Bus service to individuals with disabilities. The service is door to door and there is an application process and a fee.

**Adaptive Recreational Equipment**
Some provincial and federal parks offer adaptive recreational equipment on loan. This may include adapted beach chairs and trailrider chairs as well as volunteers to assist with the operation of them.

**Airport**
The airports in Vancouver, Calgary and Edmonton have staff ready to assist people with disabilities. Book these services in advance through the airline you are traveling with.

**Accommodation**
Smaller B&Bs in historic buildings are less likely to have accessible facilities. Larger hotels and newer-built properties should be accessible.

**Museums**
Many of the larger attractions offer mobility scooters, wheelchair or power chair rentals. It's a good idea to confirm accessibility before visiting an attraction, but most are fully accessible.

## ROCKY MOUNTAIN ADAPTIVE
Offers private lessons, guided experiences, multiday programs and camps and equipment rentals in 20 different sports and recreational activities to disabled individuals in Canmore, Kananaskis, Banff and Lake Louise.

## WHISTLER ADAPTIVE SKI & SNOWBOARD PROGRAM
This registered charity provides a range of adaptive equipment and specialized instruction from certified instructors to guests with disabilities at Whistler Blackcomb in winter. The program caters to a full spectrum of skiers, sit-skiers and snowboarders.

## RESOURCES

A list of travel resources to assist people with disabilities.

A guide for travelers with disabilities produced by The Canadian Transportation Agency.

Visit park websites to learn more about accessible trails .

Organization dedicated to removing barriers and liberating people with disabilities.

# How to See the Northern Lights

Watching the northern lights dance across a dark night sky is a magical experience. The aurora borealis can be seen in British Columbia, Alberta and the Yukon, but it's most common in the Yukon because the land lies under the auroral oval – the region with the greatest geomagnetic activity and the brightest and most frequent displays. Whether or not you are visiting the Yukon, you may have a chance to view the northern lights, if conditions are right. Here's what you need to know to increase your chances of seeing this natural phenomenon.

### Aurora Season

The aurora borealis is most visible from mid-August to mid-April, and the best time to view it is between 10pm and 3am. The Yukon is known as 'the land of the midnight sun,' because it never gets completely dark during the peak summer months, so you can't see the aurora at that time. In Alberta and British Columbia days are longer and nights are shorter in the summer. By mid-August, skies are beginning to get dark enough to see the northern lights.

### Dark Skies

Clear, dark skies are essential for aurora viewing. To see the best and brightest displays, you'll need to get away from ambient light. It's best to get out of the city. A dark sky preserve is a good place to be. A full moon also decreases your ability to see the northern lights. Avoid booking an aurora tour when there is a full moon.

### Aurora Forecast

Scientists can predict auroras based on the sun's activity, geomagnetic storms and other factors. There are several websites that provide fairly accurate northern lights forecasts. Aurora Forecast (auroraforecast.com) is a good one in the Yukon and Aurora Watch (aurorawatch.ca) is a good predictor in Alberta.

 For Yukon scan here

 For Alberta scan here

### Aurora Tours

Booking a guided aurora watching tour with an expert guide can increase your chances of seeing and photographing the northern lights. They also have warm shelters and can assist in helping you adjust camera settings to capture photographs. Even if you take a tour, there are no guarantees you will see the aurora. Conditions must be right for this magical light show to happen.

### LEGENDS OF THE LIGHTS

There are many different Indigenous cultures in Canada and each group has their own legends and stories to explain the phenomenon of the aurora borealis. Consider taking an aurora viewing tour with an Indigenous guide. You will not only get a chance to see the lights, you'll learn about some of the legends. You might also learn the legends of the lights by participating in an Indigenous storytelling experience.

# Nuts & Bolts

## OPENING HOURS

Opening hours vary throughout the year and can differ between small towns and larger centers.

**Banks** 9am to 5pm Monday to Friday

**Shops** 9am to 9pm daily in larger centers; 9am to 6pm Monday to Saturday in smaller centers

**Bars** 3pm to 2am daily

**Restaurants** 11am to midnight daily

### Public Toilets

Public toilets are available at gas stations, visitor centers, shopping centers and in national and provincial parks. Bring your own toilet paper and hand sanitizer when you are using facilities in the parks.

### Weights & Measures

Canada uses the metric system. Distances are measured in kilometers and fluids are measured in liters.

### Smoking

Smoking is not allowed in most public places. Most hotels and restaurants are completely nonsmoking.

---

### GOOD TO KNOW

**Time zone**
Most of BC is Pacific Standard Time (PST); the rest of BC, Alberta and the Yukon are Mountain Standard Time (MST)

**Country calling code**
1

**Emergency number**
911

**Population**
BC: 5.4 million; Alberta: 4.6 million; Yukon: 44,160

### Electricity
**Type A/B** 120V/60Hz

Type A
120V/60Hz

Type B
120V/60Hz

---

## PUBLIC HOLIDAYS

**New Year's Day** January 1

**Good Friday/Easter Monday** March/April

**Victoria Day** Monday between May 18 to 24

**Canada Day** July 1

**Civic Holiday** First Monday in August

**Labour Day** First Monday in September

**National Day for Truth and Reconciliation** September 30

**Thanksgiving Day** Second Monday in October

**Remembrance Day** November 11

**Christmas Day** December 25

**Boxing Day** December 26

# STORYBOOK

Our writers delve deep into different aspects of British Columbia & the Canadian Rockies life

**Traditional handmade snowshoes**
SUN_SHINE/SHUTTERSTOCK ©

# A HISTORY OF BRITISH COLUMBIA & THE CANADIAN ROCKIES IN

# 15 PLACES

British Columbia's story is one that starts long before it was given borders, Western names and currency, as there are archaeological records of thriving civilizations dating back 14,000 years. The arrival of Europeans marked a pivotal moment in the province's history, undeniably transforming the region as we understand it today. By Jonny Bierman

**AS A RELATIVELY** nascent province within a young nation, British Columbia's colonial past is complex, to say the least. Human history in the region extends back to the last ice age, far preceding interactions with Europeans. This rich heritage has been preserved through generations of oral storytelling, artistic expression and artifacts that contemporary archaeological research has carbon dated to give meaning and establish timelines. Regrettably, efforts by European empires to erase this history are an undeniable aspect of British Columbia's past – a reality that warrants acknowledgment and understanding.

While a work in progress, the British Columbia we know today has much of which to be proud. Canada's LGBTIQ+ rights movement was born in BC, the progress of reconciliation with Indigenous Peoples has been forged here and the province has been a leader in Canada's Indigenous tourism sector, helping to revitalize culture and language through enriching experiences. Conservation and sustainable land management mean over 700 provincial parks and protected areas are here for you to explore, while several destinations, museums and historic sites pay homage to the past, acknowledging both its triumphs and shortcomings.

## 1. Haida Gwaii & Triquet Island

14,000 YEARS OF INDIGENOUS HISTORY

Since time immemorial, Indigenous Peoples have thrived in what we now know as 'British Columbia.' The earliest signs of human habitation have been identified in Haida Gwaii and Triquet Island in the Heiltsuk Territory of the Great Bear Rainforest through the discoveries of stone tools and evidence of ancient fishing practices. Oral history dating back thousands of years in the Heiltsuk Territory spoke of a non-frozen strip of land during a time when most of North America was covered by glaciers – the Indigenous used this area for survival, and now archaeologists have reaffirmed that ancient knowledge, dating it back 14,000 years.

*For more on Haida Gwaii and the Great Bear Rainforest, see p143 and p121.*

## 2. Nootka Island & Bella Coola

THE FIRST EUROPEANS MAKE LANDFALL

Following the arrival of the British and Spanish to Nootka Island in the late 1700s, years of rivalry ended in a treaty for joint ownership of the small island located just off the coast of Vancouver Island. Eventually, Spanish dominance of North America began to wane, and the last Spanish ship was ordered out in 1795, marking the end of their influence. Meanwhile, in 1793, Alexander Mackenzie made the first overland trip across North America, which ended near Bella Coola. A white rock he inscribed 'Alexander Mackenzie from Canada by land 22nd July 1793' stands today at Sir Alexander Mackenzie Provincial Park.

*For more on Bella Coola, see p119.*

### 3. Vancouver Island
THE BORDER IS DRAWN

In the early 19th century, the British colonized Vancouver Island and established Fort Victoria, with the British fur-trading corporation Hudson's Bay Company playing a key role. The Oregon Treaty of 1846 established the 49th parallel as the border between British and American territories, keeping Vancouver Island under British control. The island became a Crown colony in 1849, the first to be established in British territory west of the Great Lakes. Victoria was the colony's capital, and Sir James Douglas became the governor in 1851.

*For more on Vancouver Island, see p83.*

### 4. Fort Langley & the Fraser River
GOLD FEVER ARRIVES

In 1858, Sir James Douglas sent 800 ounces of newfound gold from the Fraser River to the San Francisco Mint, triggering rumors of a new gold find. By late spring, prospectors began arriving in Victoria and New Caledonia (now New Westminster), with thousands searching for gold. After losing territory due to the California gold rush, Douglas urged Queen Victoria to cre-

ate a colonial government in New Caledonia, also asserting dominance over Indigenous Peoples. The petition was granted, and New Caledonia was renamed British Columbia. Its capital was in Fort Langley before later being moved to New Westminster due to its strategic positioning on the mouth of the Fraser.

*For more on Fort Langley and the Fraser River, see p125 and p124.*

### 5. Fraser Canyon & Barkerville
ANYTHING FOR RICHES

In the Fraser Canyon, tensions between miners and the Nlaka'pamux (Ingla-kap-ma) First Nations led to the Fraser River War of 1858. The Nlaka'pamux demanded a negotiated agreement before allowing miners to explore their territory beyond Yale. The conflict, known as the Canyon War, saw brief battles, and ransacked and burned towns with murdered men, women and children. Peace was restored with the arrival of Governor Douglas and the Royal Engineers in Yale. Miners made their way up the Fraser River as the Cariboo Gold Rush was sparked. Billy Barker later struck it rich in 1862 and Barkerville Town was established near the claim.

*For more, see Tuckkwiowhum (Tuck-we-ohm) Heritage Village on p125 and Barkerville Historic Town & Park on p128.*

### 6. Banff National Park
CANADA'S NATIONAL PARK SYSTEM IS BORN

In the course of constructing the railway through the Rocky Mountains, the discovery of hot springs in a cave led the then-prime minister to designate this area as a protected reserve in 1885. Over time, this reserve was expanded to include Lake Louise and extend north towards the Columbia Icefields. Despite a few name changes and size adjustments, Banff National Park stands as Canada's first national park and the genesis of the Canadian national park system. The Cave & Basin National Historic Site, which is open to visitors, offers a glimpse into this significant discovery and the cultural and spiritual importance it held for the Indigenous Peoples.

*For more, see Banff National Park (p207) and the Cave & Basin (p214).*

**Community Hall, Fort Langley (p125)**

ELENA_ALEX_FERNS/SHUTTERSTOCK ©

## 7. Revelstoke
THE RAILWAY REACHES BC

In 1885 the last spike was hammered into a railway tie near Revelstoke, a town in southeastern BC. This marked the culmination of a years-long project, the seeds of which were sown with the American purchase of Alaska in 1867 and fears of American further expansion. Fearing American intentions and facing financial difficulties, British Columbia had sought federal support and protection – but only if it got a railway connecting it to the rest of Canada within 10 years. After these terms were agreed upon, BC became Canada's sixth province in 1871, and 14 years later the railway reached Revelstoke.

*For more on this, see Revelstoke on p141.*

## 8. Glacier National Park
PROTECT THE SCENERY FOR TOURISTS

Following the construction of the transcontinental railway, Glacier National Park was established in 1886 simultaneously with Yoho National Park, the year after Banff National Park was created in Alberta. With tourism and the train's scenery being of the utmost importance, the government saw this as a priority. Glacier National Park was named for the nearby 'Great Glacier' (Illecillewaet Glacier) and its dominating ice.

*For more on Glacier National Park, see p160.*

## 9. Strathcona Provincial Park
PROTECTED NATURE FOR BRITISH COLUMBIANS

In 1911 Premier Richard McBride established Strathcona Provincial Park, British Columbia's first provincial park. This followed organized lobbying and public concern about the rapid logging of Vancouver Island. The park protects, among other features, Della Falls, Canada's tallest waterfall and the 16th tallest in the world. Established 26 years after the inauguration of the Banff National Park in Alberta, this park was an early indicator of the growing concern about the intersection of the natural environment with human activity, and the need to protect the former from the latter.

*For more on Strathcona Provincial Park, see p97.*

## 10. Chinatown Storytelling Centre
UNJUST DISCRIMINATION TOWARD CITIZENS

This Vancouver center recounts the history of the Chinese who played an integral role in the gold rush, building the railway, and building the country. Despite their contributions, in 1885 the Canadian government tried to stop immigration by charging a special head tax of $50. In 1923, the government went on to pass the Chinese Exclusion Act, which prevented the immigration of anyone from China and severely suppressed their rights, even if they were born in Canada. Among a long and unfair list, the Act barred them from reuniting with family, including their own spouses and children in China, and ensured they were always paid less than white people.

*For more on the Chinatown Storytelling Centre, see p61.*

## 11. Castle Pub
A CITY THAT CELEBRATES LOVE

Canada's first same-sex Kiss-In was staged in 1971 at Vancouver's Castle Pub, an establishment that refused to serve openly affectionate couples. On August 1, 1973, Vancouver's earliest pride celebrations were held and the first unofficial Pride Parade in Canada took place in Vancouver in 1978. However, in 1981, Vancouver and Montréal hosted the first official municipal Pride Parade celebrations. Vancouver had a big role to play in Canada's LGBTIQ+ rights movements, and celebrations today are among the biggest in the country.

*For more on pride celebrations in Vancouver, see p50.*

## 12. Yukon
SELF-GOVERNANCE FOR YUKON FIRST NATIONS

In 1973 the 'Together Today for Our Children Tomorrow' position paper was brought forth by Indigenous trailblazers from the Yukon to then-prime minister Pierre Trudeau, proposing a settlement that recognized local First Nations rights to self-government, economic development and control of their lands. After 20 years of negotiations, Yukon First Nations successfully reached the Umbrella Final Agreement, a treaty framework with the territorial and federal governments. Since then 11 of the 14 First Nations in Yukon

**Snowboarding, Whistler**

have entered into modern treaties and now have law-making power for their lands and citizens and are the decision-makers for projects on their Settlement Land.

*For more, visit Kwanlin Dün Cultural Centre (p186).*

## 13. Vancouver

PUTTING VANCOUVER ON THE MAP

Expo 86 transformed Vancouver, reshaping the False Creek area from an industrial wasteland into a vibrant, mixed-use urban space. The event showcased Vancouver as a must-see tourist destination, attracting mass volumes of people while spurring economic growth. The Expo infrastructure investments still thrive today – look no further than the city's SkyTrain network, Canada Place (which hosted the Canada Pavilion), BC Place, and the famous geodesic dome that housed the Expo Centre (now Science World). Hosting the successful World's Fair elevated Vancouver's international profile, contributing to its selection as the host for the 2010 Winter Olympics.

*For more on Vancouver, see p50.*

## 14. Whistler

WELCOMING THE WORLD TO BRITISH COLUMBIA

Although officially known as Vancouver 2010, much of the XXI Winter Olympics were held at Whistler Blackcomb, arguably North America's best ski resort. Canadians couldn't have wished for more than to claim gold medals in both women's and men's hockey on home soil. But what set these games apart from previous ones? These Olympics took place at the same time digital media platforms such as Facebook, Twitter and YouTube gained prominence. Respectively, Vancouver and Whistler took center stage as history unfolded before a captivated global audience and the first pivotal time the world witnessed the Games on something other than a television.

*For more on Vancouver and Whistler, see p50 and p116.*

## 15. Kamloops Indian Residential School

TRAGIC DISCOVERIES LEAD TO CHANGE

In May 2021, the tragic discovery of 215 Indigenous children's remains at the former Kamloops Indian Residential School shook Canada. It exposed Canada's residential school system's dark history and the multigenerational trauma it caused, previously unknown to many. The incident sparked national grief, outrage, and demands for further investigations, ultimately uncovering thousands more remains. In response, the Canadian government accelerated reconciliation efforts and established National Truth and Reconciliation Day to raise awareness and honor the lost children and survivors. From that point forward, Canadians have confronted historical injustices by taking it upon themselves to learn and unlearn, support Indigenous businesses, and confront the truth on the path to reconciliation.

*For more information on the residential school system, see p241.*

# MEET THE CANADIANS

Expect a warm welcome from Canadians, but don't be surprised if someone apologizes at some point. Some of the stereotypes are true. Debbie Olsen introduces her people.

**THERE ARE MANY** stereotypes about Canadians and some of them are true. Canadians really do love hockey and maple syrup. Hockey is the official national winter sport, and Canada is the world's largest exporter of maple syrup products. Canadians do apologize a lot. If you step on a Canadian's toe, they'll probably apologize for being in your way. When Canadian pro golfer Adam Hadwin was mistakenly tackled by a security guard at the 2023 Canadian Open, he apologized. Being polite is so ingrained in the culture of Canada that he couldn't help himself.

It's common for Americans to think of Canada as the place where their cold weather comes from. While Canada does have cold winters, it isn't always cold. There are four seasons. Summer weather is typically balmy and warm. But our cold winters have helped to shape the culture and people of Canada. It is reflected in Canadian art and literature, and it is prominent in pastimes like ice skating, hockey, ringette, snowmobiling, dogsledding and tobogganing. Canadians embrace the cold.

Canada has historically been both a French and a British colony, and since 1969 the country has had two official languages – French and English. French is more widely spoken in Québec than it is in the western part of the country. Canada is an independent commonwealth nation, but the British monarch is still the head of state. Pictures of Queen Elizabeth II, Canada's longest reigning sovereign, adorn the Canadian $20 dollar bill.

A country of immigrants and descendants of immigrants as well as Indigenous Peoples, Canada is culturally diverse. Canada is the second-largest country in the world and the vastness of it has contributed to its diversity. That is part of the reason why it is so difficult to generalize when it comes to explaining who Canadians are and what they are like. Being Canadian means different things to different people. Canada is united by its diversity.

If there are generalizations to be made, one could say that Canadians value freedom and diversity, and they are committed to social justice. Canada was the fourth country in the world to legalize same-sex marriage, and it is a nation committed to universal healthcare. Canada is also a peaceful nation. More than 125,000 Canadian Armed Forces members have served in international United Nations peacekeeping missions over the past 70 years.

Canadians are welcoming and friendly. If you need directions or restaurant advice or you get a flat tire on the side of the road, most Canadians will go out of their way to help you. But they might tell you they're sorry while doing it.

### How Many & How Old?

Canada has a population of just over 40 million. According to Statistics Canada, the average age in Canada on July 1, 2022 was 41.7 years. The number of Canadians aged 65 and up is higher than those under 15.

## I'M AN ALBERTAN & A CANADIAN & I'M MÉTIS – IT'S COMPLICATED

I was born in British Columbia and raised in Alberta. I grew up in a small town near Waterton Lakes National Park. Everything about the Canadian Rockies brings me peace and reminds me of home.

My birth mother's family is Indigenous from Québec. Our Wendat ancestors lived in that part of Canada for thousands of years. My father's family originally came from Wales and the United States. I identify as Métis, a French word that means I have mixed European and Indigenous ancestry. My ancestry is diverse and complicated, just like the country I proudly call home.

More than 450 ethnic or cultural origins were reported in the 2021 Canadian Census. Ethnic and cultural diversity is a point of pride in Canada. In the 2020 General Social Survey, 92% of the Canadian population aged 15 and older agreed that ethnic or cultural diversity is a Canadian value.

255

# INDIGENOUS TOURISM'S JOURNEY

Familiarizing yourself with the local culture, traditions and appropriate etiquette is an integral part of being a responsible traveler. By Jonny Bierman

**THE HISTORY OF** Canada's treatment of Indigenous Peoples is not one of which anyone is proud. Assimilation, cultural genocide, racial segregation, sterilization and forced removal from ancient territories are among a list of tragic mistreatment of Indigenous Peoples by former governments.

Among the worst was the implementation of the 'Indian Residential School Program,' which saw 131 residential schools operate between 1831 and 1996. Children were forcibly removed from their homes and taken to residential schools that were run by the church and funded by the federal government. Their hair was cut, their clothes taken away and they were punished for speaking their language. The goal of these brutal establishments was to assimilate them into Western culture and rinse them of any Indigenous cultural identity. At the same time, from 1884 to 1951, the federal government imposed a potlatch ban, which made it illegal for Indigenous Peoples to hold ceremonial potlatches that celebrated gift-giving, feasting and other traditions.

Collectively during this dark time, pride and practice of culture were made virtually impossible. Many children never returned home and it's estimated that over 6000 children died in these schools. Those who survived lost their identity, language

and cultural understanding, and grew up without nurturing parents during critical years of development.

In May 2021 using ground-penetrating radar technology and testimony from survivors, 215 unmarked graves were found at the former Kamloops Indian Residential School, sparking outrage and grief across Canada. These were the first of thousands more, which are still being discovered to this day. Canadians and the world were now waking up to the heinous acts that had long been known to survivors, but rarely to anyone else.

## A New Era of Understanding

Prior to these discoveries, most of this information was confined to Indigenous communities. It wasn't taught in the provincial education curriculums, and it was seldom talked about outside Indigenous tourism experiences. As the awareness of these tragic events began to unfold, a collective effort among Canadians escalated to learn, unlearn and embark on individual paths to reconciliation. As part of their response, the Canadian government instituted National Truth and Reconciliation Day, observed annually on September 30. Previously recognized as Orange Shirt Day in British Columbia, this event was initiated in BC in 2013 by Phyllis

Webstad, a residential school survivor from Williams Lake who had her cherished orange shirt taken away on her first day at residential school. The aim of the day is to raise awareness about the impact of residential schools on Indigenous Peoples. During this time, Indigenous tourism saw a large spike in demand as individuals realized the educational potential of these experiences and the sustainable economic impact they have for Indigenous communities that are using tourism as a means of cultural and language revitalization.

### A Catalyst for Sustainable Economic Growth

Although Indigenous tourism has long been present in Canada, it has recently experienced a surge in demand and recognition both domestically and internationally. A new wave of Indigenous entrepreneurs recognize the potential and value in sharing their culture through products and immersive experiences, resulting in a greater variety of offerings than ever before.

Additionally, increased federal funding through targeted mandates and policies acknowledges the vital role Indigenous tourism plays in revitalizing culture and language and fostering economic growth in rural and remote areas. And both for Indigenous experience providers and non-Indigenous customers, the industry presents a unique opportunity to contribute to the path towards reconciliation.

### Leading Cultural Revitalization

From coast to coast to coast, Indigenous entrepreneurs – many of whom are women – are setting an example for their communities by showing pride in their culture and embracing Indigenous identity. Historically and today, Indigenous communities are disproportionately marginalized due in part to outdated laws and the remote locations many were forced to occupy during colonization.

With the marketing and destination development support of provincial and national Indigenous tourism associations, even the most remote communities are now able to elevate their experiences and attract visitors. As the public shows genuine interest in learning about and from Indigenous communities, the younger generations are looking up to their community members with pride and confidence in embracing their Indigenous identity.

### Saving Language

At residential schools, speaking indigenous languages was strictly prohibited and met with severe punishment, such as lashings or worse. This, coupled with generational gaps where children could not learn from their parents, led to the decline of ancient languages that had existed for thousands of years. Consequently, the only individuals who retained the ability to speak these languages were knowledgekeepers and elders.

Efforts to preserve languages are being made through traditional education for younger generations and extensive digitization of these languages. Indigenous experiences also play a vital role in language preservation by providing economic support for digital adoption and attracting visitors who are eager to listen and engage in traditional conversations.

### Bringing Land & Water to Life

Since time immemorial, Indigenous Peoples have used the flora and fauna of the places you explore for their survival. The forest and flora are the medicine cabinet, the rivers, land and fauna are the pantry, and the sky is for navigation. British Columbia and the Canadian Rockies radiate an energy that

**Medicinally significant plants**

INDIGENOUS TOURISM ASSOCIATION OF CANADA ©

begs to be explored. Its rivers teem with migrating salmon, its rocky cliffs with roaming wildlife, its oceans with whales leaping from the deep, and its forests with cedars, pines, grass and ferns that rustle in the wind.

All of these natural elements that Grandfather Sun and Grandmother Moon touch on Mother Earth have significance – meaning you can only gain through an Indigenous-led experience. Some plants, for example, can be deadly when ingested improperly, but if they're boiled, they can be medicine. Embracing the wisdom of ancestral harvesting through an Indigenous experience will give the land you explore profound and new meaning.

## Your Role as Traveler

Canadians are on a journey of coming to terms with a tragic and inherited past by learning, unlearning and supporting reconciliation efforts. Following the 2021 discovery of the unmarked graves, a free course from the University of Alberta's Faculty of Native Studies called Indigenous Canada saw a surge in enrolments to better understand the history of Indigenous Peoples and their perspectives. At the time of writing, the course remained free online for anyone to take.

INDIGENOUS ENTREPRENEURS – MANY OF WHOM ARE WOMEN – ARE SETTING AN EXAMPLE FOR THEIR COMMUNITIES BY SHOWING PRIDE IN THEIR CULTURE AND EMBRACING INDIGENOUS IDENTITY

**Matricia Bauer, Warrior Women drumming group**

As a traveler, it's vital to show respect and comprehension towards Indigenous Peoples. Acquainting yourself with local customs, traditions and etiquette are keys to responsible and mindful travel. A great example of an easy way to learn online is by taking the Haida Gwaii Pledge (haidagwaiipledge.ca). In every province and territory in this region, there are Indigenous experiences, cultural centers and museums to learn from. Some of the most transformative experiences in these places are Indigenous-led and Indigenous-owned. Supporting these when traveling contributes to the collective duty of reconciliation.

## Indigenous Tourism Organizations

**Destination Indigenous** (destinationindigenous.ca) As Canada's national leader in Indigenous tourism, the Destination Indigenous non-profit provides economic development advisory services, the marketing of experiences, and support for those starting an Indigenous tourism business, while also leading the burgeoning Indigenous culinary scene (indigenouscuisine.ca). It recently launched a new accreditation program called 'The Original Original,' which aims to ensure quality in truly authentic Indigenous experiences.

**Indigenous Tourism Alberta** (indigenoustourismalberta.ca) ITA is a non-profit organization dedicated to fostering the growth and promotion of authentic, sustainable Indigenous tourism experiences in Alberta.

**Indigenous Tourism British Columbia** (indigenousbc.com) With over 200 unique Indigenous communities, Indigenous Tourism British Columbia showcases diverse experiences, including urban dining, art galleries, boutique hotels, wildlife tours, workshops and oceanside campsites.

**Yukon First Nations Culture & Tourism Association** (indigenousyukon.ca) The Yukon includes 11 self-governing First Nations groups, and its rapidly expanding array of Indigenous experiences showcases the success of this system. The Yukon First Nations Culture and Tourism Association holds the Adäka Cultural Festival in Whitehorse annually at the end of June to celebrate Indigenous culture through art, dance, song and workshops in what is one of the largest Indigenous festivals in Canada.

Electric vehicle charging station, Vancouver

# ELECTRIC BC

British Columbians are embracing EVs – what does this mean for travelers? By Carolyn B Heller

**BRITISH COLUMBIA HAS** one of the largest public electric vehicle charging networks in Canada, with more than 4300 public charging stations across the province. The government's stated goal is to have 10,000 public charging locations up and running by 2030. So how easy is it to make an EV road trip across BC right now?

## Where the Chargers Are

As in many destinations, British Columbia has the greatest number of EV chargers in the areas with the largest population, where residents with EVs make up a growing percentage of drivers. You'll find numerous EV chargers across the Vancouver metro region, in and around Victoria, in Squamish and Whistler, and in cities like Kelowna, Kamloops, and Cranbrook as you travel east. EV chargers are also plentiful along Hwy 1, the Trans-Canada Hwy, which connects the coast with the Canadian Rockies.

Increasingly, you'll find EV chargers in smaller BC towns, too. At the intersection of Hwys 1, 3 and 5, two hours east of Vancouver, the community of Hope has several banks of different types of chargers, making it convenient for a coffee and charging break before you continue east over the mountains toward the Okanagan Valley or west toward Vancouver and the Pacific Coast.

In the Okanagan, many wineries have installed EV chargers, encouraging guests to linger over tastings of pinot noir or chardonnay while topping up their vehicles; just make sure you have a designated driver if you're combining wine sampling with recharging stops. More and more hotels here, and gradually throughout the province, are installing chargers for guests. Other accommodations, particularly cabins or motels with exterior outlets, might let you plug in overnight; it won't be fast, but you'll get a decent charge.

The Kootenay-Rockies region has been making significant investments in EV technology. The Accelerate Kootenays project (acceleratekootenays.ca) is a community-driven initiative to develop cleaner transportation throughout the area by providing funding to support EV charger installations. Towns like Revelstoke, Golden and Nelson all have multiple charging options, and many communities now have at least one public charger, often at city hall or other government office, the local visitor center, a community center, or the town's library.

Another place to find chargers? British Columbia's national parks. Parks Canada has slowly been installing EV chargers at national parks and historic sites nationwide. In BC, look for chargers at the Pacific Rim National Park visitor center, at the Field visitor center in Yoho National Park and at the Rogers Pass Discovery Centre on Hwy 1 in Glacier National Park, an area that otherwise has few other services.

On Vancouver Island, EV chargers are plentiful along the eastern shore between Victoria and Campbell River and in the west coast towns of Tofino and Ucluelet. While the south and north coasts and the inland regions currently have fewer chargers, you should still be able to explore these regions in most EVs with a decent range.

Remote communities in BC's north have been slower to install chargers, although you'll find them in larger towns like Prince George, Prince Rupert and Terrace. Plan carefully as you travel north, especially where distances are greater.

### Tips for EV Drivers

Major car-rental companies in BC are renting EVs, particularly in the Vancouver area. Another option is a specialized business such as Zerocar (zerocar.ca), a Vancouver-based rental service concentrating on Tesla rentals. You can sometimes find electric vehicles through the Turo car-sharing service (turo.com).

Tesla's navigation system will find chargers and calculate how far you can go without recharging, but whatever type of EV you have, it's still useful to download apps such as PlugShare (plugshare.com), which locates charging stations, describes their type and speed, and includes user ratings and comments, often identifying malfunctioning units. A Better Route Planner (ABRP, abetterrouteplanner.com) also helps identify where you can charge as you plot your road trip.

BC Hydro (electricvehicles.bchydro.com), the provincial electricity company, operates many of the province's faster charging stations, so checking its website or app can identify their locations. Other charging networks that you'll find in BC include flo (flo.com) and Sun Country (suncountryhighway.ca). Because EV technology is evolving rapidly, it's worth checking for updates immediately before your trip to find out what networks have the most stations along your route.

Research charger availability when you investigate places to stay. If you can charge overnight at your accommodations, you'll save yourself time and possible range anxiety during the day.

Remember that the multiple mountain ranges you'll traverse as you travel across BC can drain your battery. Be sure you have a full charge before crossing the Coast Mountains on the remote, high-elevation Coquihalla Hwy (Hwy 5) between the coast and the Okanagan or when traveling Hwy 4 over Vancouver Island's mountains toward Tofino and the Pacific Coast.

For most road trippers exploring British Columbia, driving an electric vehicle has become a viable option. With EV adoption rates expected to remain high, and with increasing investment in EV charging stations across the province, EV travel should only get easier for BC travelers.

# INDEX

Map Pages **000**

Map Pages **000**

Vancouver (p50), framed by stunning seacapes, majestic mountains and towering trees, offers cycling, shopping, skiing and swimming.

The adventurous should opt for rafting on the Sunwapta River (p230), where the Sunwapta Falls throw up class III rapids.

**Mapping data sources:**
© Lonely Planet
© OpenStreetMap http://openstreetmap.org/copyright

## THIS BOOK

**Destination Editor**
Sarah Stocking

**Production Editor**
Jeremy Toynbee

**Book Designer**
Nicolas D'Hoedt

**Cartographer**
Corey Hutchison

**Assisting Editors**
Alice Barnes-Brown,
Soo Hamilton,
Simon Williamson

**Cover Researcher**
Nicolas D'Hoedt,
Lauren Egan

**Thanks** Ronan
Abayawickrema,
James Appleton, Alex
Conroy, Alison Killilea,
Charlotte Orr

MIX
Paper from responsible sources
FSC™ C021741

Paper in this book is certified against the Forest Stewardship Council™ standards. FSC™ promotes environmentally responsible, socially beneficial and economically viable management of the world's forests.

Published by Lonely Planet Global Limited
CRN 554153
10th edition – May 2024
ISBN 978 1 83869 701 3
© Lonely Planet 2024 Photographs © as indicated 2024
10 9 8 7 6 5 4 3 2 1
Printed in China